THE WALLS WITHIN

POLITICS AND SOCIETY IN
MODERN AMERICA

*William H. Chafe, Gary Gerstle, Linda Gordon,
and Julian E. Zelizer, Series Editors*

For a full list of books in this series see: https://press.princeton.edu/series
/politics-and-society-in-modern-america

The Walls Within

THE POLITICS OF IMMIGRATION
IN MODERN AMERICA

SARAH R. COLEMAN

PRINCETON UNIVERSITY PRESS

PRINCETON & OXFORD

Published by Princeton University Press
41 William Street, Princeton, New Jersey 08540
99 Banbury Road, Oxford OX2 6JX

press.princeton.edu

First paperback printing, 2023
Paperback ISBN 9780691203331

The Library of Congress has cataloged the cloth edition as follows:

Names: Coleman, Sarah R., 1983- author.
Title: The walls within : the politics of immigration in modern America / Sarah R.
    Coleman.
Description: Princeton, New Jersey : Princeton University Press, 2021. |
Series: Politics and society in modern America | Includes bibliographical references
    and index.
Identifiers: LCCN 2020043120 (print) | LCCN 2020043121 (ebook) |
    ISBN 9780691180281 (hardback) | ISBN 9780691203331 (paperback) |
    ISBN 9780691185927 (ebook)
Subjects: LCSH: United States—Emigration and immigration—History—20th century. |
    United States—Emigration and immigration—History—21st century. | United
    States—Emigration and immigration—Government policy. | Immigrants—
    Legal status, laws, etc.—United States | Illegal aliens—United States.
Classification: LCC JV6455 .C56 2021 (print) | LCC JV6455 (ebook) |
    DDC 325.73—dc23
LC record available at https://lccn.loc.gov/2020043120
LC ebook record available at https://lccn.loc.gov/2020043121

British Library Cataloging-in-Publication Data is available

Editorial: Bridget Flannery-McCoy and Alena Chekanov
Production Editorial: Karen Carter
Jacket/Cover Design: Layla Mac Rory
Production: Danielle Amatucci
Publicity: Alyssa Sanford and Kate Farquhar-Thomson
Copyeditor: Karen Verde

This book has been composed in Arno

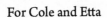

For Cole and Etta

CONTENTS

THE WALLS WITHIN

How can we show
Americans that these
restrictions hurt them?
Or to Stacy?

I'm seeking to protect
the value of citizenship,
do we factually devalue
it?

Tell me about methods &
the archives? How did
this all come together as
research was carried out?

We have focused throughout on
the state. This book
really points out the
layers of the state
apparatus.

restricting education & employment.

The erection of these intense walls. What is their effect on citizens?

Introduction

THE TOUGH QUESTION

JUSTICE MARSHALL: *Could Texas deny them [unauthorized immigrants] fire protection?*

JOHN HARDY: Deny them fire protection?

JUSTICE MARSHALL: *Yes, sir. F-I-R-E. Could Texas pass a law and say they cannot be protected?*

see Cheney

JOHN HARDY: If their home is on fire, their home is going to be protected with the local fire services just . . .

JUSTICE MARSHALL: *Could Texas pass a law and say they cannot be protected?*

JOHN HARDY: I don't believe so.

JUSTICE MARSHALL: *If they could do this [deny unauthorized immigrants access to public education], why couldn't they do that?*

JOHN HARDY: Because . . . I am going to take the position that that is an entitlement of the . . . let me think a second . . . You . . . that is . . . I don't know. That is a tough question.

—*PLYLER V. DOE, US SUPREME COURT ORAL ARGUMENT, DECEMBER 1, 1981*

legal status isn't enough; citizenship is most important

THIS EXCHANGE between the gravelly voice of Justice Thurgood Marshall and the Texas twang of John Hardy lays bare the question: what are the rights of noncitizen immigrants in the United States? The answer to this question shifted dramatically over the last quarter of the twentieth century during debates in courtrooms, in Washington, and in communities and legislative arenas across the country. The impact of these events and battles on evolving alliances cannot be understated. America's transition from a "nation of immigrants" to a country characterized by a sharpened division between those with citizenship rights and those without didn't simply shape the political landscape of those years but fundamentally shapes American life today.[1]

In recent years, federal policy toward immigrants has become hostile, yet Americans have a surprisingly thin understanding of just how that came to be. This book traces the struggle of politicians, interest groups, courts, activists, and communities to define the rights of immigrants in the United States after the passage of the historic Hart-Celler Act of 1965. A key piece of legislation in Lyndon Johnson's Great Society, Hart-Celler ended the national quota system of the 1920s and launched a new era in immigration, remaking the nation's demographic profile over the next four decades, reshaping American society and culture, and launching deep debates over the place of the immigrant in American life. In particular, political battles erupted over immigrants' access to education, labor, welfare, and civil liberties. Sometimes these battles grew so acrimonious that they dominated American politics.

Historians have not paid much attention to these battles; nor have social scientists who focused more on battles over admissions restrictions than on the rights of immigrants who were admitted.[2] For much of the period under consideration, controlling admission to the United States across its southern border proved too difficult for policymakers. Thus, the battle to control immigrants shifted from external borders to internal ones: to what extent would noncitizen immigrants receive the rights given to US citizens? Those internal borders—which focused on access to schools, to employment, and to welfare—form the subject of this book. So, too, do the various levels of government—the federal, state, and local authorities who tangled with each other over who would have the right to make the critical decisions affecting the lives of immigrants.

While initially seen as a triumph for liberal immigration policy, the Hart-Celler Act proved to be both progressive and deeply conservative at the same time. Scholars have shown how the replacement of the national origins system with equal quotas actually created new obstacles for potential immigrants from the Western Hemisphere as it ignored the particularly compelling reasons residents of some nations had for seeking to emigrate to the United States.[3] But this duality of the Hart-Celler Act becomes even more striking, as this book shows, when we consider how the act that fostered an increase in the numbers and diversity of immigrants also inspired a reactionary movement that has sought to marginalize those same immigrants inside the United States.

This new anti-immigrant sentiment was notably different from the anti-immigrant sentiment of the late nineteenth and early twentieth centuries, in large part because the nation itself was notably different.[4] Racism and nativism had become less reputable in American society, while the United States had embraced and expanded a welfare state with a variety of new benefits. As a result of these changes, the new restrictionists rejected overtly racist arguments and instead charged that immigrants unduly burdened the state and its citizens.[5] In this new rendering, immigrants took government benefits and jobs away from working- and middle-class Americans in an era when the new service-oriented, low-wage economy left many citizens economically insecure.[6] Working- and middle-class White *and* Black citizens sometimes viewed the massive growth of Latino and unauthorized populations (all too often seen as one and the same group of people) as the causes of the inequality and displacement associated with the new economy.[7] The movement grew by forging unusual alliances between groups from different sides of the political spectrum. Many unions warned that immigrants would undercut the wages and access to jobs for citizens of the United States. Environmental activists drew upon population control arguments to oppose immigration. More traditional nativists warned of the immigrants' deleterious implications for "American" culture and society. At the same time, the rise of a broad-based conservative movement against "big government" also fueled restrictionist rhetoric that objected to the success of immigrants' rights groups in defending government support for immigrants in the 1970s and early 1980s. For their own reasons, each of these groups sought to restrict the rights of immigrants and together worked to undermine the idealistic vision of the United States as a nation of immigrants that John F. Kennedy had celebrated and that Lyndon Johnson had made part of his Great Society.

These diverse anti-immigrant groups pursued a multifaceted strategy to restrict immigrants' rights, engaging the courts, Congress, state legislatures, ballot initiatives, and other forums to press for political change. Their movement created new cleavages in the electorate and facilitated a redistribution of power within both political parties. The Democrats were divided by a desire to accommodate both anti-immigrant labor unions and members of an emerging centrist faction, Third Way New Democrats, while still appealing to the party's proponents of an expansive and inclusive New Deal welfare state. The party was also split between its pluralist and humanitarian wing that favored opening borders and absorbing immigrants into the mainstream of American society as quickly as possible and those who worried that increases in the labor supply would be so large that the wages of all working-class Americans would suffer. The Republicans were riven by a different divide, one between restrictionists on the one hand and business conservatives on the other, whose commitment to free enterprise and deregulation (and an ample supply of immigrant workers) caused them to support permeable borders.

This book highlights the constellation of institutions and activists that together thwarted restrictionist efforts through the 1970s and 1980s, providing a perhaps surprising example of liberal persistence during a period generally understood as an era of conservative ascendency. First, the modern civil rights movement had fostered expansive notions of the Equal Protection and Due Process clauses of the Fourteenth Amendment, which gave immigrant rights advocates access to resources and networks that expanded their claims on the state. Second, in a nation increasingly committed to deregulation and the free movement of capital, goods, and labor across nation-state boundaries, anti-immigration hard-liners struggled to gain power and shape policy within both parties. Third, restrictionists also struggled to navigate the complexity of the United States' fractured legislative process and regulatory structures at the federal, state, and local levels. Altogether, the particular politics of immigration after 1965 divided the parties internally, set potential allies against each other, and created significant difficulties for those seeking to forge the unusual alliances needed to enact policy change. In the end, however, the obstacles to restrictionist reform and repeated failures to pass restrictive immigration policy during the 1970s and 1980s only strengthened the resolve of anti-immigrant activists and helped fuel popular restrictionist sentiment through the decades.

The anti-immigrant movement of the 1970s originated in a rejection of state toleration for *unauthorized* immigrants, but by the 1990s, the increasingly polarized debate, with an emboldened restrictionist movement, had begun to question rights for *all* immigrants, including authorized immigrants and green card holders. The 1990s proved to be a pivotal decade. Citizenship status became the litmus test for basic rights. Anti-immigrant activists successfully limited the access of both authorized and unauthorized immigrants to key welfare programs, including federal welfare benefits, Medicaid, and food stamps. At the same time, they built on the conservative shift in policymaking from the federal to the state level to empower state and local law enforcement officers as the front-line enforcers of immigration policy.

———

This book reveals the centrality of debates about the rights of immigrants to the politics of immigration policy in the United States. The focus on border and admissions policy after 1965 has obscured fights over the rights of immigrants already in the United States. While placing alienage rights in the nation's interior at its core, this project never loses sight of the importance of the external border.[8] The intersection between border enforcement and domestic rights is always dynamic because, as legal scholar Linda Bosniak writes, noncitizens are "deportable by definition." Regardless of whatever civil, social, or economic rights they enjoy in society, their status as deportable "will always circumscribe their lives, making absolute sphere separation . . . a practical impossibility."[9] While potential expulsion is always present in noncitizen immigrants' lives, this work focuses on the increasing role that alienage rights played in immigration control and policy at the end of the twentieth century.

As the rights of immigrants in the United States loomed larger and larger, so, too, did the dispersed character of power in the American federal system. This study looks at the entire scale of policymaking that is pertinent to immigrants, showing how local, state, and federal actions shaped policy implementation and politics in distinct ways. From its founding to the late nineteenth century, the federal government played only a limited role in regulating immigration. State and local authorities dominated, creating immigration control regimes with distinctive and uneven patterns in enforcement and influencing popular attitudes toward immigrants well before the era of federal exclusion.[10] In the late nineteenth century, responding initially to the growth of Chinese immigration on the West Coast, federal officials began to control immigration, winning support for their new powers from the US Supreme Court in two cases, *Chy Lung v. Freeman* (1876) and *Henderson v. New York* (1875).[11] For the rest of the nineteenth century and much of the twentieth century, the Supreme Court remained committed to federal preemption in immigration enforcement as largely settled legal doctrine.[12]

However, as federal policy appeared increasingly directionless in the 1970s and 1980s, states and local government began taking more decision making about immigrants into their own hands. In doing so, local and state action in turn pressured federal officials either to delegate authority to the states or to conform federal immigration policy to state preferences. By driving immigration policy during the 1990s, states and localities ushered in a new era of immigration federalism.[13] By 2010, states were shaping immigration policy in numerous ways, with some states pushing increasingly restrictive legislation while others sought to pass laws to increase immigrant integration.[14] The shift to the states that got under way in the 1990s also represents an important step in the larger trend of devolution of authority to the states seen across many policy arenas during the period.

To understand late-twentieth-century immigration history is to gain a more refined understanding of the end of the twentieth century in the United States. The political debates over immigrants' rights intertwined with debates over large-scale structural changes in the new economy, including those generating unemployment and underemployment, stagnating wages, and deindustrialization. Those who sought to restrict immigration increasingly sought to roll back the expanded notion of social and economic citizenship that had been forged through the Progressive Era, the New Deal, and the Great Society. Immigration history is central to the history of the American state.

The history of immigration restriction in the late twentieth century also brings important new insights to an understanding of the conservative revolution. Many historical works describe a collapse of liberalism in the 1960s and a political shift to the right that took hold in 1970s.[15] In contrast, this book shows how many liberal reforms endured the so-called Reagan Revolution and how the conservative agenda actually achieved more success in the 1990s under the Clinton administration. But liberalism never disappeared. As the evidence here shows, the institutional factors and political activities that thwarted restrictionist efforts kept those liberal visions of social and economic rights alive.

By focusing on the persistence of liberalism even during the supposed triumphant moment of conservatism and the passage of immigration restriction under a Democratic administration, this book is able to join a larger move "Beyond the Red-Blue Divide."[16] Rejecting a narrow focus on partisan politics and election cycles that seem to make the red-blue divide real, the approach to immigration history taken here examines the intersection of political culture, electoral politics, and political economy in ways that allow us to see clearly the divisions that endured within parties and the alliances that formed across party lines during this supposed period of party homogenization and hyper-partisanship.

Finally, in explaining how the rise of restrictionist energy often yielded less than many hoped, or feared, *The Walls Within* puts the Tea Party and Trump-fueled anger that has emerged since 2008 in the context of this three-decades-long history of anti-immigrant activism. Restrictionists have had reason to be unsatisfied, and to become ever more radical, as the policies that have diminished the rights of immigrants have not diminished the growing size of the foreign-born population.

Any study of immigration at the end of the twentieth century requires that one grasp how fundamentally the Hart-Celler Act changed the demographic profile of the United States. Passed in 1965, Congress established a preference system that first favored family reunification and then gave preference to employment-based migration. The 1924 Immigration and Nationality Act, also known as the Johnson-Reed Act, had previously defined immigration for a half century. Wartime hysteria, fears of working-class radicalism, the rise of the eugenics movement, as well as the maturing of the industrial infrastructure which reduced the need for unskilled labor led to the passage of the Act in the early 1920s. Its chief aim was to drastically reduce immigration, and with its passage, Congress sought to use "immigration law as an instrument of mass racial engineering" in order to produce a nation that was heavily white and of northern and western European descent.[17] The 1924 Act set immigration at no more than 2 percent of what the US total for each nationality had been in 1890, when immigrants arriving were predominantly from Western and Northern Europe, drastically cutting immigration from Southern and Eastern Europe. Additionally, the Act banned immigration by people "ineligible to citizenship," which, when paired with a series of court decisions in the early part of the twentieth century that had ruled Asians were ineligible to become citizens based on their race, largely ended legal immigration from Asia, and especially from South and East Asia. But the 1924 Act made much less of an attempt to stem immigration from Mexico. Agricultural labor needs in the Southwest and American foreign policy concerns blocked the restriction of Mexican immigration. As a result, Mexico and other countries of the Western Hemisphere were not subject to either the numerical quotas or the "ineligible to citizenship" ban that targeted Asians, as under naturalization law at the time, Mexicans were deemed to be White.[18] Nonetheless, while not formally excluded through quota by the 1924 Act, Mexicans were considered readily deportable and faced deportation, administrative exclusion, and repatriation campaigns throughout the 1924–1965 period of restriction.[19]

Following this period of severe restriction, the passage of the Hart-Celler Act in 1965 drastically remade the nation's immigration patterns and its racial composition more broadly. Approved by Congress under an ethos of civil rights and fairness and as part of the Great Society, the Act set a uniform cap on all nations at 7 percent of the annual total. In its rejection of national origins, and its replacement with a system that on its face was race neutral and based on egalitarianism, the 1965 immigration act can be seen as part of the larger civil rights movement, passed the same year as the Voting Rights Act, and just a year after the Civil Rights Act of 1964. "We have removed all elements of second-class citizenship from our laws by the [1964] Civil Rights Act," Vice President Hubert Humphrey noted. "We must in 1965 remove all elements in our immigration law which suggest there are second-class people. . . . We want to bring our immigration law into line with the spirit of the Civil Rights Act of 1964."[20] At the time, few of the bill's supporters or opponents anticipated that the legislation would result in a demographic transformation of the United States, with a transformed population of unprecedented diversity emerging.

In an effort to promote uniformity, the Hart-Celler Act also introduced for the first time a cap on immigration from the Western Hemisphere. Thus, while the overall cap rose, the volume of legal immigration from Mexico actually fell, leading to a sharp increase in deportations, as Mexican migrants increasingly became recast as "illegals."[21] As a result, there has been a rising perception of immigration as an "invasion" by a lawbreaking population seen as non-assimilating in a threatening way. In addition, the 1965 immigration law required tracking of previously largely informal migration by Central and South Americans, creating a significant increase in immigration regulation and bureaucracies that have continued expanding ever since, with immigration status serving as a proxy for certain kinds of racial discrimination. While there have been incremental changes to the numbers allotted to the preferences established in 1965, the general structure of immigration regulation created by the Hart-Celler Act still governs admission today.

As a result of these new admissions allocations, the demographic composition of the United States has shifted significantly over the last fifty years. Of the approximately 59 million immigrants that arrived in the United States between 1965 and 2015, approximately half came from Latin America and one-quarter from Asia.[22] Whereas in 1965, 84% of Americans were classified as non-Hispanic Whites, by 2015 that share had declined to 62%. The Hispanic share of the population grew from 4% in 1965 to 18% in 2015. Asians also saw their share rise, from less than 1% in 1965 to 6% in 2015. New immigrants, their children, and grandchildren have driven much of the population growth in the United States since 1965, adding 72 million people to the nation's population, accounting for 55% of the population growth.[23]

This work focuses on the changes in immigrants' rights during and in the wake of these demographic changes and in particular looks at education, labor, and welfare rights and civil liberties protections, four key arenas where the state touches individuals' lives. The first half of the book covers roughly 1965–1990, the period when new arguments over immigrants' rights emerged and efforts at restriction were met with mixed success. The second half addresses 1990–2000, a time when anti-immigrant activism began to make consequential gains and states began to play a significant role in immigration policymaking. The debates over the rights of noncitizen immigrants in the United States in the 1970s were undoubtedly shaped by the perception of many native-born Americans that they faced increasingly limited opportunities for economic mobility and that the political and social means to achieve their own aims and aspirations had narrowed.

The debate over opportunity and access was inherently linked with arguments over what acceptable "entitlements" were and to what extent the government had to "promote the general welfare, and secure the blessings of liberty."[24] During the 1970s, twenty years after the famous *Brown v. Board of Education* desegregation decision, school segregation and inferior educational opportunities remained at the forefront of public discourse. As seen in the *Swann* and *Milliken* Supreme Court decisions over busing policy, as well as the violent anti-busing protests in Boston, arguments over integration raged across the country. Educational equity and school financing disparities were contested in local communities and came before the Supreme Court in the 1973 case *San Antonio Independent School District v. Rodríguez*.

Part of this larger national dialogue over access to quality public education included a fight over immigrants'—particularly unauthorized immigrants'—access to public education. Chapter 1 explores how during the 1970s, several local school districts in Texas, with the backing of the Texas state legislature, began to charge tuition to unauthorized students. A group of unauthorized students and their parents sued the school board, and a team of activist lawyers took the case to the Supreme Court in *Plyler v. Doe* (1982). Chapter 2 traces the federal government's role in the case, under both the Carter and the Reagan administrations, and addresses how the federal government's arguments were deeply influenced by political and policy concerns. In the end, the Supreme Court's 1982 landmark decision extended the rights of the Equal Protection Clause of the Fourteenth Amendment to unauthorized children, expanding the rights afforded to those with anything less than citizenship status to new bounds.

While education was one key component of the social contract, so too was access to fair labor and employment. In what some social scientists have dubbed "the fading American dream," 92 percent of Americans born in the 1940s earned a higher salary than their parents by the time they turned thirty, but only about half of those born in the 1980s could say the same.[25] This regression of Americans' ability to do better than their parents was tied to significant changes in the economy with the rise of post-industrial labor, including the impact of stagflation, the oil crisis, and changes in the labor force. Chapters 3 and 4 explore the debate over immigrants' access to employment during this period of tumultuous change in the American economy.

Studying the passage of employer sanctions for hiring unauthorized immigrants under the 1986 Immigration Reform and Control Act shows how cracks began to emerge within the liberal coalition as the new economy created active rifts in the pro-immigration alliance. But they also show how the strength of neoliberalism and a commitment to free movement of capital, goods, and people reigned in Washington and across the nation. As a result, even as the architects of the 1986 bill set out to punish employers who gave unauthorized immigrants jobs, all enforcement mechanisms were successfully removed from the bill before passage. The measures to deny jobs to unauthorized immigrants were thus rendered toothless; in addition, the bill granted a road to citizenship for three million unauthorized immigrants. Though framed as an act of immigration control, the 1986 Act actually did little either to seal the border or to punish unauthorized immigrants themselves or employers who gave them jobs. These chapters also help us to reconsider the labor history of this period. A declension narrative focused on outsourcing dominates labor history of the end of the twentieth century.[26] By turning away from that narrative, this project shines a light on those who came to the United States for work, as well as the economic stagnation and part-time service economy that they encountered. Noncitizen immigrants' success in gaining access to education and labor rights was matched by success in other policy areas, the gains driven in part by the growth of Latino and Mexican American activism. While these efforts were not uniformly successful, there was a notable expansion of immigrants' rights during this period.[27] This expansion would not remain true for following decades, as seen in the second half of this book.

The long simmering ambivalence toward social welfare in the United States entered a new era during the 1990s, and its confluence with the changing immigrant population had dramatic constricting effects on immigrants' rights as well as on the broader social contract. During the 1960s and early 1970s, the War on Poverty and the welfare rights movement made gains in expanding social welfare and opportunity for minorities and the poor in the United States.[28] As a result, the meaning of citizenship and the social contract had expanded, fueling the growth of the conservative right. Chapter 5 explores how by first mobilizing at the state and local levels, these conservative anti-welfare forces were successful in slashing some services during the 1970s, including notably in California under then-Governor Ronald Reagan. Unauthorized immigrants were made ineligible for many welfare programs as a result of these efforts. These anti-welfare campaigns, combining with the rising tide of conservatism and changing party politics, achieved even greater success and remade the American welfare state during the 1990s.[29] Immigrants in particular saw dramatic shrinkage in their access to benefits. California voters overwhelmingly supported a ballot initiative, Proposition 187, which sought to prohibit unauthorized immigrants from accessing public benefits including health care, education, and other social services. While federal courts invalidated many of the Proposition's provisions, the measure's popularity drove national policy. Following California's anti-immigrant lead, the 1996 Welfare Reform Act disallowed access for millions of authorized immigrants to Supplemental Security Income (SSI), along with food stamps and other means-tested programs. As a result, in the realm of federal welfare, the rights of immigrants in the United States largely depended on citizenship status instead of whether such immigration was legally authorized.

While border state California led the way in blocking immigrants' access to the welfare state, it was in the nation's landlocked core that immigrants' civil liberties began to be challenged in dynamic ways during the 1990s. In Iowa, a murder in a small town and the broader region's changing immigration patterns spurred the creation of the 287(g) program by Congress as part of the 1996 Immigration Reform and Immigrant Responsibility Act. This program allowed the federal government to deputize state and local law enforcement to assist in federal immigration enforcement. Chapter 6 explores the roots of this program and the shifting role of state and local law enforcement in immigration enforcement, beginning in the mid-1970s and culminating in the implementation of 287(g). This program effectively ended a century of exclusive legal federal control over immigration enforcement, and it created a new set of civil liberties concerns. While this was a major government policy shift, the program's implementation was highly contested at the local level, demonstrating again the dynamic role that local governments played in implementation as well as the limits of restrictionist pressure.

Taken together, these chapters show that the politics of immigration reform and immigration restriction were powerful not only at the country's edges, but at its core. Debates over education, labor, and welfare rights and civil liberties for noncitizen immigrants revealed the growing strength of the restrictionist movement in the United States. In the aftermath of the civil rights movement, anti-immigration activists forged a new restrictionist movement with rhetoric drawn from the language of rights, benefits, and burdening the state. Pivoting its tactical approach during the 1990s, this modern anti-immigrant movement made inroads, coming to dominate national politics and ushering in a new era of immigration federalism.

Immigrants in the United States entered the twenty-first century with few of the governmental benefits that they had enjoyed thirty years earlier. Locally, they continued to carve spaces to live, work, and thrive in the face of shifting political winds. At the beginning of the twenty-first century, while many in the United States still referred to the country as a "nation of immigrants," it was more accurately a nation of citizens and noncitizens, in which the benefits of citizenship had been both narrowed and denied to a very significant population living permanently in the United States.

1

The Rose's Sharp Thorn

TEXAS AND THE RISE OF UNAUTHORIZED IMMIGRANT EDUCATION ACTIVISM

JUST BEFORE 6 AM ON September 9, 1977, a group of children and their parents were ushered through the side door of the federal courthouse in Tyler, Texas. Fearing deportation if their identities became public, the Robles, Lopez, Hernandez, and Alvarez families slipped through the side door to attend a very early morning hearing, the timing of which was also set to help them maintain their anonymity. The Lopez family arrived with their car packed with their most valuable belongings, in case they had to go back across the border quickly.[1] Two young lawyers, Larry Daves and Peter Roos of the Mexican American Legal Defense and Education Fund (MALDEF), represented the families as they stood before US District Court Judge William Wayne Justice in order to challenge a fee imposed by the local school board on those students who could not provide documentation of their legal immigration status. What began that morning as a hearing in a small town in East Texas emerged as a landmark Supreme Court case, *Plyler v. Doe*, which would expand the rights of noncitizens in the United States.

That this case grew to change the law of the land was no accident, as it was the capstone of several key developments that began building in the 1960s. One of these developments was the passage of the Hart-Celler Act in 1965, which profoundly altered the demographic profiles of communities across the country by increasing their diversity due to immigration. These changes also inspired opposition movements that worked with state and local governments to craft laws that would restrict immigrants' access to public services and benefits. It was this broader oppositional movement that produced laws and covenants, like the Tyler school fee, to block unauthorized immigrants' access to public education.

In response to this increase in restrictive laws, in the 1970s, a group of activist lawyers formulated a broad legal strategy to expand immigrants' educational rights. To do so, they built upon the legacy of the civil rights movement by mobilizing established professional networks and tapping funding sources that had supported many similar efforts and by embracing the legal strategies and notions of "rights" that had been successfully employed in the civil rights movement. Specifically, they sought to strike down restrictive statutes like the Tyler fee, which were fiercely defended by local and state officials and conservative public interest groups.

Indeed, just as the liberal legal challenges were borne of societal and political changes in the 1960s, so too was the opposition they would engender, as conservative legal activism emerged largely in reaction to the rights revolution of the 1960s. Conservative legal activism used the networking connections forged during the welfare reform efforts in California to build their organizations and borrowed some of the language of the 1978 taxpayer revolt in order to mobilize support around a different notion of "rights." Given these competing forces, *Plyler* grew into a landmark case because all sides saw it as one front in a larger battle over rights, both in terms of who was entitled to them and what specific benefits were correspondingly granted.

From the beginning, given the high stakes of defining whether one's immigration status would exclude one from the protections of the Equal Protection Clause of the Fourteenth Amendment, both sides assiduously sought the support of the federal government. As the case wound its way to the US Supreme Court, the federal government's role in the case was highly contested within both the Carter and Reagan administrations, whose positions were deeply influenced, not just by constitutional arguments but by political and policy concerns. Efforts to maintain the support of key political constituencies, the hard-fought 1980 presidential election, and concerns over the expansive growth of federal benefits all impacted the government's positions. The voices concerned with the expansion of benefits for immigrants that emerged in *Plyler* were the early roots of a movement that would come to dominate the immigration debate in the following decades. In the end, the Supreme Court's 1982 decision extended the rights of the Equal Protection Clause of the Fourteenth Amendment to unauthorized persons, expanding the rights afforded to those with anything less than citizenship status to new bounds.[2]

The expansion seen in the *Plyler* case is one key moment in a longer history of alienage rights. Throughout American history, the distinctions between

cyclical
↑ increase ↓
) contraction

citizens and noncitizens have cyclically increased and contracted. During periods of labor recruitment, including the turn of the twentieth century when Mexicans supplanted Asian workers in the West, distinctions between citizens and noncitizens were loosened in response to economic priorities. After World War I, economic contractions led governmental officials and citizens to demand that Mexican laborers return to Mexico with families that included many US citizens. This pattern of restriction repeated itself with the depression in the 1930s, and the repatriation campaigns that followed. During World War II, the border with Mexico was reopened, the Bracero program responded to labor shortages, and citizenship-based distinctions were submerged. Operation Wetback and the McCarran-Walter Act represented another swing toward restrictions and the sharpening of distinctions based on citizenship.

During these ebbs and flows, noncitizen immigrant residents and activists made claims upon the state. Beginning in the 1880s, the Supreme Court began to recognize "a sphere of constitutional protections for aliens beyond the domain of immigration regulation."[3] In *Yick Wo v. Hopkins* (1886), the court struck down a San Francisco ordinance that made it illegal to operate a laundry in a wooden building without a permit from the Board of Supervisors. While on its face race-neutral, when the regulation was applied, every Chinese laundry owner in the city was denied a permit, while every White-owned laundry was granted one. The court held that, notwithstanding their alienage, resident aliens were protected by the Equal Protection Clause of the Fourteenth Amendment.[4] Throughout the late nineteenth and early twentieth centuries, states and localities at various points continued to try to legislate or regulate alienage rights within their state bounds.[5] Other scholars have shown that even in ages of rising restriction, immigrants at times have been able to successfully access the benefits of the welfare state when certain actors have recognized their "belonging" to and legitimate rights claims on American society despite their tenuous technical legal status with the state.[6] The *Plyler* case, and the larger expansion of alienage rights during the 1970s and 1980s, as well as the subsequent restriction during the 1990s, fit into a much longer pattern in the history of alienage rights.

Early Roots

While the *Plyler* case would not reach the Supreme Court until 1981, many of its roots can be traced to the late 1960s and early 1970s. These years saw the emergence of demographic trends, rising anti-immigrant sentiment, and corresponding pro-immigration activism that would continue to frame the debate for the decades to come.

Beginning in 1968, legal Mexican immigration to the United States had become increasingly restricted as a hemispheric cap was imposed for the first time, forcing Mexicans to compete with immigrants from the Caribbean and Central America for 120,000 available visas. Rapid population growth and a declining economy in Mexico in the late 1970s fueled an explosion of unauthorized immigration from Mexico to the United States. There was a 40 percent drop in legal immigration from Mexico by 1977.[7] Immigration and Naturalization Service (INS) apprehensions of Mexican nationals grew from 55,340 in 1965 to 99,883 in 1977.[8] Between 1965 and 1986, an estimated 28 million Mexicans entered the United States as unauthorized immigrants.[9]

There was an increase in concern with unauthorized immigration as towns and cities across the nation began to grapple with their changing demographic profiles. In 1965, when Congress had passed the Hart-Celler Act, immigration was not a major concern for most Americans, and most felt immigration should be kept at similar levels or were ambivalent about it. A poll taken that year showed that 39 percent of Americans felt immigration levels should be kept the same, 20 percent were unsure, while 7 percent wanted it increased, and 33 percent wanted it decreased.[10] By the early 1970s, sentiment was starting to change.

Immigration to the United States increasingly was portrayed in popular discourse as an "invasion" by a threatening non-assimilating population.[11] The popular media sensationalized the immigration shifts. A headline in *U.S. News and World Report* heralded a "Surge of Illegal Immigrants Across American Borders," and the accompanying story highlighted that "[n]ever have so many aliens swarmed illegally into the U.S.—millions, moving across the nation."[12] According to other news reports, "Great waves of Latin-American immigrants appear well along the way to accomplishing what their Spanish ancestors couldn't: the 'conquest' of North America."[13] The *Los Angeles Times, San Francisco Examiner*, and other outlets warned of the "growing peril" of immigrants.[14] This invasion narrative was heightened by rhetoric that increasingly portrayed the fertility rate of Mexican women as abnormally high and menacing.[15]

According to the popular media, the problem was not just the number of immigrants arriving; it was also that these immigrants were unassimilable outsiders causing problems. The *New York Times*, for example, ran stories that blamed the "character" of arriving Mexicans for urban problems like crime and poverty, claiming that immigrants in San Francisco "did not fit into the traditional lifestyle set by the long-time residents."[16] The *Los Angeles Times* ran a story in 1977 which argued that the image of an unauthorized immigrant as "a servile person who stays out of trouble" was no longer accurate as, according to the LAPD, "illegal aliens commit 50 percent of all pickpockets, 30 percent of all hit-and-run accidents, 25 to 30 percent of all shoplifts, 20 to 25 percent of all burglaries, 20 percent of all auto thefts and 5 percent of all homicides."[17] Beyond crime and poverty, immigrants were depicted as a public health threat due to their supposed high rates of communicable diseases and drug use.[18]

These narratives and discourse about immigrants permeated the political sphere as well. In 1973, INS commissioner Leonard Chapman stated, "The problem [of immigration] is serious. But we are seeing the beginning of a flood—a human tide that . . . is going to engulf our country, unless something is done to stop, or at least slow it."[19] The US Supreme Court increasingly began to address unauthorized immigration from Mexico during the 1970s, labeling it "a 'colossal problem' posing 'enormous difficulties' and 'formidable law enforcement problems.'"[20] Some justices called the immigration from Mexico "virtually uncontrollable" and argued it was creating law enforcement problems of *"titanic proportions."*[21]

While anti-immigrant sentiment was growing nationwide and across all three branches of government, so was the effort to expand immigrants' rights, and in particular, rights for unauthorized immigrants. The late 1960s and early 1970s were a period of rights expansion more broadly. Moving beyond the passive desegregation and voting rights fights of earlier years, the rights battles now focused on government expansion of affirmative action, active integration through busing, and the birth of the welfare rights movement. At the same moment in the early 1970s, a varied group of activists began to mobilize for the rights of unauthorized immigrants, both at the grassroots level and through legislative and legal challenges, replicating the approach taken by the African American civil rights movement.[22] This growth of support for the rights of unauthorized immigrants was a recent development, as previously many Mexican American organizations and most of the mainstream organized labor groups often had directly opposed unauthorized immigrants in their claims on state and society.[23] This chapter focuses on one of the legal challenges, but grassroots mobilization also occurred across the nation, as seen in the work of groups like the Maricopa County Organizing Project. Seeking to improve conditions for unauthorized migrants working in the citrus fields, MCOP successfully organized a series of work stoppages at Barry Goldwater's Arrowhead Ranch between 1977 and 1979 that resulted in a labor contract that included housing, paid vacation, health insurance, health and safety rules, and pay increases for its workers.[24]

Deep in the Heart

In Texas, many nationwide trends were evident in the early 1970s. Between 1970 and 1980, the US Census's conservative estimates (encompassing only authorized admissions) show that the Hispanic population in Texas grew by more than a million people, and by 1980, Hispanics made up approximately 21 percent of the population statewide.[25] Locally, between 1970 and 1977, Tyler's Hispanic population grew almost 15 percent.[26] The anti-immigrant sentiment that was growing nationwide was also becoming a larger part of the Texas political landscape, and in 1975, Eagle Pass, Texas, a town 500 miles southwest of Tyler on the banks of the Rio Grande River began blocking unauthorized students from gaining entrance to their schools.[27] Later that spring, in response to a request from the board on the legality of the school board's action, Texas Attorney General John Hill issued an opinion holding that all children, regardless of their immigration status, were entitled to attend public schools within the district of their residence.[28]

At the time of Hill's opinion, the Texas Education Code held that all children between six and twenty-one years of age were entitled to attend the public schools of the district where they resided.[29] The following month, the Texas legislature voted to modify the Education Code to allow public state schools to begin charging tuition for unauthorized children to attend. There is scant legislative history of the amendment, but its timing suggests it was made in direct response to the Attorney General's opinion.

Lawsuits against the statute arose quickly. In the spring of 1977, the statute was first challenged by Peter Williamson, a Houston immigration attorney, who asserted that the law violated both the due process protections of the Fifth Amendment, which provides that no State shall "deprive any person of life, liberty, or property, without due process of law," and the equal protection guarantee of the Fourteenth Amendment, which states that no state shall deny to any person within its jurisdiction the equal protection of the laws. The case was promptly dismissed and Williamson's appeals denied.

For the first year and a half following the passage of the amended statute, Tyler officials had ignored the changes to the state Education Code. Parents continued to register their children by showing their residency status through a housing lease or bill but were not required to show documents proving their right to remain in the United States. "I guess I was soft-hearted and concerned about the kids," Superintendent Plyler later testified. But the school board feared that the district would become "a haven" for unauthorized families, and thus announced in 1977 that unauthorized students would only be able to attend Tyler schools if they paid a tuition fee of $1,000. Soon thereafter, school authorities began to inform parents that their children would not be able to attend school in the fall tuition-free without providing their immigration papers. At the time, fewer than 60 of the 16,000 students in the Tyler school system were thought to be unauthorized.[30]

Humberto Alvarez was one of the parents in Tyler who was informed that spring by Douglas Elementary School authorities that his children would not be allowed to attend in the fall without proper documentation. José Robles first heard of the new policy from a teacher in the spring, and in the late summer, the principal at Bonner Elementary in Tyler told Robles that his children would need either an American passport, a birth certificate issued by a US hospital, or proof of legal residency status in order to register without cost.[31] Scores of parents in Tyler soon faced identical warnings from local school officials.

As families struggled with the new policy, several contacted a local Catholic outreach worker, Mike McAndrew, who connected them with Larry Daves and Bobby Rodkin, two young civil rights lawyers who worked in the area.[32] After the families were referred, the lawyers interviewed eight families and entered into an agreement to represent four of them in challenging the constitutionality of the Texas statute and corresponding Tyler fee. As McAndrew noted, it was hard to find willing families, as the families were fearful of being deported.[33]

The four families who went forward with the case, the Robles, Lopez, Hernandez, and Alvarez families, shared similar patterns of immigration and employment. For three of them, the male wage earner had first arrived in the United States in the late 1960s or early 1970s, to be followed several years later by the rest of his family. The families had lived in the region continuously since their arrival in the United States, with the parents working at either the local Tyler Pipe Company, the Loggins Meat Company, or at the local nurseries, and paid federal income taxes.[34] For example, Lídia Lopez crossed the border from Mexico in 1975 to join her husband Jose who had entered several years earlier, and both had found work at a local nursery.[35]

Many of the children in these families had been born in Mexico, while other siblings were born in Tyler at one of the two local hospitals and thus had American birth certificates. The families were active members of the community and most rented their homes but owned their vehicles.[36]

When these families reached out to the public interest legal community in Tyler, they encountered one small part of a nationwide effort that had undergone extensive development in the prior fifteen years. This growth would profoundly shape the *Plyler* case in terms of the people involved, the legal strategies and tactics used, and its base of support.

Formal efforts to provide civil legal support for underserved populations had existed since the late nineteenth century, but the 1960s marked a new era in the expansion of legal services in the United States. Passage by Congress of the Economic Opportunity Act in 1964 for the first time provided federal funding for legal services to the poor and created new funding streams to encourage graduates of the top law schools to pursue a career in public legal services. In turn, groups like the Ford Foundation began devoting significant funding to legal services. As a result of this support, over the next decade, legal services grew, increasing by 650 percent between 1963 and 1971.[37] Many of the litigators who pursued careers in legal services through these new channels of support in turn embraced a form of legal advocacy pioneered by the National Association for the Advancement of Colored People (NAACP) and the American Civil Liberties Union (ACLU), which were aggressive in challenging existing laws on due process and equal protection grounds of the Fifth and Fourteenth Amendments.[38]

Across the country and throughout Texas this type of legal advocacy grew significantly during the 1970s. East Texas Legal Services opened eight offices between 1978 and 1981, and at its peak employed forty full-time attorneys.[39] Conservative communities around Texas fought the presence of these legal advocates and the legal activism they practiced. The response to legal activism in Hereford, in West Texas, was typical of many towns in Texas. A group of young lawyers working for Texas Rural Legal Aid in Hereford brought a range of civil rights–related cases, including challenging farm labor abuses, racial discrimination in school board appointments, and voting apportionment. The lawyers, who were not local to Hereford, were branded by the conservative community as "carpet baggers," and as one paper noted, "[i]t might be styled as Harvard vs. Hereford, for it involves several brash, young, Harvard trained lawyers and a citizenry angry and alarmed." Local officials charged that the lawyers were "hurting our county and dividing our people." In particular, the fact that the legal services that these public interest lawyers provided were funded by the government was a source of frustration to many White residents. As Bruce Coleman, a wheat farmer and ranch farmer, noted, "I got my taxes fighting my taxes . . . I'm paying on both ends to fight myself, so you see why I'm upset." Sherriff Travis McPherson argued, "It's a gross misuse of taxpayers' money."[40] Closer to Tyler, East Texas Legal Services was a "widely hated set of initials in East Texas."[41]

It was one of these advocacy-based projects that first drew Larry Daves to East Texas and specifically to Tyler. Daves had grown up poor, moving around the southwest as his father worked in mining and eventually ending up in Amarillo, where his mother worked as a typist. Tall and athletic, he was a standout playing football in high school and won a scholarship to the University of Washington. While at the University of Washington, Daves read about the work of the California Rural Legal Assistance and was inspired to become a lawyer. Daves returned to Texas for law school at the University of Texas at Austin. In his second year, he began work on a voter registration project in Black communities near Nacogdoches run by the Texas Civil Liberties Union and American Federation of Labor and Congress of Industrial Organizations (AFL-CIO), work that culminated in litigation challenging county and federal legislative apportionment.[42] After law school in 1971, Daves tried to establish a legal aid office in Nacogdoches but because of lack of funding went into solo practice taking civil rights cases on his own.[43] Daves and the groups that he worked for originally on the apportionment project came to Texas not only because of the great need for legal services for the underserved in the area, but also for the same reason that MALDEF would be drawn there several years later in the *Plyler* case: Judge William Wayne Justice.[44] These groups would seek cases in Judge Justice's jurisdiction because it was one of the most liberal in the Fifth Circuit.

Judge Justice was not a popular man in Tyler by 1977 following a series of controversial rulings. His finding in 1970 that Tyler Junior College's prohibition against long hair for men was unconstitutional drew the wrath of the White majority in Tyler, and his desegregation order of Tyler public schools—a plan that entailed significant busing and the closure of the Black high school— enraged many people in the community. The desegregation ruling was assailed not only in Tyler, but across the region, and Judge Justice was quickly viewed by White East Texans as "heretical, a native son who had turned on tradition and who threatened the underpinnings of the social order."[45] His ruling in favor of the unauthorized students in the *Plyler* case would only bolster this view.

Judge Justice was born in 1920 about 35 miles to the west of conservative Tyler in the more liberal town of Athens and was part of a long tradition of Texas Democratic populist liberalism. His father, Will Justice, was a lawyer, a dedicated progressive Democrat, and a childhood friend of Senator Ralph Yarborough. Justice received his undergraduate and law degrees from the University of Texas, and after serving in the US Army, he returned to Athens, where he practiced law and was involved in Democratic politics, including supporting Senator Yarborough. After a patronage skirmish with then Vice President Lyndon Johnson, Senator Yarborough persuaded President John Kennedy to appoint Justice as the United States Attorney in the Eastern District of Texas in 1962. Six years later, President Johnson named him a federal district judge.[46]

One of the strategies of the legal interest groups operating in Texas and across the nation was forum shopping: devising a compelling constitutional case, but then bringing it in a federal district where plaintiffs could hope to land before a sympathetic judge who would be more predisposed to rule in their favor and against socially restrictive laws. Sitting in a geographically sprawling jurisdiction, Justice was the only sitting judge in four of the six divisions of the district court. Consequently, getting a case assigned to Judge Justice's docket was merely a question of filing in the right region of the district.[47] Implementing this approach themselves, Daves and Rodkin brought their challenge knowing that Judge Justice was all but certain to hear it.

Following their meeting with the parents of the children excluded from Tyler schools, Daves and Rodkin reached out to the MALDEF offices in San Antonio, who referred them to Peter Roos, the director of education litigation at MALDEF in San Francisco. MALDEF was a relatively new group in the legal advocacy field, founded less than a decade earlier as an outgrowth of the Chicano movement but deeply rooted in the civil rights movement. MALDEF sought to build upon the successful expansion of rights for African Americans during the 1960s by achieving the same federal support and protections for the rights of Mexican Americans during the 1970s.

MALDEF emerged in the late 1960s when Pete Tijerina, a leader of the civic organization League of United Latin American Citizens (LULAC), began exploring the possibility of establishing an organization similar to the NAACP Legal Defense Fund (NAACP LDF), but with a focus on the plight of Mexican Americans. Jack Greenberg of the NAACP helped connect Tijerina with the Ford Foundation, and within a year, MALDEF was incorporated in 1968 with a $2.2 million five-year grant to implement a series of legal service programs.

In its strategic approach it was explicitly modeled after the NAACP LDF, with Greenberg sitting on its board of directors and LDF attorney Vilma Martinez, who would later become executive director of MALDEF, serving as a liaison between the two organizations and assisting with the initial Ford grant application.

For its first few years, MALDEF struggled on many fronts. Inundated with routine legal aid cases that would be settled out of court, it struggled to bring cases that would trigger affirmative litigation over access and civil rights. While the initial plan included a desire for the organization to be staffed with many Mexican American attorneys, there were few experienced Mexican American civil rights lawyers on staff at its inception, a situation the Ford Foundation sought to address in the long term by establishing thirty-five scholarships for Mexican American law students, but which in the short term meant relying on non–Mexican American attorneys.

Finally, some of its San Antonio staff, including Tijerina, were deemed "militant" and openly feuded in the press with the board, a perception that caused the Ford Foundation to send in outside evaluators to examine MALDEF's activities in the 1970s, leading to the relocation of the main office to San Francisco and the replacement of Tijerina as executive director.[48] Its new executive director, Vilma Martinez, set up an education litigation project where MALDEF pursued cases addressing bilingual education and school desegregation.[49] Soon, the organization began to gain traction with cases before the Supreme Court. Initially focused exclusively on the rights of Mexican Americans, MALDEF had recently expanded its mission to pursue protections for Mexican Americans and Mexican immigrants regardless of immigration status.[50]

After committing to this expanded effort to demand rights for immigrants regardless of immigration status, MALDEF began looking for cases regarding educational rights for unauthorized children, believing they represented the strongest channels through which to challenge restrictive legislation. The organization hoped to get a case before Judge Justice, as MALDEF was well familiar with his left-leaning jurisprudence, or another more left-leaning judge. When Daves called, Roos immediately headed to Tyler.[51]

Like Daves, Roos was part of a new generation of young law school graduates involved in the burgeoning legal services movement during the 1960s. He became engaged in the issues surrounding the educational challenges of poor children as a young law student at the University of California, Hastings, and gained his experience in education litigation at two legal aid offices in

California. After a few years at the Center for Law and Education at Harvard where he worked on educational rights for handicapped children, he joined MALDEF in 1975, overseeing both the development of education litigation and the formulation of the organization's broader advocacy strategies.[52]

Soon after Roos arrived in Tyler, he and Daves filed the *Plyler* case on behalf of the plaintiffs. With the case set to be heard by Judge Justice as they had hoped, Roos and Daves also moved for a closed hearing and an injunction to have the plaintiff families' identities kept secret. Judge Justice allowed the use of the anonymous designation in the caption of the case, and although he would not allow the hearing to be closed, he scheduled it to begin at 6 am and arranged for the plaintiffs to enter through a side door to lessen the chances of their identities becoming public. Roos and Daves also sought a protective order to keep the INS from deporting their clients because of their participation in the case, but Judge Justice refused to grant the request.[53]

From the beginning, Judge Justice, Roos, and others understood the larger political issues at stake. Roos reached out to federal officials to gain their opinion and Judge Justice invited their participation with a brief. Michael Wise, a young trial attorney in the Civil Rights Division of the Justice Department, was assigned to examine the case and later recalled his supervisors telling him that Judge Justice had contacted them and asked them to participate as well, and due to his progressive nature, "we try to do something if he asks us to do it." Wise's supervisors wanted to be helpful and were worried that the US Attorney for the Eastern District might try to deport the unauthorized children given the political climate in East Texas. Ultimately, the Justice Department decided to participate in the case, and Wise was sent to Tyler to represent the department's view and ensure that the local officials did not attempt to deport the unauthorized children.[54] Once in Tyler, the local officer assured Wise "that the INS would not take any steps to obtain the names of the plaintiffs nor would it take any special action in their respect."[55]

Outside the courtroom there was a lot of confusion with regard to the implications of the injunction keeping the plaintiffs' identities secret. Local newspapers incorrectly reported that the injunction was a blanket protection order to prevent deportation of the plaintiff families under any circumstances. Local residents expressed their anger. "These people are illegal aliens," a restaurant owner fumed, "violators of the laws of the land, yet a judge can protect them against that law."[56] News reports surfaced that US Attorney John Hannah "had reviewed the Tyler matter and referred it to Dallas immigration authorities," and rumors began circulating in the newspapers that Hannah was seeking to deport the plaintiffs and conduct an immigration sweep in Tyler for the purpose of intimidation of the Mexican American community.[57]

In response to these news reports, Roos immediately wrote on September 13 to Leonel Castillo, the Commissioner of the INS, on behalf of his clients. Roos demanded that any "[g]overnmental retribution against those who seek the aid of the courts to protect the civil rights of their children should not be countenanced by your office," and warned that any such action would "be a clear effort to deny these persons an opportunity to vindicate their civil rights through the Courts." In addition, Roos noted the foreign policy implications of any deportations in response to the suit, noting that Mexico would oppose the actions.[58] Several days later, William Chambers, director of the Dallas district of INS, announced it would not try to deport those involved in the case. Chambers said that his position would not change unless he was told by the Department of Justice to do otherwise.

While MALDEF began its litigation efforts in Tyler, it also began to look for similar cases around the country as part of a broader strategy to address similar types of educational discrimination. For example, on September 15, MALDEF staff attorney Morris Baller reached out to a legal services attorney in Chicago who had sued the Chicago Board of Education, challenging its exclusion of unauthorized schoolchildren on equal protection grounds. Baller discussed the complexity and difficulty of the legal arguments implicit in the challenge and expressed his interest in sharing strategies and assistance.[59] Baller also responded to John Serrano of the Maricopa County Legal Aid Society in Arizona who had written to MALDEF seeking resource files on making legal challenges to the exclusion of immigrant children from public schools. Baller wrote that they were "extremely interested in the issue" and asked if there was any means by which MALDEF might assist.[60] Peter Roos followed up on a possible litigation lead in Tucson, Arizona where the local school superintendent had recently announced that the school district would begin requiring either a birth certificate or a permanent resident alien card for each student. Roos expressed interest in joining with a group of Arizona plaintiffs challenging the order.[61]

As seen through the litigation MALDEF was pursuing in Arizona and Illinois, the barring of access to public education for unauthorized students was becoming more commonplace in many areas across the country and was an issue of natural interest to MALDEF. In California, reports that some districts were excluding students if they could not provide documentation of legal residency status prompted Wilson Riles, the California superintendent of public instruction and director of education, to write to all district and county superintendents in defense of unauthorized students' access to public education. Riles reminded them that the California education code did not make a distinction between legal residents and unauthorized students.[62] Even after Riles's reminder, the issue continued to arise and in Oakland later that year, rumors again surfaced that certain schools were checking immigration status at registration. This prompted the district's legal advisor, Sandra Woliver, to remind the superintendents of the district's duty to provide free public education to all students.[63]

As the issue was being weighed in communities in California and across the country, back in Tyler, Judge Justice reached a decision. MALDEF's careful strategy of forum shopping paid off. In finding for the plaintiffs, Judge Justice wrote that the Texas statute violated the Fourteenth Amendment in denying the students equal protection under the law. He also ruled that the statute and policy were preempted by federal immigration law as well as the Protocol of Buenos Aires, a multilateral treaty to which the United States was a party.[64]

MALDEF lawyers were delighted with the decision. From the beginning of MALDEF's participation in the case, Vilma Martinez and others understood the potential of a favorable ruling to set precedent against similar legislation and school practices in other jurisdictions as well as to potentially open the door for expanding the rights of immigrants more broadly. But despite MALDEF's plans to extend the ruling to other states and use it as a positive precedent, there was little time to celebrate as the decision was promptly appealed by the state of Texas to the US Court of Appeals for the Fifth Circuit.

The Debate Spreads

Sparked by Judge Justice's decision, within weeks cases were filed around Texas by additional legal services lawyers challenging the same statute. Ultimately, the various complaints filed in the state's four federal districts were consolidated into a single pleading, *Texas v. In Re Alien School Children*, which was assigned to Judge Woodrow Seals of the Southern District of Texas based in Houston.

Judge Seals had a similar path to the bench as Judge Justice, but unlike Justice had a reputation for unpredictability. Born in Louisiana, Seals had moved to Texas to attend law school after serving in World War II. During the

1950s he was involved in state politics and was Harris County Democratic Chairman, later serving as John F. Kennedy's campaign manager in the area in 1960. With Senator Yarborough's support, President Kennedy named him a US Attorney in Texas in 1961, and President Johnson appointed him to the district court in 1966. Judge Seals was deeply religious, and his faith was well entwined with his jurisprudence. A devout Methodist, he served as a lay leader in his congregation and pushed the church to become more involved in some of the pressing political and social justice issues that were roiling the nation. As chair of the Methodist Conference Board of Christian Social Concerns in 1971, he created debates about abortion and the Vietnam War, a striking form of activism.

The legal strategies used by both sides in the consolidated cases before Judge Seals were similar to those in *Plyler*. While the students' attorneys challenged the constitutionality of the new state law, attorneys for the school districts noted that the schools were struggling to address just the influx of legal immigrant children.[65]

Attorneys for both the students and the state sought to bring in outside support to their cause. The Texas Attorney General's office contacted the Mountain States Legal Foundation, one of several new conservative legal services groups, and asked them to participate in the case.[66] These conservative legal activists sought to frame the case as an example of the growing intrusion of the federal government into the right to self-government and feared that the courts would use it and other cases to create an even wider notion of personal rights that was anathema to the larger conservative community beyond Texas.

Just as the 1960s created numerous groups in pursuit of expanding the gains of the Warren court and the Great Society, so too did it engender the growth of the conservative movement in reaction to the rights revolution of the 1960s. One part of the conservative opposition was a new public interest law movement. This legal movement was born from the larger conservative movement, particularly in California, where the election of Ronald Reagan in 1966 ushered in significant reforms to the welfare system that tightened eligibility, reduced benefits, and increased work incentives. The battle over welfare reform in California during Reagan's eight years in office was fierce, and the changes he helped create had been thoroughly attacked by liberal reform groups and legal aid societies. In response, many of Governor Reagan's advisors and many conservative activists, including Edwin Meese, began to discuss the need for a public interest law group that could play an oppositional role to the liberal groups in litigation.[67]

The first such group, the Pacific Legal Foundation (PLF), was founded in 1973 by a group of Reagan staff members and conservative activists from across California. William French Smith, who later served as Attorney General in the Reagan presidential administration, was a key supporter and helped secure funding for the group by connecting the activists with John Simon Fluor, a California industrialist frustrated with the environmental movement, who served as PLF's first chairman of the board.[68]

Growing out of the success of PLF, the National Legal Center for the Public Interest was founded in 1975 with the goal of replicating the PLF model across the country, including through the formation of the Mountain States Legal Foundation (MSLF). As MSLF argued, there was a need for their advocacy as "[t]he voice of the silent majority had been silent too long while the forces of the few learned the value of achieving in the courts what they could not achieve through negotiation or legislation."[69] The MSLF Board in 1977 included key Reagan supporters such as Joseph Coors Sr., president of the Coors Brewing Company and a founder of the Heritage Foundation, and James Watt, who was MSLF's president and chief legal officer and later served as Secretary of the Interior in the Reagan administration.[70]

For the MSLF, the cases in Texas were a microcosm of the broader issues that had midwifed their own existence: the gross expansion of the rights revolution of the 1960s, the creation of a higher tax burden to pay for this government expansion that was placed on the backs of regular Americans, and the trampling of rights of local and state institutions by an overreaching federal leviathan. In support of its small government beliefs, the MSLF filed an amicus brief in *In Re Alien Schoolchildren* in support of Texas's right to determine for itself whether to educate unauthorized students.[71]

In addition to its legal activism, the MSLF drew attention to the case through articles in its newsletter, *The Litigator*. The group's appeal echoed the rhetoric and language that was common to conservative activists in the tax revolt movement of the late 1970s. MSLF asked their membership to question if those illegally in the United States "have a federally guaranteed right to an education paid for by state taxpayers?"[72] But more than that, the MSLF and its allies argued the case was an important battle in the ongoing larger war over whether the rights of individuals growing out of the rights revolution trumped the state's rights, and that the ultimate outcome would decide "whether the states' sovereignty [over educational policy] may be defeated by the identification by a federal court of a hitherto unidentified fundamental educational 'right.'"[73]

In sum, like MALDEF, the MSLF believed these cases could have a much broader impact than determining education policy in a few Texas districts, and they rallied their membership by warning that a positive decision for the students that would allow unauthorized students and their families to receive a state education had the potential to create other fundamental rights to which unauthorized immigrants, and by extension others, would be entitled.[74] The MSLF made clear to its supporters that a great deal was at stake in the Texas case for conservatives nationwide.

To bolster their case against this strong organized opposition, the lawyers for the plaintiffs in the *In Re Alien School Children* cases sought consolidation with the *Plyler* case. But as it was preparing its appeal, MALDEF had no interest in consolidation. MALDEF hoped that by preserving its independence in the Tyler case, it could more effectively use *Plyler* as part of a larger move to expand the constitutional rights of unauthorized immigrants. Roos feared consolidation would allow the opposition to buttress their weak record, as at the district court the opposing counsel had not effectively built their argument with supporting evidence. Consolidation also risked the opposition bringing in better and more well-funded opposing counsel.

Roos further believed that the narrow confinement of the case to Tyler, and no other districts or the state as a whole, would make it easier for the appeals court to rule in their favor as "the stark Tyler facts almost demand a ruling in our favor while a broader factual setting might be disturbing to the court." In other words, *Plyler* would be an easier pill for the court to swallow, but one that could eventually be implemented as a means of extracting more expansive rulings. "[O]nce we have a Tyler victory, we will have started down a slippery slope which will make it impossible for the court to legally or logistically limit the ruling to Tyler."[75] But the other parties involved were persistent and throughout 1979 made motions to try to consolidate the cases that MALDEF continually rebuffed.[76]

While Roos and MALDEF struggled to hold their ground against those seeking to consolidate in order to pursue their own ambitious legal strategy, the main focus of their time was on getting ready for the appeal. In the run-up to the Fifth Circuit arguments, both sides worked to secure additional support from outside groups to bolster their respective positions, and Roos turned to other national groups involved in education and immigration.[77] Roos worked with some of the groups to align the briefs with MALDEF's priorities. For example, he worked with the National Education Association to raise a challenge in an amicus brief to the tuition aspects of the Texas statute.[78]

But it was the support of the federal government that was most important. After its success at gaining federal support in the lower court, MALDEF anticipated that the Justice Department would again weigh in for them in front of the circuit court. In reality, however, the government's support was far from certain. Roos soon voiced his concern to Assistant Attorney General for the Civil Rights Division Drew Days on March 28, 1979, writing, "[i]f support were withdrawn now, it would be worse than if the Department had remained silent from the beginning."[79]

—the legal and
political organization
on the right & left

MALDEF   vs.   PLF
(Pacific Legal
Foundation)

&

MSLF
(Mountain States
Legal Foundation)

2

"A Subclass of Illiterates"

THE PRESIDENTIAL POLITICS OF
UNAUTHORIZED IMMIGRANT EDUCATION

PETER ROOS'S CONCERNS about the potentially wavering support of the Carter administration were not unfounded. In Washington, the administration was actively grappling with its participation in *Plyler* as the case represented a nexus of tenuous issues. *Plyler* brought together the politicization of the Justice Department, the administration's foundering immigration policy, and its shaky commitment to civil rights.

In the wake of Watergate, President Jimmy Carter had campaigned on the platform of depoliticizing the Department of Justice and, as Attorney General Bell interpreted it, "[t]he administration's views on matters of the law . . . were to be decided at the Justice Department not 1600 Pennsylvania Avenue."[1] This focus on independence meant that during the early years of the Carter administration, the Attorney General was reticent to share information with the White House, and Attorney General Bell sought to isolate Solicitor General McCree and others at the department from the political players at the White House. But over the previous two years, the Attorney General and the White House had skirmished over department decisions and by 1979, the White House and the Justice Department had a complicated relationship with regard to political influence in the department's proceedings. One such disagreement between the White House and the department was over the 1973 killing of Santos Rodriguez, a case of particular importance to Latino interest groups. Rodriguez, a twelve-year-old boy, was shot point blank by a Dallas police officer while handcuffed in a police car, and the Department of Justice refused, even when pressured from the White House, to prosecute the officer for the shooting under federal civil rights statutes after the officer had been convicted under state statutes.[2]

Plyler also came at a vexing point in the administration's efforts to reform immigration policy. By the time of the Fifth Circuit arguments, the Carter administration's record on addressing immigration issues was one of failure. Two years earlier, in 1977, Carter had proposed a comprehensive plan for addressing illegal immigration, which was quickly introduced in the House and Senate. Largely crafted without the input of congressional leadership or even any key constituencies, the proposal immediately became mired in conflict. It languished, and eventually the White House and other congressional leaders formed the Select Commission on Immigration and Refugee Policy (SCIRP) in 1978, also known as the Hesburgh Commission after its chair, Reverend Theodore Hesburgh. The Hesburgh Commission was tasked with developing a comprehensive immigration and refugee policy plan that would have broader consensus support than the administration's failed plan.[3]

The Plyler case not only highlighted the Carter administration's immigration policy weakness, it also brought to light the administration's reluctant commitment to civil rights. Carter was in a unique position; as a white southern governor, he had campaigned as a centrist outsider in the wake of Watergate, and his success was dependent upon receiving continued support from a diverse coalition. Elected largely because of his popularity in the new south and industrial north, Carter won 63 percent of the union vote and two-thirds of the bottom income spectrum.[4] However, he also needed to maintain the support of traditional democratic strongholds of minority voters. Carter was in a precarious position, wavering from the path of rights expansion seen in his predecessors, looking to avoid any issues that might fracture his base even further.[5]

With these three issues at hand: DOJ's politicization, the administration's failing immigration policy, and its uncertain commitment to civil rights, the administration's various arms began to argue over the scope of the government's position and brief. Far from being based solely on the merits of the legal arguments, political and related policy concerns played key roles in shaping the government's position in the *Plyler* appeal. Just as the plaintiffs and the defendants understood it, administration actors saw *Plyler* as potentially having much wider implications for federal benefits and other rights and thus sought to craft a position that was both bureaucratically practical and politically defensible. In the end, the Carter administration's brief reflected the changing nature of the Democratic Party at the time: still committed to the rights revolution of the 1960s but increasingly influenced by those in the party committed to restraining the growth of entitlement programs—a faction whose power was at a nadir in the 1970s but whose power within the party would increase drastically over the next two decades.

From the beginning of the Fifth Circuit appeal process, it became clear that the government was not comfortable with the reach of Judge Justice's opinion. Immediately following the district court's decision, counsel staff at the Department of Justice, the Department of State, and the Department of Health, Education and Welfare (HEW) all analyzed Judge Justice's findings. In post-trial internal memos, the Department of Justice argued that the state's legislation violated the Equal Protection Clause, but they rejected the argument that federal immigration law preempted the state law and thus invalidated it.[6]

While the Department of Justice and the White House ultimately formed the administration's position, other agencies that were potentially impacted by the case weighed in. Internally, HEW counsels agreed with the DOJ assessment and further questioned the plaintiffs' case, noting that not only did the plaintiffs lack the specific characteristics that the Supreme Court had outlined as warranting strict scrutiny but they also considered advocating that the government stay out of the case entirely, suggesting that it "constitutionally requires, a political solution."[7] HEW officials struggled with finding a middle ground between supporting the children in their case without committing to an expansion of rights for unauthorized adults. For that reason, HEW ultimately supported "relying heavily on plaintiffs' status as minor children, and the fact that the defendants' acts harm them directly," so that the government could support their claims "without unduly expanding the rights of adult unauthorized aliens in relation to the States, and without foreclosing the options of the political branches of the Federal government." HEW wanted to retain the right to deny unauthorized adults access to many social welfare programs.[8]

The State Department too debated whether and how the administration should weigh in on the appeal. The department's Deputy Legal Advisor, William T. Lake, dismissed the plaintiffs' argument that international treaties preempted the Texas state statute on legal technicalities, but nevertheless advocated that the government's commitment to the right to education in the United States compelled the administration's involvement on behalf of the students.[9]

With the reactions to Judge Justice's ruling expressed by various agencies to the Justice Department, Drew Days began to formulate the federal participation in the case at the Fifth Circuit. Days, a former attorney for the NAACP LDF and the first African American to head the division, had been appointed by President Carter in an attempt to pacify activists upset by Carter's tapping of Griffin Bell for attorney general, whose record in pushing integration was seen by many as weak.[10] Days's appointment was also notable because up to that point, the division had always been headed by attorneys who were not identified with civil rights work or activism before their appointment, generally signaling the caution of past administrations to wade too deeply into civil rights questions. The naming of Days to the important post broke decades of legal tradition.[11]

Emerging as a key voice pushing the administration to chart a bold course in involving itself in civil rights matters, Days prepared a memorandum for Solicitor General Wade McCree urging the continued participation of the department at the Circuit Court level. On a moral and constitutional level, Days argued for intervention. In his memo to McCree, he noted that while he felt most legislation "is entitled to a degree of judicial deference on the premise that the populace will act to rectify unwise or improvident legislation," in this case, and others where the legislation is "based on hostile intent toward an identifiable group," the "courts must carefully protect those subjected to disparate treatment." That is, on such an important question, the Justice Department could not simply wait for the states passing these forms of legislation being challenged in *Plyer* to come to their senses or for the electorate to respond with their vote. Days felt the legal arguments that compelled the department's support for the plaintiffs were that the children were entitled to protection by both the Equal Protection Clause and Due Process Clause, and that the Texas statute created an unconstitutional and discriminatory classification.

Recognizing that the administration's participation was going to be based not just on the case's constitutional question, Days outlined an array of practical and political reasons for intervention. He argued the department ought to express its opinion because there was a high potential in *Plyler* that the court would opine on when ostensibly neutral classifications were actually based on national origin status. In doing so, the court could either expand or constrain the scope of suspect classifications, impacting future litigation brought by the Civil Rights Division. Days also argued participation in the case would strengthen the department's commitment to ensure that both disadvantaged and non–English speaking students receive adequate education, including access to bilingual programs.[12]

Turning to foreign policy, Days outlined a twofold reason for intervention. First, he noted that the department had been tasked with investigating any possible violations of the country's human rights obligations under the Helsinki Accords. But an even more compelling reason for intervention, Days argued, was that discrimination by a state toward foreign nationals could impact foreign relations with their home nations, echoing the *Chy Lung* decision of a century earlier.[13] Finally, Days pointed to the administration's own immigration policy position as a reason for intervention. If Congress were to pass the president's immigration plan, many unauthorized children would become legal residents, yet they would have been denied an opportunity for a basic education.[14]

Nevertheless, while Days argued for overturning the Texas statute, he did not endorse unlimited protections and rights for unauthorized immigrants. Understanding how the case could be used as a precedent for the expansion of other benefits, including welfare, Days was careful to maintain room for both the states and the federal government to impose some forms of regulation and restriction based on immigration status, but with greater latitude for federal regulation due to the "Federal responsibilities over international affairs." This regulation was admissible for Days because under the Equal Protection Clause, courts are not required to secure "for illegal aliens all the protections to which citizens, or legally admitted aliens, are entitled."[15]

Days's memo set off debate within the department about the legal merits and political aspects of the government's continued role in the case. Deputy Solicitor General Louis Claiborne was critical of many of Texas's assertions. He disputed the claim that unauthorized students were a greater educational burden than those with authorization, and highlighted how "Texas welcomes the presence of 'illegals'—for the cheap, unorganized labors they provide and the taxes they pay—while preferring not to have their children attend her schools."[16] But neither was Claiborne entirely satisfied with the strength of the students' case.[17] Nevertheless, Claiborne urged the Solicitor General to file an amicus brief on behalf of the students. Given the administration's earlier participation in the case, Claiborne argued, "there is some momentum in favor of staying with the case" in the Fifth Circuit but suggested potentially staying out of the matter should it eventually make its way to the Supreme Court.[18]

Leading the opposition to intervention was Sara Beale, an assistant to Solicitor General McCree who had clerked for him on the Sixth Circuit. Beale argued that the government should take a more conservative position, either by arguing that the Texas statute was constitutional or, if the foreign policy considerations raised by the State Department were judged compelling, to not participate in the case at all.[19] Beale believed that there was a rational basis for the statute as it was a "partial solution for the educational problems caused by the influx of Mexican immigrants."[20] Beale rejected Days's argument that "illegal aliens" were a suspect classification and argued that there was a significant difference between the rights of legal versus unauthorized immigrants, contending that given the Supreme Court's recent Fourteenth Amendment jurisprudence, equal protection was likely limited to "lawfully admitted aliens."[21]

Underlying all of these internal memos at DOJ was an awareness of the case's potential implications for broad federal policy, an issue also raised by HEW. Many at DOJ were wary that any arguments made in *Plyler* could be used to challenge the federal government's own citizenship and residency restrictions on the disbursement of benefits and entitlements. In 1978, federal statutes excluded unauthorized immigrants from federal social welfare programs, including food stamps, Supplemental Security Income, federal unemployment compensation, and Medicare, and while Congress had not excluded unauthorized immigrants from Aid to Families with Dependent Children (AFDC) or Medicaid, HEW regulations limited these programs to citizens and legally admitted immigrants.[22] Claiborne in particular engaged deeply on this issue.[23] He argued that the federal programs with alienage restrictions were of a significantly different nature than those of Texas because they were distributed to a family, whereas the educational benefits that Texas was challenging went directly to students. Recognizing the potential fallibility of his differentiation between federal and state programs, Claiborne still urged the Justice Department's participation in the case, saying "it is questionable how far we should be deterred from urging a sound result in a case . . . merely because our own house is not in the best order."

All of the internal debates within the department caught the attention of Phil Jordan and Nelson Dong, staffers in the Attorney General's office who had been tasked with watching for cases that had the potential to ignite larger public or political debates. Noting that while McCree was "leaning toward taking no position at all" on the appeal, both men urged the Attorney General to weigh in.[24] After hearing from Dong and Jordan, Attorney General Bell immediately expressed interest in weighing in on the case, but sought to limit the extent to which he was seen as ordering McCree to take a position.[25] Bell expressed his "private views" to Solicitor General McCree that "it would be better to stand mute unless asked to participate by the Fifth Circuit." If the department was asked to participate, then Bell would decide whether to consult with the White House on the administration's position or to just decide on his own.[26]

While Attorney General Bell urged McCree not to participate, the pressure from around the administration continued to mount. In a critical move, MALDEF lobbied other agencies to weigh in on the students' behalf. HEW Secretary Joseph Califano wrote to McCree arguing that the Texas statute violated the Equal Protection Clause and that education "is central to our way of life in the United States." Califano attacked the statute for penalizing the children for their parents' conduct, arguing it was "contrary to the basic concept of our system that legal burdens should bear some relationship to individual responsibility or wrongdoing."[27]

Califano urged participation not just because of the impact on the children of Texas, but because unchallenged, the Texas statute could spawn similar restrictions and negative consequences across the nation. "Over twenty-five years ago, the Supreme Court acknowledged these consequences when it observed that 'education is perhaps the most important function of State and local governments,' [in] *Brown v. Board of Education*." Califano argued that if the students, already disadvantaged because of their poverty and lack of English-speaking ability, were denied an education, "they will continue to be locked into the lowest socio-economic class with all of the consequences to our society."[28]

MALDEF also reached out to the State Department, and Deputy Secretary of State Warren Christopher urged McCree to file a supportive amicus brief. He expressed his belief that not only was federal involvement justified for legal reasons, but that foreign policy concerns called for "deal[ing] in an enlightened and humane way" with those who were in the United States to work without authorization. Christopher reminded McCree of the president's repeated public statements and commitments to the human rights of unauthorized workers, including in a recent speech to the Mexican Parliament.[29]

Under pressure from various parts of the administration, the Solicitor General sought additional guidance from Attorney General Bell. Bell reiterated his opinion that the department should stay out of cases at the appellate level unless asked by the Fifth Circuit and reached out to the White House for further direction.[30]

DOJ sent materials on the case to the White House and at the top, Phil Jordan noted that there was some discomfiture regarding the department's position.

As I told you on the phone . . . there are some strong arguments against the illegal aliens on the law (although, in fairness, the Civil Rights Division and Louis Claiborne believe a pro-illegal alien argument is winnable), and it seems a bit awkward for the Federal government to contend that Texas cannot burden illegal aliens when the Federal government itself is charged with keeping illegal aliens out of the country.[31]

Jordan raised one of the more difficult subjects at issue—the case's potential impact on other federal programs. Jordan wrote, "Food is at least as imp[ortant] as educ[ation]—If so could Cong[ress] deny AFDC benefits or life-sustaining assistance. Problem is this sticks it to certain districts and NOT others.—But Cong[ress] has banned Fed support (for aid to illegal aliens) to state systems."[32]

At the White House, Franklin White, associate director of the Domestic Policy Council, analyzed the case and wrote a recommendation for Stuart Eizenstat, director of the Domestic Policy Council, that looked at the legal arguments but also placed the case within the broader political landscape. Legally, White felt there was a strong case against the administration's participation. White believed that "the Court will not extend the benefits of the Equal Protection Clause to illegal aliens" as education has "traditionally been viewed as a matter of state and local concern." White also felt that Congress's policies and "the logic of immigration laws" allowed for alienage restrictions. In particular, given that Congress required states to verify lawful status when administering federally financed programs, White felt "it makes no sense to prohibit them from also limiting their own state funds for education to persons here lawfully." He also felt that if the students were successful in their claims, it would be hard to deny them access to AFDC. Thus, White felt the legal and policy implications suggested that the administration should not file a brief.

But while White felt the legal and policy background called for staying out, he believed the administration had to reckon with the larger domestic political forces at play. One of the primary concerns was that, given DOJ's earlier participation, failing to participate again would "be seen as an act of betrayal by Hispanic groups," because *Plyler* is viewed as a "critical case by MALDF [*sic*]." The Carter administration's immigration reform plans and lack of commitment to civil rights concerns had already strained the administration's relationship with Latino groups and constituents. These tensions had continued to escalate as the Latino constituency was angered that the Department of Justice had recently decided not to bring charges in the death of Larry Lozano, a twenty-seven-year-old who was allegedly beaten to death in a jail cell in Odessa, Texas, as well as with the nomination of Benjamin Civiletti to Attorney General.[33] White noted that with this souring of relations as background, "our abandoning [Plyler v.] Doe at this point would run the risk of destroying our credibility with them."[34] For White, the political concerns ultimately outweighed the legal arguments so he urged Eizenstat to tell DOJ that "Justice should continue to support the plaintiffs by seeking leave to file an amicus without awaiting a request from the [Circuit] Court."[35]

Eizenstat agreed with White that it was unlikely that the Circuit Court would rule for the plaintiffs, but disagreed with White's conclusion.[36] Eizenstat was concerned with filing because "This will (a) impose big costs on school districts (b) go contrary to DeCanas. Rich H. [Hutchinson, Staff Secretary] didn't mention this as a big Hispanic issue." Ultimately Eizenstat favored restraint, arguing "I'd wait until Fifth Circuit asks us before filing. We can say we made our position known in the lower court . . . Tell Phil we would leave it up to their discretion."[37] And with that note, the issue was punted back to the Justice Department.

It wasn't until after the deadline for filing in the Fifth Circuit, in a meeting with the LULAC leadership, that new Attorney General Benjamin Civiletti announced the department would file a brief which "only would be an interpretation of the law and not a filing on behalf of the parties in the suit" as they had in the Southern District before Judge Seals.[38]

Once the Department of Justice submitted its brief to the Fifth Circuit in the fall of 1979, MALDEF praised the move.[39] Internally, Roos was deeply relieved that the Department of Justice had filed a supportive brief given the resistance within the administration. His notes to the MALDEF Executive Committee shed some light on what had swung the pendulum in favor of the students. Calling it a "major effort" to "coax a supportive brief," Roos attributed their success to the support MALDEF had secured from HEW and the State Department "which has resulted in a breakthrough."[40] At the end of the day, political concerns and pressures from elements outside DOJ had prevailed in the Carter administration's position in the Fifth Circuit filing. But it was highly contested, as conservative elements with a focus on restraining the growth of entitlement programs had forced a debate on the merits of the case across the department and the administration.

Seeing the Plyler plaintiff's success in securing the federal government's participation with an amicus brief in the Fifth Circuit, the plaintiffs in In Re Alien School Children urged similar participation in their case before Judge

Seals in the Southern District of Texas. Emerging again as a liberal force within the department, Drew Days wrote to the Attorney General urging participation and going a step further by filing as a party plaintiff instead, "because of the state-wide impact of the action, the additional procedural advantages we would enjoy, and the greater weight that might be given to the government's views."[41] Days succeeded in convincing the Attorney General, and the department filed a motion to join the suit as plaintiffs, positing that the Texas law "invidiously and irrationally" discriminated against immigrants.[42] This position drew the ire of opponents, including the criticism of Susan J. Dasher, the Assistant Attorney General for the state of Texas. Dasher rebuked the actions of the DOJ, saying "Regulating the flow of illegal immigration is a federal responsibility . . . We have no power to regulate the flow, and since it's a federal responsibility, they ought to come up with some of the money. They aren't, and then they have the nerve to come in as plaintiffs."[43]

Decisions and Reactions

While *Plyler* was still pending before the Fifth Circuit, after a brief trial in Houston, Judge Seals reached a decision in *In Re Alien Schoolchildren* in July 1980. With many similarities to Judge Justice's decision in *Plyler*, Seals decided for the plaintiffs, holding that the Texas statute violated the Equal Protection Clause and ordering the schools involved in the litigation to admit the unauthorized students without a fee.[44] Texas Attorney General Mark White immediately vowed to appeal and attacked the federal government's position in the case by returning once more to a fiscal argument, saying it told the state "to pay for the failures of the Justice Department." White argued that the states were being forced to pay for the inability of the federal government to control immigration.[45]

Concerned with the significant political ramifications of the case, G. G. Garcia, one of Governor Bill Clements's aides, urged Clements to direct White not to appeal the decision. Garcia implored Clements to consider how "politically damaging" pushing the case forward would be to his important relationship with the government of Mexico, and also to Ronald Reagan's efforts in the Latino community.[46] Despite Garcia's warning, Governor Clements publicly denounced the decision and vowed to appeal.

Echoing the dismay expressed by White, Clements, and other Texas officials, MSLF senior attorney Maxwell Miller, who had filed a brief in the case, responded to Seals's decision by turning again to the incendiary rhetoric that had been so effective in the California tax revolt in 1978. He wrote in the widely circulated MSLF newsletter that the ultimate losers in the case were Texas taxpayers, who he argued had to pay for benefits for those who were subject to deportation, as well as the children of Texas who would suffer as Texans' tax dollars would be "stretched to pay for . . . children of persons who frequently do not pay those taxes." But to Miller, the defeat at the district court level signaled an even greater loss, namely that "[t]he 'rule of law' to which we have avowedly been dedicated since the founding of the republic also lost."[47]

While the governor, the state attorney general, and MSLF vowed to fight the ruling, others in Texas were pleased with Seals's decision. News outlets like the *Dallas Times Herald* and the *Dallas Morning News* praised the decision, and leaders including former Senator Ralph Yarborough and Judge Justice were delighted with Judge Seals's opinion, with Justice writing to Seals, calling it "Miracles of miracles!" and Yarborough hailing it as "statesmanship to the highest order on the part of the court."[48]

For Yarborough, the decision meant that unauthorized children would not be "condemned to be a generation of alien, non-citizen, non-educated, unopportunitied people." Like the MSLF attorneys, Yarborough also saw the decision as a creation of rights, but he praised the way in which Seals had "granted rights to one group of people without taking away the correlative rights from another." For Yarborough, it was this aspect of the *In Re Alien School Children* decision that "reflects the spirit and vision of America."[49]

When Texas appealed the *In Re Alien School Children* decision to the Fifth Circuit where *Plyler* was pending, they also sought a stay of the Seals order so that the school districts involved in the litigation would not have to admit unauthorized students to school until the litigation was concluded. The Fifth Circuit granted the stay on August 12, 1980, but several weeks later, on September 4, Supreme Court Justice Lewis Powell, the sitting justice for the circuit, dissolved the stay pending the decision of the Fifth Circuit, and the school districts were required to admit the unauthorized students for school that fall.[50]

Collectively, these actions put the issue of education of unauthorized students, which had remained largely quiet after the government's decision to file in the *Plyler* appeal and as a party plaintiff in *In Re Alien School Children*, back on the administration's radar. But ultimately, it was events outside the courtroom that drove education for unauthorized immigrants to the forefront of the White House's agenda and influenced the resulting policy debates.

Searching for Political Solutions

During the fall of 1980, rising domestic political pressures including the impending presidential election led the Carter administration to publicly address the issue of unauthorized students' access to education in a way that differed significantly from its positions espoused in court. While White House staffers continued to seek out discrete policy solutions that would help to diffuse the issue, on the campaign trail, Carter and others embraced more neutral and vague positions, distancing themselves from the positions they had taken in court.

Political pressure on the Carter administration began to mount after the schools were ordered to admit the unauthorized students while the litigation was pending, as it gave states new fodder in a long-running debate over school construction funding. For some time, local and state officials from several states had been complaining that rising numbers of students were causing overcrowding in schools and lobbied the federal government for more funding for school construction. Immediately after Judge Seals's decision, several Texas officials met with Stuart Eizenstat to urge the White House to approve more school construction funding in border communities.[51] Eizenstat began to explore the possibility of the administration potentially supporting a bill sponsored by Senator Bentsen of Texas which sought to provide additional school funding through existing aid programs. The Bentsen legislation was developed in response to the Supreme Court's 1972 ruling in *San Antonio Independent School District v. Rodríguez* which held that the San Antonio Independent School District's financing system, based on local property taxes, was not an unconstitutional violation of the Fourteenth Amendment's Equal Protection Clause even if it caused inter-district expenditure disparities. Bentsen's legislation aimed to provide greater funding for schools in poorer school districts.

Adding pressure to the situation was the fact that Texas was of critical electoral importance to President Carter in 1980 as he sought to win reelection. It had long been a solidly Democratic state, and no Democrat had won the presidency in the twentieth century without winning Texas.[52] However, Texas had been trending toward the Republican Party for some time, and by 1980 it was a battleground state. While Reagan had been polling widely ahead there during the summer of 1980, by September, news outlets were suggesting that polls were narrowing and a *Texas Monthly* survey released at the end of September showed President Carter with an eight-point lead.[53]

Perhaps the two most pronounced groups at the center of the state electoral battle were moderate Republicans found in areas like the affluent suburbs on the west side of Houston, and Mexican Americans centered mainly around San Antonio and in South Texas. Democratic strategists felt Carter would not be able to win unless he garnered solid Mexican American support, and James Baker, a senior Reagan strategist, echoed them when he declared, "The election in Texas is going to turn on the Hispanic vote."[54] Just four years earlier in 1976, when 480,000 Hispanics were registered to vote in Texas, Jimmy Carter had garnered 76 percent of the Hispanic vote and won the state by fewer than 150,000 votes.[55] Given the importance of that growing segment of the Latino population, both candidates worked hard to woo Latino voters that fall.

Facing a tough battle, President Carter followed his advisors' suggestions and sought to distance himself from the government's role in the case and instead embrace a neutral position which would alienate neither Latino voters nor moderate Republicans who were drawn to the fiscal rhetoric used by conservative activists. When President Carter traveled to Texas on a campaign swing shortly after Justice Powell had ordered the state to enroll the unauthorized students, his staff gave him talking points and background information on the case and its political implications in the state.

In briefing him, Carter's staff noted the concerns local officials had raised about overcrowding and lack of resources and informed the president of an upcoming administration announcement supporting Senator Bentsen's school construction funding legislation. But turning to the recent court actions and Justice Powell's order, they noted that, although Texas's Latino population would probably support the ruling and order, it had the potential to alienate some suburban moderates. Nevertheless, given division over the issue across the state, Carter's staff suggested that the president stick to a vague statement supporting some federal support along the lines of Senator Bentsen's bill to alleviate some of the strain on local communities.[56]

Carter was asked about the *Plyler* case and Judge Seals's decision in *In Re Alien School Children* at a campaign stop on September 15 in Corpus Christi. Carter punted, responding without mentioning the Justice Department's role in the cases, and sought to distance himself from the controversial cases by saying that "[t]his is a matter that is in the Federal courts. It would not be proper for me as President, because of the separation between the Executive and the Judiciary, to involve myself in it." As to funding, Carter ignored the impending announcement of White House support for Senator Bentsen's bill and instead argued that impact aid should not be given to Texas schools as, he argued, it was meant to support areas surrounding military bases where the federal government had caused an influx of students and not border states just "because the state government happens to disagree with the Federal Government on an issue."[57]

Governor Reagan was unable to avoid the issue when he campaigned in 1980. Early in the primary, during an April primary debate in Houston with George H. W. Bush, both were asked about education for unauthorized students.[58] Governor Bush responded first and called on the government to address unauthorized immigration more broadly in a way that would be "sensitive" to both labor and human needs, because the current situation was "creating a whole society of really honorable, decent family-loving people that are in violation of the law . . . and exacerbating relations with Mexico." Speaking more directly to the issue of unauthorized immigration, Bush thought "I would reluctantly say I think they would get whatever . . . the society is giving to their neighbors." He didn't want "to see a whole—think of six- and eight-year-old kids, being made, you know, one, totally uneducated and made to feel that they are living . . . outside the law."

When the moderator turned to Governor Reagan, he voiced his support for an open flow of individuals and a recognition of the issues in Mexico; he claimed 40–50 percent unemployment was driving people to cross the border. Rather than put up a fence, as was being floated, Reagan suggested, "Why don't we work out some recognition of our mutual problems, make it possible for them to come here legally with work permits, and then, while they're working and earning here, they pay taxes here. And when they want to go back, they can go back. And they can cross, and open the border both ways by understanding their problems."[59]

But, like Carter, when the polls showed the race tightening that fall, Reagan gave a more nuanced and conservative response. When he returned to Texas that fall for the general election, he was asked about the issue during a campaign stop in Brownsville. He noted that he was "disturbed that the Carter administration has allowed this problem to become a burden to your district's taxpayers." But, like Carter, Reagan demurred from taking any stance on the issue, instead promising that the issue would be carefully reviewed were he to be elected.[60]

While the president and Governor Reagan sought to avoid the issue, the increasing pressure of campaign efforts to woo voters in Texas kept it front and center. White House aides sought to manage the situation by keeping both sides satisfied. Fearing the potential backlash from an endorsement of funding education for unauthorized immigrants, but seeking to mollify many Latino communities, the administration did more to highlight its support of Senator Bentsen's legislation, which would fund border schools more broadly, by showcasing its support with an event held along with Vice President Mondale.

Even after the administration came out publicly in support of the Bentsen bill, the issue of funding for the education of both documented and unauthorized immigrant schoolchildren remained controversial to many in Texas, to the consternation of White House officials. In preparation for the home stretch of the campaign, Jim Dyke, Vice President Mondale's domestic policy advisor, outlined the status of the various court proceedings and encouraged Mondale to stress the "complexity of the entire undocumented worker situation," suggesting that Mondale sidestep specifics by answering that the Hesburgh Commission would be preparing recommendations.[61]

The growing concern with government spending that was a major issue in the campaign left the White House feeling vulnerable regarding its position on the Bentsen bill. Fiscal conservatives argued the Bentsen legislation was a back-door approach to funding free public school for unauthorized students and thus would lead to even more government spending. Staff advocated that if Carter was asked on the campaign trial, he should respond that the bill's funding mechanism was based on the number of legal immigrant children, so the government was not going to fund unauthorized students' education under the bill.[62]

The White House staff also worried about another fiscal-based attack, but this one alleged that the Carter position was an unfunded mandate; that is, how could the federal government ask the people of Texas to bear the entire cost of children who were not in the country legally?[63] Here again the White House staff suggested stressing the complexity of the issue and punting.[64] Nowhere in the campaign preparation materials was there any suggestion that the president reference the position the Carter administration had taken in either of the cases. With the pressures of the 1980 election to win moderate voters and address government spending, the administration's role as party plaintiff in *In Re Alien* and the amicus brief before the Fifth Circuit in *Plyler* were removed from public view, replaced by broad statements of support for funding legally admitted immigrant students and broad generalities about the difficult nature of the situation.

While publicly distancing themselves from the Justice Department's support of the children in the *Plyler* case and referring the broader issue to the Hesburgh Commission on the campaign trail, White House officials privately began to investigate ways to neutralize the issue by working on policy prescriptions outside the court system, beyond support of the Bentsen legislation, which would not allow them to fund schools for unauthorized students. At the direction of Eizenstat, Deputy Director of Domestic Affairs Bert Carp, Domestic Policy staffer Debbie Hyatt, and the Department of Education began to look into both the "feasibility and desirability" of funding schools for unauthorized students through funding streams at the Department of Education.

When Hyatt reached out to the newly independent Department of Education (DOE), she discovered that just as the issue of free public education for unauthorized children was divisive in the public domain, the Department of Education itself was divided on the issue.[65] DOE staff believed that while the unauthorized immigrant students and their school districts needed fiscal support, they were uncertain about whether the state or the federal government should provide it.[66] Hyatt presented four options to Eizenstat; three of them involved addressing the issue via legislation and the fourth used the secretary's discretionary authority to fund a program for unauthorized immigrants' education, which Hyatt preferred as it would be quicker since it did not involve passing legislation.[67]

But the White House senior domestic policy staff dismissed all four proposals from the Department of Education and instead debated either simply restating support of the Bentsen legislation or proposing entirely new legislation.[68] Carp was adamant that any remedy needed to paint broad strokes about the population the funding would support, and felt they might be able to avoid being seen as funding unauthorized immigrants. Bill Fisher, a staffer in the Department of Education, weighed in, arguing that while there was a clear need on the ground and political support from the two Texas senators for funding unauthorized students' education, he warned that addressing the larger issue was technically and politically difficult.[69] He agreed with Carp that in order to make the program politically viable, it would have to be billed as a transitional program with a focus on assisting the school districts rather than a program that would help the unauthorized students. Even so, he feared this "distinction could easily be lost on those with strong views on the 'problem' of Mexican nationals in Texas."[70]

After weighing all of the advice, Eizenstat decided the administration should not do anything new, determining that simply restating support for the Bentsen legislation seemed like the best option.[71] The vice president's remarks during an appearance in Laredo, Texas on October 25 reflected this decision to avoid staking out a politically vulnerable position, as Mondale simply restated the administration's support for Senator Bentsen's bill.[72] White House aides, while interested in finding funding mechanisms to relieve some of the pressure from a volatile situation, were not willing to risk public support in the election over the issue of the education of unauthorized students.

By the late fall of 1980, the Carter administration had effectively back-tracked from its earlier support in the briefs for education rights for unauthorized students, as electoral pressures pushed the White House to adopt nothing beyond a vague position of supporting increased funding for school districts with many legally admitted students.

Yet, while the Carter administration sought to maintain as neutral a position as possible before the election, on October 20 the Fifth Circuit finally handed down its decision in the *Plyler* case. The Court of Appeals affirmed Judge Justice's ruling that all "aliens," even those illegally within territorial boundaries of the United States, were entitled to equal protection and that the Texas statute violated the Fourteenth Amendment, whether under a mere rational basis standard or some more stringent standard, though the court overruled Judge Justice's ruling that the statute was pre-empted by federal laws or international agreements.[73] In February 1981, the Fifth Circuit issued a summary affirmance of the district court's opinion in the *In Re Alien* cases, merging them with the *Plyler* case, and on May 4, 1981, the Supreme Court agreed to hear both cases. The Fifth Circuit decisions guaranteed the issue would remain part of the national debate for the incoming Reagan administration.

Wavering Support

As soon as the Supreme Court agreed to hear the cases, Roos began to adjust his legal strategy for arguments before the high court. Recognizing the national stage, he sought to broaden his base of support among Washington activist groups, manage grassroots support, and maintain the support of the federal government under the leadership of the new Reagan administration—no small feat.

Roos, understanding that many of the amicus briefs being sent to the court supporting their position were from groups known for providing immigration assistance, sought to build support for the cases among additional varied activist groups, including the American Civil Liberties Union, the American Jewish Congress, and the Western Center for Law and Poverty.[74] MALDEF specifically sought additional support from within the education community and procured briefs from the California State Board of Education, as well as from Edgewood, Texas Independent School District, which MALDEF targeted because it was one of the poorest school districts in Texas. MALDEF urged Edgewood to hold "legal arguments . . . to a minimum" in their Supreme Court brief in order to focus on the human and economic side of the case.[75]

While Roos sought to build support for the case overall, he was cognizant of the ways in which grassroots support for a wider swath of benefits might trigger a public backlash that could harm their chances in the Supreme Court. Writing to Norella Beni Hall, a California resident who sought to develop community support for the plaintiffs in *Plyler*, Roos noted that "focus must be narrowly on the issue of education for undocumented children or at most, coverage under the Equal Protection Clause. It is clearly not in the best interest of the case to use it as a rallying cry for the expansion of other services to undocumented persons. Each pyramid must be built one brick at a time."[76]

While building broad support was one area of focus for MALDEF, Roos believed that continued support from the federal government was of critical importance.[77] However, the Reagan administration's public commitments to both fiscal and social conservatism and reducing government spending, when paired with a new leadership and driving ideology at the Justice Department, would make gaining the government's support an uphill battle.

MALDEF undertook a significant effort to get the Reagan administration to weigh in on behalf of the students. Mirroring the approach taken with the Carter administration, MALDEF reached out to the leadership of departments beyond the Reagan Justice Department to influence the government's position. Initially, MALDEF ally Edward Aguirre, former US Commissioner of Education under President Ford, contacted William Clohan, an Undersecretary at the US Department of Education. Soon after, Roos reached out directly to Clohan to ask for the department's support in the case. Roos noted the government's support in both the *Plyler* and *In Re Alien Schoolchildren* cases to raise a precedent of continued support and entreated Clohan to continue its support in the Supreme Court as he argued denying education to children "who are without any culpability for their condition" would be tragic not only for the students but also for society.

Given the Reagan administration's commitment to reducing government expenditures in social welfare, Roos aimed to head off concerns about the possible use of the case to expand benefits for unauthorized immigrants in other areas by noting that "There is no legal or practical reason why this should be so." The arguments for educating unauthorized children were "uniquely compelling," and he suggested that "Even if undocumented aliens are protected by the Equal Protection Clause, their rights to other benefits would have to be weighed against the justifications advanced for their denial. . . . The briefs filed by the United States in the Fifth Circuit clearly keep government options open in this regard."[78]

Restraint was not only a theme in government spending for the Reagan administration, but also in its approach to judicial activism, posing another challenge to MALDEF's efforts. The election of President Reagan brought a whole new wave of political appointees to the Department of Justice. They embraced a judicial ideology that sought to narrow and constrict the role of the federal courts. The new Attorney General William French Smith, who had been involved with Pacific Legal Forum, laid out the new approach in a speech he gave that fall. "We believe that the groundswell of conservatism evidenced by the 1980 election makes this an especially appropriate time to urge upon the courts more principled bases that would diminish judicial activism." Smith went on to describe how Solicitor General Rex Lee was working to identify "key areas in which the courts might be convinced to desist from actual policy-making."

One area particularly impacted by these new approaches was the work of the Civil Rights Division. According to Smith, the courts' "analyses of equal protection issues have often trespassed upon responsibilities our constitutional system entrusted to legislatures." Smith and others in the new administration believed "this multiplication of implied constitutional rights—and the unbounded strict scrutiny they produce—has gone far enough." Smith promised that the Department of Justice under his leadership would "attempt to reverse this unhealthy flow of power from state and federal legislatures to the federal courts—and the concomitant flow of power from state and local government to the federal level."[79]

Reagan had nominated William Bradford Reynolds as Assistant Attorney General for Civil Rights, the position Drew Days held in the Carter administration. With good credentials including spending several years working in the solicitor general's office during the Nixon administration and a reputation as a moderate (one that would later be proven false), Reynolds was appointed to the post after various candidates for the job were considered too controversial.[80]

Following the elevation of Smith and Reynolds, the Civil Rights Division began undergoing significant changes reflecting the appointees' preference for judicial restraint. And this approach was felt even in smaller matters, as even routine filings were reviewed more closely by high-level political aides. As one Justice Department official commented of the Civil Rights Division at the time, "There are people who are sympathetic to a very, very unbounded conception of where civil rights enforcement leads. We need the review to make sure something isn't smuggled through."[81]

The Reagan administration's opposition to judicial activism would influence the way it viewed the *Plyler* case. Regardless of the changes at the top of the Justice Department, career staff in the Civil Rights Division continued to urge participation in the case, and in August 1981 began drafting a proposal for the government advocating a position similar to the one taken by the Carter administration. As summarized by Walter W. Barnett, the deputy chief of the Appellate Section of the Civil Rights Division, under the argument, the department would assert that the Texas statute did not meet a rational basis test and the statute could not be justified as a way of addressing the rising number of unauthorized immigrants.[82] After several intradepartmental meetings, the task of drafting a brief ultimately fell to Senior Deputy Solicitor General Lawrence G. Wallace.

Wallace was a longtime career staffer in the solicitor general's office known for seeking to counterbalance the ideological shifts of the various administrations during his time in the department. An academic standout as editor-in-chief of the *Columbia Law Review*, Wallace had clerked for Justice Hugo Black and served as a professor at Duke University School of Law before being hired to work in the solicitor general's office in 1969. No stranger to high-profile civil rights cases, Wallace had drawn criticism during the Carter administration from Drew Days and others within the department for urging the administration then to oppose the University of California's affirmative action policy in the *Bakke* case, a position that the Carter White House overruled when it directed the solicitor general to file on behalf of the University of California.[83]

In a memo to Solicitor General Lee, Wallace urged adopting a "somewhat enhanced judicial scrutiny" standard which relied on the fact that unauthorized aliens were a "particularly vulnerable 'insular minority.'"[84] This middle approach, Wallace argued, would allow flexibility if the state were to change its justification, and would allow the department to avoid "adhering to or specifically repudiating the arguments we made below [in the 5th circuit]." Additionally, such an approach, Wallace posited, would avoid "negative implications for some other (e.g., welfare) uses of the same classification."

In crafting this recommendation, Wallace noted a close resemblance, even a relationship, between legislation like the one being challenged and pre–Civil War racist legislation that outlawed teaching slave children, legislation that was later invalidated by the Thirteenth Amendment. Wallace wrote that while he recognized that there were some differences between the Texas law and the pre–Civil War prohibitions on educating slaves, the Texas law was "as close a counterpart to those laws as we realistically can expect to encounter in our own time, with much the same tragic consequences."

Wallace argued that the current case was not a "judicial usurpation of policymaking," which would have gone against the administration's embrace of judicial restraint, and he ended his argument for the administration to support the students with an impassioned plea:

> We should remember that our reason for participating in these cases was to foster civil rights (and to assure federal supremacy in the making of immigration policy and protect other federal interests), rather than to gang up with the State against an insular minority seeking equal treatment under the law . . . I believe that continuing, on narrow grounds, to espouse the civil rights claim in these cases would be truer to our constitutional history.[85]

Yet, when the Justice Department's brief representing the government's views was filed on September 8, 1981, it reflected few of the ideas seen in the drafts that Wallace had circulated. The government's brief argued that unauthorized immigrants were "persons" within the meaning of the Fourteenth Amendment, but told the court that the United States would "leave to the parties directly affected the arguments concerning whether the Equal Protection Clause requires Texas to educate alien children who were not lawfully admitted into the United States." Solicitor General Rex Lee later added, "This is an issue that is the state's interest, not the federal government's."[86]

While judicial ideology played a big role, so too, allegedly, did political favoritism and bargaining. While the Department of Justice called the move away from the position advocated by the government in the Fifth Circuit appeal nothing more than a "straight lawyering decision," many news reports at the time tied the switch to extensive lobbying by Texas Governor William P. Clements.[87] Department leaders at the time said that Clements had met with Attorney General Smith and asked him to shift the government's position in the *Plyler* case.[88] But others such as Ruben Bonilla of LULAC charged that the change of position was part of a larger political deal, namely that Clements would temper his criticism of President Reagan's proposed immigration policy in exchange for the department's shift of position in the *Plyler* case.[89] MALDEF's Vilma Martinez scorned the administration for the alleged political deal, asking, "Has the President placed his friendship with the Governor of Texas above the future opportunities of innocent children?"[90]

Similar to the inner workings of the Carter administration, political concerns as much as legal arguments played a key role in shaping critical positions in the Reagan Justice Department. The Reagan administration's position in the case reflected the influence of conservative party politics and the emerging strength of judicial restraint. Nevertheless, the administration's brief, which, while backing away from attacking the Texas statute still argued that equal protection rights extended to unauthorized individuals, demonstrating that the Reagan revolution was bounded by some strands of persistent liberalism.

While it was not a complete reversal of the Carter position, it limited federal intervention and thus Governor Clements of Texas praised the Justice Department's new stance as "the federal government getting out of the state's business. It's a healthy sign and one that confirms President Reagan's pre-election position on all these matters of delegating more responsibility to the states."[91] The Governor's General Counsel David Dean saw the Reagan administration's position as standing for the principle that the case was a matter of state's rights and he noted that the federal government's new perceived neutrality could be a "big plus" for the state when the case was argued.[92]

Predictably, Latino groups were unhappy with the Reagan Justice Department's brief, with LULAC calling it "another in a long series of retreats by this Administration on issues dealing with the protection of rights of minorities."[93] Indeed, *Plyler* was just one of many shifts undertaken by the new president in the area of civil rights. In the same week as it announced its position in *Plyler*, the Department of Justice also urged the Supreme Court to uphold a Washington State law that sought to end local desegregation efforts through busing.[94] Other policy changes within the department included the approval of a school desegregation plan for Chicago that the department had rejected a month before as incomplete because it would not achieve desegregation. It had also declined to pursue a cross-district busing plan in Houston.[95]

In the *Fort Worth Star Tribune*, an editorial cartoon by Eric Harrison summarized many activists' interpretations of the Reagan administration brief.

FIGURE 2.1. *Fort Worth Star-Telegram* editorial cartoon, published September 18, 1981.
© 1981 by McClatchy. All rights reserved. Used under license.

In it, as a man pulls a child labeled "illegal alien children" out of a school-house while snarling, "come back outa there you little brat and get back to work," President Reagan, dressed as a sheriff, stands watching and remarks, "looks like a states' rights issue to me." The cartoon stressed Reagan's blind eye to Texas's suppression of immigrants' rights and its concurrent reliance on immigrant labor.

Oyez

Including the government's brief, eighteen amicus briefs were filed with the Supreme Court by a wide range of civic, governmental, and religious organizations.[96] Other groups in the conservative public interest legal movement, including the Pacific Legal Forum, submitted briefs similar to the one submitted by MSLF before the Fifth Circuit. When the case finally came before the Supreme Court for oral arguments in December 1981, the individual school districts were represented by local education attorney John Hardy and the state by Richard Arnett, the Texas Assistant Attorney General. As the cases had been consolidated into one argument by the court, Peter Roos and Peter Schey, one of the lead counsels in the *In Re Alien* case, split the oral argument for the students.[97]

The court the men argued before had undergone a transformation from the liberal Warren court that heard many of the famous Fourteenth Amendment equal protection cases during the 1950s and 1960s. The Warren court had expanded the notion of fundamental rights and interests protected by the Equal Protection Clause to include such points as the right to an appeal in a criminal case, the right to travel from state to state, and the right to vote.[98] It had also begun to move toward an expanded definition of suspect classifications to include those based on wealth, such as when Justice William Douglas wrote in *Harper v. Virginia Board of Elections* (1966) that the "lines drawn on the basis of wealth or poverty, like those of race, are traditionally disfavored."[99]

But the Burger court that Roos and Schey faced was new. Six of the nine justices had been appointed in the past twelve years. Following Chief Justice Warren's retirement in 1969, President Nixon appointed Warren Burger to the Chief Justice's seat, and the seats occupied by Hugo Black, William O. Douglas, Abe Fortas, Potter Stewart, and John Harlan during the Warren court were now held by Nixon appointees Lewis Powell, Harry Blackmun, and William Rehnquist, Ford appointee John Paul Stevens, and new Reagan appointee Sandra Day O'Connor. William J. Brennan, Thurgood Marshall, and Byron White were the three holdovers from the old Warren court. At first, the Burger court seemed to be following the lead of the Warren court's activism. In March 1971, in its *Griggs v. Duke Power* ruling, the court held that the congressional intent in the 1964 Civil Rights Act included not only barring overt discrimination but also actions that are discriminatory in operation. A month later it also embraced the legacy of the Warren court in *Swann v. Charlotte-Mecklenburg Board of Education*, where the court declared district-wide busing was a permissible means of achieving racial balance in systems where de jure segregation prevailed.

But by the time *Plyler* came before the Burger court a decade later, it had already begun to signal a new direction on federal education policy, specifically around the issues of school segregation, busing, and educational financing. In *Miliken v. Bradley I*, a divided court struck down the lower court's decision to allow the busing of mostly African American students from Detroit across district lines to suburban schools with much larger White student populations and vice versa. Texas had witnessed many school segregation debates first-hand. In *San Antonio v. Rodriguez*, for example, the court found no con-stitutional basis for mandating funding equity among school districts within the same state. In doing so, the court also found no evidence that education was a "fundamental" right protected by the Constitution. While the Burger court did little to stand in the way of reversing national momentum to end de jure segregation in the nation's schools, its decisions left de facto segregation largely intact.

In *Plyler*, the questioning by the justices was long, going well over the scheduled one-hour limit, with all nine justices asking questions.[100] Recordings of the oral arguments reveal the pointed nature of the questions from the bench. Justice Stevens asked the state if it preferred the students be educated or uneducated. Other justices questioned what access unauthorized immigrants had in the state to other services such as obtaining driver's licenses and owning property. As noted in the opening to this work, Justice Thurgood Marshall wondered aloud if the state could deny fire protection to unauthorized immigrants. Hardy began to answer Marshall by saying fire protection was "an entitlement" but then shifted, conceding "That's a tough question." Justice Sandra Day O'Connor asked how the state could "punish children for having something over which they have no control," their parents' illegal entry.[101] From the questioning, the inconsistent application of alienage restrictions in Texas became clear, as did several justices' views that the students were being targeted for their parents' actions.

With the oral arguments completed, a decision was expected before the end of the court's term in June. Justice Brennan's case history notes reveal a tense and spirited debate during the justices' conference. Chief Justice Burger began the discussion by arguing that unauthorized immigrants should not be entitled to receive welfare but conceded that immigrants were "persons" within the meaning of the Fourteenth Amendment and was joined by Justice White. Brennan and Marshall felt the Constitution extended equal protection to all persons, regardless of their immigration status. Justices Blackmun and Powell joined Brennan's side. Justice Rehnquist argued that many of the children demanding an education were not five or six years old but, rather, those who'd come to the country on their own, and in doing so referred to them as "wetbacks." Marshall exploded at Rehnquist, who attempted to defend himself by saying that in his part of the country the term *wetbacks* still had "currency," as Brennan recalled it. Marshall fumed that by the same reasoning, he'd long been called a "*nigger*."[102] Just as in America more broadly, the issues of racial discrimination were contentious at this level.

On June 15, 1982, the Supreme Court handed down a narrow 5 to 4 decision with Justice Brennan writing for the majority, with Justices Marshall, Blackmun, Powell, and Stevens joining. The majority opinion struck down the Texas statute. The court reaffirmed its earlier decisions that unauthorized persons were protected by the due process provisions of the Fifth Amendment and extended those rights to the Equal Protection Clause of the Fourteenth Amendment. In doing so, the court dismissed Texas's claim that those illegally residing there were not "within its jurisdiction" and thus not entitled to equal protection, as Brennan wrote that there was "no support for the suggestion that 'due process' is somehow of greater stature than 'equal protection' and therefore available to a larger class of persons."[103]

The majority rejected the argument that unauthorized alienage was a suspect class, as "their presence in this country in violation of federal law is not a 'constitutional irrelevancy.'" The five justices defended the state's ability to act with respect to unauthorized immigrants but limited this authority to when "such action mirrors federal objectives and furthers a legitimate state goal," which the opinion stated was not present in the *Plyler* case. In fact, the opinion noted, "It is difficult to understand precisely what the State hopes to achieve by promoting the creation and perpetuation of a subclass of illiterates within our boundaries."[104]

Many court observers posit that in order to win the support of swing Justice Powell, Justice Brennan explicitly reaffirmed an earlier decision authored by Powell that found public education was "not a 'right' granted to individuals by the Constitution."[105] Nevertheless, Brennan's opinion argued, "[b]ut neither is it merely some governmental 'benefit' indistinguishable from other forms of social welfare legislation. Both the importance of education in maintaining our basic institutions, and the lasting impact of its deprivation on the life of the child, mark the distinction." Justice Powell joined the majority opinion but also wrote his own concurrence, stating that "[a] legislative classification that threatens the creation of an underclass of future citizens and residents cannot be reconciled with one of the fundamental purposes of the Fourteenth Amendment."[106]

In his dissenting opinion, Chief Justice Burger, joined by Justices White, Rehnquist, and O'Connor, argued that the Texas statute held "a relationship to a legitimate state purpose," the only necessary test of constitutional muster. Burger also expressed concern about the larger impact of the decision on other benefits and entitlements. Burger's dissent is notable for the way in which it echoed many of the demands for judicial restraint expressed by Attorney

General Smith and others in the conservative movement. Burger assailed the majority opinion as it allowed the court to "assum[e] a policymaking role," and asserted that the *Plyler* decision was an example of the "justly criticized judicial tendency to attempt speedy and wholesale formulation of 'remedies' for the failures . . . of the political processes." Chief Justice Burger criticized the majority opinion for cobbling together "pieces of what might be termed quasi-suspect-class and quasi-fundamental-rights analysis" as it saw fit to get the result that it wanted in the case.[107]

Reactions and Legacies

Chief Justice Burger's argument that the court was overreaching in its policymaking found support throughout the administration. At the Department of Justice, the leadership was disappointed with the decision and viewed the case as a missed opportunity for the department to encourage the court to pursue a course of judicial restraint.

Two special assistants to the attorney general, John Roberts (who would become Chief Justice of the US Supreme Court twenty-four years later) and Carolyn Kuhl, wrote the attorney general a summary of the decision and highlighted for Smith the missed opportunity. They suggested that if the solicitor general's brief had taken a position on the equal protection issue in this case, "It is our belief that a brief filed by the solicitor general's office supporting the State of Texas—and the values of judicial restraint—could well have moved Justice Powell into the Chief Justice's camp and altered the outcome of the case. In sum, this is a case in which our supposed litigation program to encourage judicial restraint did not get off the ground, and should have."[108]

At the White House, the communications office prepared materials on the administration's reactions to the court's decisions at the end of the term. Commenting on the holding in *Plyler*, the White House again echoed a desire for judicial restraint, saying the case was a "Difficult call for Court to make. . . . Tough to second guess this; but RR wishes this issue could have been left to Congress instead of having the Courts decide it."[109] Education Secretary T. H. Bell reluctantly supported the decision because "it's the law of the land," but he noted that he had some concerns about "imposing on the State of Texas certain policies that I think ought to be decided by the State of Texas and the Legislature and the school boards down there."[110]

Given all of the earlier public conversations about the larger impact of the case, it is not surprising that the news reports and commentary that followed the decision immediately began assessing the impact that the case might have in other arenas, such as welfare and other entitlement programs.

Many people on both sides of the issue saw the case as the first step in a long path to an expansion of rights for unauthorized immigrants. Conservatives saw it as an overreaching expansion of rights and feared that alienage status restrictions on access to other federal and state programs would soon be targeted. One Justice Department staffer commented that "I fully expect now that illegal alien groups will make attempts to go further."[111] Many warned of the economic burden that would be created by extending broader social welfare benefits to the unauthorized. Texas Education Commissioner Raymond Bynum said the decision "may encourage a move to make local and state governments provide food stamps, welfare payments and Social Security benefits to illegal aliens," which Bynum said would "create a tremendous burden."[112] Robert Conner, the Executive Director of Federation for American Immigration Reform (FAIR), which had filed an amicus brief supporting Texas and the school district, called the case "a major setback in efforts to delimit the rights of illegal immigrants," and he predicted "there will be floods of litigation in coming years that will rely on this decision as a precedent to open many more state and local benefits and programs to illegal aliens."[113] A *Washington Post* editorial, while calling the Texas statute "unwise," also tacitly endorsed a principle of restraint and fired a warning shot against expanding *Plyler*, noting that "the courts would be wise to attach great weight to the decisions of elected legislatures. Judicial expansion of entitlement programs to millions of illegal aliens will be a lot more controversial than providing public education to 20,000 young children. And it's a good bet that these more difficult questions are just around the corner."[114] These rhetorical arguments used in the wake of the *Plyler* decision that immigrants were a burden on the economic well-being of the state because of their use of social welfare programs would grow over time.

On the liberal side, activists saw the decision as a huge opportunity, an opening salvo, and began devising ways to use it to address other areas. Peter Roos and other immigrants' rights lawyers suggested that the *Plyler* decision's impact was most likely to be found in challenging state regulations regarding social services. Providing examples of where the *Plyler* decision might be useful, MALDEF's John Huerta pointed to restrictions to state-funded medical care.[115] MALDEF's Morris Baller observed that a recent New York decision holding that the state could not deny day care to unauthorized children was apparently influenced by the *Plyler* rationale, noting that it demonstrated the ways the case was already influencing the national legal movement.

In the months following the decision, MALDEF began to explore other areas of possible litigation based on this success. Staffer Norma Solis wrote to Jose Garza suggesting denial of food stamps, limitation of health services, and barring of access to continuing education as areas where they might direct their efforts and seek to apply the *Plyler* decision to overturn restrictive statutes.[116]

While MALDEF lawyers in 1982 viewed their victory in *Plyler* as the first step in an effort to expand rights both in terms of who was entitled to them and what specific benefits were correspondingly granted, the road toward achieving these gains turned out to be far rockier than they envisioned. Soon MALDEF and other liberal groups would find themselves on the defensive, as battles over restricting social welfare benefits, limiting employment discrimination protections, and removing civil liberties protections would be the focus of debate at the local, state, and national levels. The next decade would be marked by a larger debate over the rights held by noncitizens. And just as it did in *Plyler*, the federal government would continue to play a key role in shaping these debates and defining these rights.

While *Plyler* is a key turning point in the shifting definition of rights, it also illuminates several larger debates about the period. Most of the scholarship on *Plyler* focuses on its legal legacy, but looking at it through a lens of political history illuminates several new themes and challenges some dominant theories ascribed to the period.[117] While the 1970s are often viewed by immigration scholars as an era of "political stalemate" between the action points of the 1965 Hart-Celler Act and the Immigration Reform Control Act of 1986, the history of *Plyler* shows us that by shifting our focus from the legislative to the executive branch and the courts, the 1970s and early 1980s were anything but stagnant.[118] It was a period of political action as both the Carter and the Reagan administrations assessed and wrestled with the political and policy implications of the shifting demographics.

The *Plyler* case also points to the ways in which liberalism evolved between the Great Society and the Reagan Revolution, a period often relegated in historical scholarship to the narrative of the rise of the conservative right. While liberal activists and the judiciary were successful in extending rights to new populations, examining the government's briefs in *Plyler* also shows new dimensions of the rise of conservatism in the Democratic Party. Often portrayed as emerging during the 1980s with the growth of the Democratic Leadership Coalition and with the "ending of welfare as we know it" under President Clinton, the *Plyler* case demonstrates how conservative elements with a focus on restraining the growth of entitlement programs were present and forceful within the Carter administration. As the effects of the neoliberal economic restructuring became more apparent over the next two decades, these voices calling for restraining entitlement spending would become even more powerful and focus their opposition on not only unauthorized immigrants' benefits, but benefits for all. Finally, the Reagan administration's brief, which while backing away from attacking the Texas statute still argued for extending equal protection rights to unauthorized individuals, illustrates how liberal notions continued to frame the political discussions of the day. Over the following decades, the expansive nature of rights for unauthorized immigrants upheld in the *Plyler* decision would continue to come under attack from all sides and lead to a shift in the notion of rights for all immigrants, regardless of legal status.

3

"Heading into Uncharted Waters"

CONGRESS, EMPLOYER SANCTIONS, AND LABOR RIGHTS

IN 1970, the nation entered a severe economic recession. Real GNP declined for the first time since 1958, corporate profits and industrial production fell, and unemployment hit a seven-year high.[1] Many Americans, searching for stability in a shifting economic world, feared that immigrants would take jobs from citizens in an increasingly competitive employment market. This unfounded fear fueled a movement to restrict access to employment for unauthorized immigrant laborers by passing laws to penalize businesses that employed them, a category of restrictions known as "employer sanctions." These efforts were one part of a growing restrictionist sentiment toward immigration that gained strength both in public discourse and in national politics in the 1970s. While the rapid growth of anti-immigrant sentiment would suggest that immigration reform was likely, an unusual confluence of forces from the left and right combined with the fragmented American governing system to block the passage of any major federal legislation during the decade. While federal legislative policy remained unchanged, the battles over it during the decades had a significant impact, shaping the way forward for the immigration policy developments of the 1980s.

The restrictive push for employer sanctions was initially driven by an alliance of traditionally liberal legislators supported by organized labor, African Americans, and legal aid groups. At first, these activists targeted states and used the federal courts to push for employer sanctions in the early 1970s, but by the middle of the decade they turned to the federal government, where they were stymied by legislative barriers, presidential inaction, and agricultural interests which prevented any comprehensive action.

61

In the late 1970s, some thought that the Carter administration might create an opportunity for change as the rural populist Democratic president began pushing for an immigration proposal that included employer sanctions. Simultaneously, changes in committee leadership eased the way for legislation to clear the House of Representatives. Yet, despite these changes, obstacles remained. Carter's failure to understand the politics of immigration, as well as his inability to work with Congress—a lingering problem throughout his presidency—hindered these efforts. Moreover, a growing and increasingly powerful Latino immigrants' rights movement opposed employer sanctions and effectively entrenched employer sanctions in legislative gridlock for the rest of the decade. For many of these Latino interest groups, immigration policy was not simply an important subject of interest, but an existential issue. At stake in these debates were not only policies, but also their leadership standing among the interest groups.

Rapidly shifting debates over employer sanctions reflected significant political realignments that were underway in American politics in the 1970s. Cracks formed in the liberal coalition that had passed the Hart-Celler Act as the rise of an economy in which more and more workers would be steered into non-union, low-wage, service-sector jobs destabilized the politics of immigration. Labor unions, the NAACP, and other civil rights organizations that had lobbied for the liberal expansion of immigration in 1965 now turned toward restriction.[2] The strength of restrictionist anti-immigrant forces grew significantly during this period, as many Americans blamed immigrants for mounting inequality and insecurity. They saw immigrants competing for opportunity as contributing to the massive economic changes that proved costly to their own lives. By the late 1970s, anti-immigrant sentiment and activism swept through Washington politics, forcing Democrats and Republicans to navigate tricky new waters. Some of the key Democratic constituencies of organized labor and ethnic lobbies were split. Both parties sought immigration restriction, even as Democrats struggled to consolidate the support of the growing Latino constituency, and Republicans fostered an ideological and political base of free market idealism. Immigration policy has long been an issue that simultaneously fractured the parties from within and brought strange bedfellows together in viable policy compromises.[3] The politics of employer sanctions was no different. Crucially, the divides created within the parties, and the unusual alliances required to pass sanctions, have endured until the current day.

The birth of employer sanctions provides insight into an important moment in the decades-long shift from the pro-immigration successes of the 1970s, as in the *Plyler* case, to the anti-immigrant convergence in US politics in the 1990s. It was a moment when immigration began to play a larger role in national politics. Much of the harsh rhetoric and vitriolic anti-immigrant tropes that would become commonplace in later debates infected the national political conversation. These early battles over employer sanctions also show how, even at this moment of rising conservatism, growing restrictionist efforts were thwarted by a combination of institutional factors, interest group opposition, and shifting political alignment.

New Problems, New Opportunities, and Old Hatreds

In the early 1970s, the United States entered an era of dramatic economic disruption and transformations. After the longest sustained period of economic growth and increasing economic equality in the nation's history, unemployment doubled from 3.5 percent to 7.1 percent between 1969 and 1977.[4] Income and economic inequality also returned with a vengeance. Beginning in 1973–1974, real individual earnings began to stagnate and then fall.[5] Real incomes for families increased marginally, but only because more family members worked, and workers took on longer hours to make up for lower wages. Even as unemployment skyrocketed, the inflation rate remained high, baffling economists' understandings of the modern relationship between economic stagnation and inflation. Facing both an inflation rate of 9.25 percent and an unemployment rate of 8.5 percent in 1975, economists identified a new dilemma that became known as "stagflation." Policymakers did not know what to do to stop the simultaneous increase of both inflation and unemployment, though they could measure what they came to call the "misery index," which hit highs of 17.5 percent.[6]

Stagflation hit the working class the hardest as corporations and investors sought to protect themselves. More than 38 million workers lost jobs in the United States "through private divestment." Unionized manufacturing jobs, which had created the postwar phenomenon of the "blue-collar middle-class," seemed to vanish almost overnight. Employment in the heavily unionized steel industry—the central pillar of the postwar economy—dropped by 20 percent between 1960 and 1978.[7] US corporations increasingly automated production, outsourced their supply lines, and moved their manufacturing

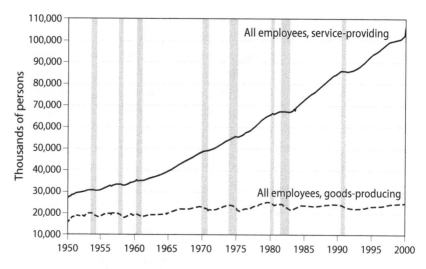

FIGURE 3.1. Manufacturing and service job growth data. From the Federal Reserve Bank of St. Louis, https://fred.stlouisfed.org/series/SRVPRD, June 24, 2020

operations abroad. At the same time, corporate leaders centralized management in US offices in new suburban office parks and, ultimately, in redeveloped urban centers, which experienced a demand for highly paid white-collar managers and low-paid service-sector workers to meet the needs and desires of the growing professional class.[8] Part-time work proliferated in the commercial and service industries, meaning low pay and few benefits for more and more workers. People seeking full-time jobs with benefits had to settle for part-time jobs with wages lower than their parents' generation had earned.[9] Altogether, these disruptions created rapidly growing income and wealth inequality, along with a combination of longer hours and less security, a combination that US workers had not seen in the postwar period.

The transformation of the US economy during and after the 1970s, broadly speaking, also overhauled employment opportunities for immigrants in particular. While agricultural jobs had always been a draw for Mexican immigrants to come north, changes in the post–World War II economy had opened up a large number of low-paying service and light manufacturing jobs to migrant workers. Forty-five percent of Mexican workers in the United States in 1965 worked in agriculture, but by 1985 that number had fallen to only 25 percent.[10] Beginning in the 1970s, immigrants increasingly found jobs in fields that traditionally had been viewed as "women's work" in the service industry, such as cleaning, cooking, and waitressing, as well as childcare. The feminization of immigrant labor continued during the 1970s as white women worked more and more outside their homes and employed immigrant labor with low wages to do the household work they had traditionally performed.[11]

As immigrants moved from working in seasonal agricultural work to year-round labor in service industries and light manufacturing, migrants began to move toward opportunities in new ways. Rather than seasonal migrant workers coming alone to work in the United States and returning to their families back home, immigrant families began to settle permanently in the United States. In addition, as crossing the border became more difficult during the 1980s, immigrants were less likely to risk multiple border crossings. Instead, they stayed for years at a time, a trend that would escalate even further in the 1990s. Employment sector changes meant immigrant destinations within the United States changed as well. Consequently, it was jobs in sunbelt cities, including Los Angeles, that provided work for immigrant labor migrating north in search of steady wages. Other cities like New York and Chicago also continued to turn to immigrants to provide low-wage, low-skilled labor in restaurants, hotels, and hospitals.[12]

The shift from agricultural work to service and light manufacturing and the related move from rural fields to urban centers made Mexican migrants more visible and more conspicuous to those in the media and politics, who viewed them as a threat.[13] In 1976, Gallup polled Americans, asking, "What problems, if any, result from the presence of illegal aliens in this country?" Fifty-one percent of respondents answered that migrants took jobs away from residents, and another 20 percent said that they were used for cheap labor.[14] Editorials in major newspapers during this time began blaming immigration for the economic challenges confronting the nation and, particularly, cities. The *Chicago Tribune* argued in 1977 that there was a one-to-one relationship between lost jobs for "legal" workers and those taken by the unauthorized population. "Illegal aliens are reaching a critical point in the United States," the *Tribune* warned. "There are about eight million illegal immigrants here now—roughly equal to the number of our unemployed." The *Tribune* continued, joining the anti-immigrant chorus who suggested that these immigrants, unlike previous newcomers to the United States, would be unassimilable. "Fearful of detection and deportation . . . their very fears prevent their absorption in the American mainstream . . . and lead to the perpetuation of ethnic enclaves that aggravate the problems of big cities."[15] Politicians joined the chorus, with Senator Strom Thurmond declaring, "Our wealth is not boundless, and the current unacceptably high level of domestic unemployment clearly shows that we do not have a general excess of available jobs."[16] The implication was that the nation faced an unavoidable conflict between immigration and the prosperity of US workers. Calls for limiting immigration admissions and increasing enforcement became more strident.

In addition to limiting immigration outright, the blossoming restrictionist movement sought to limit the pull of opportunity north of the border by imposing penalties on employers who hired unauthorized workers. Initial support for employer sanctions came from many on the left who viewed employer sanctions as a way to protect domestic labor markets and anti-poverty campaigns from an influx of low-income people. The archetypical liberal Minnesota Senator Walter Mondale advocated in 1970 for employer sanctions as a way to stem the arrival of "a massive poverty population" from Mexico.[17] Mondale and other traditionally liberal politicians won the support of key constituencies, including organized labor and African American organizations. Leonard Carter, the NAACP's western regional director, claimed that as a result of unauthorized immigrants, "the poor have been deprived of 100,000 jobs for which they might have been qualified."[18] For much of organized labor, this newfound support in Washington promised the advance of a policy they had been advocating for nearly two decades. At their 1950 national convention, for instance, AFL delegates called for legislation that would have imposed a criminal penalty on employers who hired unauthorized immigrant labor.[19]

Those calling for employer sanctions faced a steep uphill battle. These interests had long been stymied from passing such legislation by the strength of agriculture interests whose demand for cheap labor, even if it was undocumented labor, pushed the passage in Congress of the "Texas Proviso" in 1952, a federal law that protected employers of unauthorized immigrants from any legal penalties.

Starting in the States

As unemployment spiked in the early 1970s, organized labor renewed calls for employer sanctions. Many liberals and labor unions advocated for sanctions as a way to target unscrupulous employers, and as an alternative to mass-deportation tactics that were unpopular among left-leaning constituencies. By the early 1970s, the AFL-CIO had mobilized a legislative department in Washington to craft and pass sanctions legislation.[20] Other unions such as Cesar Chavez's United Farm Workers (UFW) supported employer sanctions, arguing that illegal immigration made organizing farm workers more difficult because unauthorized workers were used as scab labor during strikes.[21]

While organized labor pushed for employer sanctions in many states and at the federal level, they first gained traction in California. Unemployment was particularly high in California, where rates rose from 4.4 percent in 1969 to a thirteen-year-high of 7.4 percent in 1971, well above the national average.[22] Such conditions emboldened those pushing employer sanctions to take action, assuming there would be more widespread support.

In 1970 in Sacramento, Senator Lewis F. Sherman, a Republican from Alameda, introduced Senate Bill 1091 which would impose a $500 fine on employers who hired unauthorized workers. While supported by the County Federation of Labor, the NAACP, California Rural Legal Assistance (CLRA), and MALDEF, the bill failed to pass.[23] The rapidly shifting politics of immigration meant that support for employer sanctions grew significantly within just a year. The following year, Republican Assemblyman Dixon Arnett introduced a bill that went even further and sought to criminalize the employment of unauthorized workers, and was supported by the same groups as the earlier bill as well as by the California Federation of Labor (AFL-CIO) and the UFW. They faced the usual opposition of business groups, including the California Manufacturer's Association, California Conference of Employers, the Agricultural Council of California, and other growers' groups.[24] Arnett's bill worked its way through the majority Democratic California Assembly and was signed into law by Governor Ronald Reagan.[25]

Chicano rights organizations including CASA (Center for Autonomous Social Action) and MEChA (Movimiento Estudiantil Chicanx de Aztlán) held protests against the bill.[26] The law did not last long. Immediately after Reagan signed it, employers challenged the Arnett law in multiple suits. In one case, *Dolores Canning v. Howard*, three California business owners argued that the law would require them to violate civil rights laws in questioning employees, that it put an unfair burden on employers, and claimed that it interfered with Congress's exclusive power over immigration. In 1974, the California Court of Appeals unanimously upheld the business owners' argument, and the state dropped its defense of the law.[27]

Advocates for employer sanctions continued to defend the law. In February 1976, the US Supreme Court heard a different case, originally filed in 1972, that challenged the Arnett law. In *DeCanas v. Bica*, the Supreme Court maintained federal regulation of immigration, but concurrently clarified that regulation of employer-employee relationships was valid under state jurisdiction if those laws were harmonious with the objectives and execution of federal laws. The court remanded it back to the state for a determination of whether the state law in question impeded federal law.[28] By the time the case came back to the state, the political situation had changed and there was little interest in pursuing the case. As Dixon Arnett noted, "When it was remanded, everybody ran for cover . . . The Attorney General, at the time considering running for Lieutenant Governor, needed this issue like he needed a hole in the head."[29] In addition, the UFW and CLRA, who had played key roles in bringing the case initially, did not want to pursue it, as their views had shifted and they now saw the plight of their constituencies as being tied to that of unauthorized workers.[30]

Following the *DeCanas v. Bica* decision in 1976, there was a wave of state-level efforts to enact employer sanctions introduced in at least seventeen states across the nation with varying degrees of success.[31] While many efforts failed to overcome competing interests and strong opposition, employer sanctions laws were passed in Montana, Florida, and Vermont in 1977, Massachusetts in 1978, and Virginia in 1979.[32] However, they remained largely unenforced as state officials lacked political will and resources to regulate employer hiring at this scale.[33] As liberals became more concerned with discrimination against vulnerable workers, and employers remained committed to securing access to cheap labor, the burgeoning push for sanctions lost steam.

As the politics of employer sanctions were hashed out at the state level, the growing restrictionist movement began to push for action at the federal level. In the 1960s, a liberal civil rights–oriented coalition dominated the federal politics of immigration, pressing for the repeal of national-origin quotas and Asian exclusion. Slowly but surely, restrictionists began fracturing this coalition in the 1970s.

Beginning in the early 1970s, several groups in organized labor, including the AFL-CIO and the International Ladies Garment Workers Union (ILGWU), who were looking to Congress to put an employer sanctions bill on the legislative calendar, reached out to Congressman Peter Rodino of New Jersey, the chairman of the House Subcommittee on Immigration and Refugee Affairs. Rodino had been born in the Little Italy section of Newark, New Jersey, and after becoming an attorney, serving in World War II, and being an active member of the Essex County Democratic organization, had been elected to Congress in 1948. Rodino's constituency in Newark had been primarily Italian and Portuguese, but by the mid-1970s had a significant number of Black residents.[34] A visit from eleven top members of organized labor convinced Rodino of the need for action on employer sanctions.[35] Rodino held a series of subcommittee field hearings around the nation that revealed the deep and diverse support for employer sanctions. Acting on such support, Rodino introduced the first major federal immigration proposal of the decade in August 1972, including employer sanctions and a penalty scale consisting of monetary fines and possible imprisonment.

While there was deep and varied support for employer sanctions, there was also significant opposition. Some of the opposition to employer sanctions did not argue that discrimination based on alienage status was in fact illegal (as the Supreme Court had recently ruled in the 1973 *Espinoza v. Farah Mfg. Co* that there were "compelling reasons" to believe that when Congress had written Title VII, they had not intended the term national origin to include citizenship requirements).[36] Instead, they voiced their concern that employers, seeking to avoid the sanctions and problems of documentation, might simply refuse to hire any alien or applicant who did not appear to be white, thus violating Title VII. Others opposed to employer sanctions argued it would lead to worker exploitation and linked their opposition to the struggle against the Bracero program in previous decades.[37]

Leading the congressional opposition to employer sanctions were liberal members of Congress with significant Latino constituencies. Most notably, opposition came from New York Congressmen Ed Koch, Herman Badillo, the first Puerto Rican–born representative, and California Representative Edward Roybal, who was elected to Congress in 1963 as the first Latino member from California since 1879. Roybal's emergence as an opponent of employer sanctions would be particularly important, as he would go on to be a major voice in immigration policy debates for the next twenty years as a leading Latino voice in Washington, founding the Congressional Hispanic Caucus in 1976 and co-founding the National Association of Latino Elected and Appointed Officials (NALEO) soon after.[38] Even with this opposition, Rodino's bill passed the House in September 1972 with moderate Republican backing and broad Democratic support.

In the Senate, the measure encountered a roadblock in the form of the formidable Senator James Eastland of Mississippi. Eastland was a wealthy cotton planter who had first been appointed to the Senate in 1941 and gained notoriety for his steadfast opposition to the civil rights movement. As an agriculture subcommittee chairman and member of the Farm Bureau, Eastland was a friend of the growers who depended on cheap immigrant labor and he used his position as chairman of the Judiciary Committee to block hearings on Rodino's measure, effectively killing the bill. Undeterred, Rodino reintroduced the measure in 1973 and the pattern repeated itself, with the measure easily passing the House over opposition and hitting the Eastland roadblock in the Senate.[39] As Farm Bureau lobbyist C. H. Fields later said, "He got that bill from the House and stuck it right in his drawer."[40]

Though there was not much he could do to push back against the likes of Eastland, Rodino set out to respond to growing liberal concerns over the possibility for discriminatory effects of employer sanctions. When Rodino introduced a bill for the third time in 1975, he included measures to increase Department of Justice responsiveness to discrimination resulting from employer sanctions. While the bill made it out of the House Judiciary Committee, the growing strength of opposition, buoyed by civil rights groups and growers, forced the leadership not to bring the bill to the floor, and Eastland remained an obstacle in the Senate.[41]

While Rodino and others in Congress began to engage on employer sanctions and immigration policy, the executive branch remained largely unengaged. President Nixon created a Special Study Group on Illegal Immigrants from Mexico following a state visit with President Echeverria of Mexico in 1972.[42] But the study group led nowhere. Following Nixon's resignation, President Ford established a cabinet-level committee to examine immigration issues. While it did not propose the development of any legislation, the Ford committee did create a set of recommendations for the president that included employer sanctions, but still Ford took no action.[43] With little presidential engagement from the Nixon and Ford administrations, strong opposition from growers and emerging civil rights opposition, and the institutional block of Judiciary Committee Chairman Eastland, the early 1970s were marked by federal inaction on these issues that even the powerful political influence of organized labor could not overcome. These early skirmishes over employer sanctions at both the state and federal levels exposed cracks in the once-united liberal coalition. The new economy was creating rifts, moving the coalition away from its earlier pro-immigration agenda, presaging what was to come as conservative restrictionist elements gained even greater strength within the Democratic Party.

New Opportunities and New Allies

In the late 1970s, close observers began to believe that legislators might move more urgently to pass federal immigration restriction broadly and employer sanctions more specifically. The bottleneck of legislation in the Senate Judiciary Committee was removed when Senator Eastland retired in 1978 after serving thirty-five years in the chamber. More generally, the national economic outlook in the country went from bad to worse toward the end of the decade. By 1975, unemployment had reached 8.5 percent, up from only 3.5 percent in 1969. In 1979, twenty automobile plants closed, eliminating 50,000 jobs at those plants, and approximately 80,000 more at many of their suppliers. Between 1975 and 1979, one in six jobs in Philadelphia disappeared.[44] The worsening economic outlook only increased the support for employer sanctions from labor unions and liberals seeking to protect the domestic labor market for their constituencies. This new support was reflected in an early 1977 Gallup poll that showed Americans favored making it illegal to employ a person without proper immigration papers by a margin of six to one.[45]

As the economy faltered, the restrictionist movement began to expand and drew support from new sources, including the growing environmental and population control movements. Eugenicists had played a key role in immigration restriction during the early twentieth century and would again during the 1970s. Paul Ehrlich's 1968 book, *The Population Bomb*, spurred many activists to seek to limit population growth and its potential impacts.[46] Such concern inspired the founding of the Commission on Population Growth and the American Future, which was put forth by the Nixon administration under the lead of Daniel Moynihan, created by Congress and chaired by John D. Rockefeller III.[47] The body's interim report heightened fears of overpopulation by projecting massive growth, suggesting that immigrants would account for a quarter of all growth between 1971 and 2000, and then nearly half of the increase in population expansion in the subsequent century.[48] While its membership was divided on the issue, in its final summation, the group noted that some of its members favored a gradual reduction of immigration levels by 10 percent per year over five years. The commission's members more readily supported employer sanctions, with civil and criminal penalties for employers of unauthorized workers.[49]

In the wake of the commission's warnings, some active members within environmental groups including the Sierra Club began to push for their organizations to take a more active stance on reducing immigration. One of those pushing for restriction was John Tanton, a member of the board of Zero Population Growth and chair of the Sierra Club's population committee. Frustrated by the unwillingness of these groups to get involved in the immigration debate, Tanton and Garrett Hardin, a neo-Malthusian ecologist, formed the Federation for American Immigration Reform (FAIR) in 1979. FAIR focused exclusively on immigration issues, with a goal of setting federal immigration quotas at extremely low levels and preventing all illegal immigration. To achieve these goals, FAIR began assembling a lobbying organization in Washington and reaching out to key politicians in order to shape immigration legislation. They hired Roger Conner, a young lawyer from Michigan who was involved in the environmental movement as the group's executive director. Some of the initial funding for FAIR came from Jay Harris, a noted environmental philanthropist from Philadelphia who also served in the leadership of the Sierra Fund, and from Sidney Swensrud, the president and chairman of Gulf Oil.[50] These individuals and their funding represented a new strand of support for the restrictionist movement.

Early in the founding of FAIR, Hardin and Tanton reached out to someone who would have an outsized impact on the modern restrictionist movement for generations—Cordelia Scaife May. Tanton and Hardin were acquainted with May through work with another group, the Environmental Fund.[51] May, heiress to the Mellon banking and industrial fortune with funds of a half-billion dollars, had just become active in immigration reform. Initially interested in the birth control and environmental movements, she eventually synthesized these issues in her belief that discouraging offspring altogether would best help preserve the environment. May went on to serve on the board of the Population Council, a group founded by John D. Rockefeller III that emphasized family planning along with economic development in order to lower birthrates worldwide. By the mid-1970s, she grew frustrated with the group, leaving her board position because she did not believe they were aggressive enough, and calling for the United States to seal the border with Mexico in order to stop the immigration she blamed for overpopulation in the United States. When Tanton reached out to May with a nine-page proposal for funding FAIR, he noted, "We plan to make the restriction of immigration a legitimate position for thinking people." May provided $50,000 to get the group off the ground in the fall of 1978. Over time, May's views on immigration would become more and more extreme and she would go on to bankroll three of the largest restrictionist groups, FAIR, NumbersUSA, and the Center for Immigration Studies, along with many smaller groups.[52]

While the restrictionist movement was mobilizing and gaining institutional support, the opposition movement also began to grow. Several groups who supported employer sanctions earlier in the decade shifted their position. These groups increasingly came to see the plight of their constituencies, not in competition with unauthorized immigrants, but instead linked to that of unauthorized immigrants because they both faced continued discrimination from Anglo-Americans.[53] During the mid-1970s, pressure from urban Mexican

Americans and Chicano activists forced the UFW and Cesar Chavez to make a complete reversal and announce their opposition to the Rodino bill and employer sanctions more broadly, with Chavez arguing that "the law would shift the burden too quickly from the employer back to the alien or the Chicano, and it does not address itself to the problem of strikebreakers."[54] Soon after, the ILGWU announced that it was dropping its support for employer sanctions and would instead campaign to unionize unauthorized workers.[55]

In addition to the UFW and ILGWU, organizations central to the Latino rights movements more widely had begun changing their positions. Three of the largest Latino interest group organizations, LULAC, the National Council of La Raza (NCLR), and MALDEF, reversed their earlier support of employer sanctions during the second half of the 1970s. These groups would forge new strength in Washington as they came together and found solidarity across immigration statuses. This unity would eventually prove to be fleeting as their varying responses to the same politics of the 1980s would reflect some of their historical differences.[56]

LULAC, founded in 1929 in Corpus Christi, Texas, was the oldest of the three main Latino rights organizations, and it had traditionally been a quiet, conservative group representing the Mexican American middle class, and originally required its members to be native-born or naturalized citizens. At its founding, LULAC's goals had included assimilation, it opposed illegal immigration, and in 1954 the group had supported Operation Wetback, a federal effort to drive unauthorized immigrants back to Mexico. During the 1970s, under the leadership of Presidents Ruben Bonilla and Tony Bonilla, LULAC began to adopt more inclusive positions, admitting all Latinos residing in the United States to its membership and beginning to shift away from its earlier support of employer sanctions.[57] Signaling a more aggressive political posture, in 1979 the organization opened a Washington, DC office.[58]

The National Council of La Raza was founded in 1968 under the name of the Southwest Council of La Raza. Originally located in Phoenix, most of its early efforts focused primarily on the Southwest. With significant financial support from the Ford Foundation, NCLR undertook a more national role in 1970 with the opening of an office in Washington, and its hiring of Raul Yazaguirre. Yazaguirre, a veteran of the GI Forum and the Office of Economic Opportunity, took over as national director in 1974 and began laying the groundwork for a major reorganization.[59] NCLR began to broaden its mission to serve "Chicanos and other Hispanics" in addition to Mexican Americans, as well as to increase its involvement in public policy.[60] Within two years of Yaza-guirre's arrival, NCLR had a strong presence in Washington and was producing policy papers and information that was widely cited in congressional hearings on immigration. While in earlier debates over employer sanctions, the council board had been divided and "somewhat detached" on the issue, NCLR had hardened its position against employer sanctions by 1977.[61]

MALDEF would represent the more aggressively liberal wing of these interest groups. After initially focusing on the legal civil rights cases of Mexican Americans as discussed in the previous chapter, MALDEF began to shift its focus to the formulation of public policy and grew their lobbying efforts during the 1970s. They opened a Washington office in 1972, and by 1977, the organization's board approved a comprehensive immigration law project and began to engage with other interest groups and political leaders that shared a like-minded immigration agenda.[62] Like the other groups, MALDEF had initially supported employer sanctions in the early 1970s, arguing that "illegal aliens are taking vital jobs away from poor Mexican Americans."[63] Over the decade, MALDEF's position shifted toward opposing employer sanctions because of the arbitrary provisions that would harm Chicano citizens or permanent residents. Consequently, over the next few years MALDEF began to embrace a more explicit defense of both unauthorized and legal immigrants' rights. Several other organizations, including the ACLU and religious groups, joined the Latino lobby in opposition to employer sanctions. The United States Catholic Conference emerged as a strong force opposing employer sanctions on civil rights grounds.[64]

President Carter's new immigration proposal in 1977 helped to draw these individual activities and groups into a coordinated immigrant rights effort in Washington. While much of the energy to pass employer sanctions in the early part of the decade had come from the legislative branch, soon after his election President Carter set about developing a comprehensive immigration plan. The question of immigration had popped up several times during the campaign, most often in the key electoral states of California and Texas. Carter had begun to signal his position during the campaign, when during a July campaign stop with Mexican Americans in Texas, Carter noted that while he favored extending some sort of legal status but not citizenship to unauthorized immigrants, he also favored heavily penalizing employers for hiring unauthorized workers. On the Republican side, vice presidential nominee Senator Robert Dole had voiced the Ford campaign's opposition to employer sanctions because it was a burden on businessmen.[65]

Once in the White House, Carter's immigration policy development took shape largely at the Cabinet level by a task force with the participation of Secretary of State Cyrus R. Vance; Health, Education and Welfare Secretary Joseph A. Califano Jr.; Attorney General Griffin B. Bell; and Labor Secretary Ray Marshall.[66] While Vance and Califano were old Washington hands, having served in several previous administrations, Marshall was an academic and new to Washington.

The son of a Mississippi tenant farmer, Marshall had been raised in a Baptist orphanage after the death of his mother, and he left school after eighth grade. Lying about his age in order to join the US Navy at age fifteen, Marshall served as a radio operator in the Pacific before entering junior college, eventually earning advanced degrees at Millsaps College in Jackson and at Louisiana State before moving on to Berkeley, where he earned a PhD in economics. Marshall first taught at the University of Mississippi, where he drew the ire of the White Citizens Council for supporting integration, and then became a professor of economics at the University of Texas.[67] While sitting on the Task Force on Southern Rural Development, he met Jimmy Carter, and they became friends in part because, as Marshall would recount, "I can talk Baptist to Jimmy." When Carter ran for president, Marshall served as an advisor, writing position papers.[68] Carter surprised Marshall—and many others—when he appointed Marshall to the post of Secretary of Labor.[69] Marshall took his opportunity seriously, approaching the immigration task force as a chance to "deal with this crucial problem" of unauthorized immigration. If they did not get undocumented immigration under control, he believed, "everything we do about our own unemployment problem could be swamped by the influx of illegal workers from foreign countries."[70]

Immediately, internal divisions appeared within the Carter task force because Secretary Marshall and Attorney General Bell advocated limited amnesty and a card for all that would verify work eligibility, while Immigration and Naturalization Service (INS) Director Leonel Castillo and numerous White House aides opposed a work eligibility card and supported a more liberal amnesty.[71] Task force members also disagreed on the employer sanctions proposal, as Attorney General Bell did not think employers should be penalized for not keeping proper records of hiring practices and Secretary Marshall felt that keeping records for all applicants was the best way to prevent racial discrimination.[72] Ultimately, the group circulated a draft proposal for the president that included employer sanctions with civil but not criminal penalties.

A copy of the report from the Carter task force on immigration was sent to Annie Gutierrez, the Associate Director for justice and civil rights on the Domestic Policy Staff. Gutierrez had previously worked for the California Agricultural Labor Relations Board and was well versed in how employer sanctions split Democratic constituencies. She immediately raised concerns with DPS Director Stu Eizenstat. She argued that the task force had not properly explored the sanctions issue, noting that there was "no examination of the fiscal impact, no discussion with experts as to the feasibility, cost or timing problems." She warned to "expect an outcry" from outside groups against the proposed employment ID system and from employers against the sanctions policies. Gutierrez also called into question the feasibility of the plan, noting that enforcement would be difficult. Gutierrez urged Eizenstat to insist that the administration "should not adopt a fixed policy" and instead should have a group study the feasibility of certain proposals.[73]

Disregarding Gutierrez's warnings, the task force submitted the proposal to the president on April 27. President Carter reviewed the recommendations, approved the employer sanctions proposal, and urged that the proof of work eligibility status "be strict" and not just require a driver's license or birth certificate.[74] Feeling political pressure to address illegal immigration, President Carter quickly rejected any proposal of further studies, commissions, or policy development on immigration and instead urged that the proposals be expedited into law so the public would understand "the seriousness of a growing problem."[75] His haste and lack of thorough policy development with interest group buy-in would come back to haunt him.

With the proposal already formulated, the administration set up briefings to review it for a few key members of Congress, along with leaders from the AFL-CIO, Latino interest groups, and business groups.[76] The limited meetings on the Hill with Rodino, Kennedy, Cranston, Eastland, and Eilberg exposed lukewarm support for the Carter plan.[77] Eizenstat's briefings with the major Latino organizations drew an even more negative response. The groups expressed their opposition to the employer sanctions proposal, as well as the Eilberg and Rodino bills, as they worried about employment discrimination resulting from all three of the proposals.[78]

Disregarding all of the Hill's concerns voiced to top White House staff, President Carter's formal immigration proposal sent to Congress on August 4 included employer sanctions with civil penalties. In issuing the policy, the president acknowledged the possibility of discrimination, calling it "intolerable," but argued that the proposal was designed to minimize discrimination.[79]

Predictably, reactions within Washington varied widely and reflected the lack of consensus-building and consultation that marked the Carter policy proposal. Among Washington interest groups, there was widespread opposition to the Carter proposal. MALDEF and the Mexican American Political Association (MAPA) attacked employer sanctions as discriminatory.[80] Business interests largely rejected the Carter proposal, with the US Chamber of Commerce testifying that its employer sanctions proposal would be burdensome.[81] Unions criticized the Carter proposal, with AFL-CIO President George Meany labeling it "much too weak," and called for tougher employer sanction penalties.[82]

The Carter proposal also received a cool reception on the Hill. There was a backlash among many members for what they perceived as the administration's cursory and half-hearted consultations with the legislature on the issue.[83] Carter's failure to understand how policymaking was as much about politics as it was about policy was a significant blow. Ultimately, Rodino, Eastland, and Kennedy all reluctantly introduced their versions of Carter's proposal and begrudgingly scheduled hearings. As Deputy Associate Attorney General Doris Messiner noted on the delay, "Bell had to basically sell his soul just to get Eastland to hold a hearing."[84] The hearings unveiled the fatal flaw in the Carter proposal—a lack of policy consensus. Some members believed Carter's plan did not go far enough, while others felt it was overly punitive.

Many members, in particular those with large Latino constituencies and from border states, raised concerns with the legislation. Aware of the "political ramifications of supporting legislation many Chicanos believe is inimical to their interests," Senator Dennis DeConcini of Arizona spoke out against the "problematic" legislation, calling for revisions.[85] The Congressional Hispanic Caucus was fragmented over the Carter proposal. Congressman Roybal argued that while he viewed the employer sanctions proposal as it currently stood as not harsh, he feared it would open the door for stronger amendments to the proposal.[86]

Congressman Roybal was worried about the lack of organized activity from many Latino groups in reaction to the legislation. In meeting with leadership of several Latino organizations to discuss the Carter proposal, Roybal admonished the groups for a lack of a cohesive lobbying effort, specifically, an effort "staffed by competent and dedicated persons . . . and one that has paid members and a constituency that is real. An organization the Hill will listen to." Roybal called for a national Latino organization summit and he entreated the Latino organizations to get more involved and form a substantial new outreach campaign that targeted members of Congress with sizeable

Latino constituencies, as we "cannot go on talking to ourselves and to other liberals."[87]

But Roybal's admonishments to work more closely together rankled the leaders of many of these organizations. The politics of immigration and employer sanctions raised by the Carter proposal exacerbated rivalries between organizations seeking to distinguish themselves on the national stage. In particular, MALDEF and NCLR vied to be considered the premier Latino lobbying organization and saw the fight over the Carter legislation as the means through which to achieve prominence within a larger jurisdictional turf battle.

At this moment in 1977, MALDEF was already strategizing how it could cement its position as a leader on immigration issues both in Washington policymaking circles and also within the larger Latino community.[88] Washington staffer Al Perez argued to MALDEF president Martinez that MALDEF had achieved their first goal, as they were seen as the leading Latino immigration organization in broader Washington because they were viewed as the "most potent Hispanic opposition" driving conversations with the White House on these issues. But Perez felt they still were not recognized as the leading group on immigration policy by Latino organizations throughout the country because they had been hampered by their communications effort. Perez noted, "It makes no difference what MALDEF does; if people don't know about it, no proper credit or recognition will be forthcoming." Perez saw NCLR as MALDEF's main rival for leadership among the Latino organizations, saying they were "trying to be king of the barrio" on immigration.[89] Pointing to NCLR's larger media and communications team, Perez pushed Martinez to improve and expand MALDEF's media relations work. In addition, in order to reduce NCLR's influence, he pushed Martinez to influence staffers at the White House to ensure that MALDEF, and not NCLR, would be seen as facilitating an upcoming meeting between Latino groups and the White House.[90]

NCLR was having similar strategy sessions in order to gain greater recognition within the DC policymaking community and among the Latino organizations. Looking to gain more national visibility, NCLR began writing public position papers, gave congressional testimony multiple times, and sought to use NCLR board member Leonel Castillo's appointment as director of INS to further cement the group's stature in Washington. As a means of fortifying its leadership role within the Latino community in Washington, NCLR pushed for the establishment of various coalition groups, and then took leadership roles in all of them. These groups included the Ad Hoc

Coalition to meet with INS, which ultimately became a permanent advisory committee to INS and the Forum of National Hispanic Organizations, for which NCLR served in its leadership role. Later in the 1980s, NCLR would play a key role in the formation of the Hispanic Coalition.[91]

Working to eliminate some of these divisions within the Latino lobbying community, many Latino groups came together in San Antonio for the First National Chicano/Latino Conference on Immigration and Public Policy in October 1977. There they passed joint resolutions calling for an extension of full constitutional rights to resident aliens and amnesty for unauthorized workers.[92] Following the conference, these groups continued to work together to mobilize opposition to the Carter proposal during the winter and spring of 1977–1978 and engaged in significant lobbying on the Hill. The groups also began to reach out to other organizations such as the ACLU, the Church World Service of the National Council of Churches, and the National Immigration, Refugees, and Citizenship Forum to discuss legislation strategy and to exchange information on lobbying efforts and materials. The unified efforts among these groups would last for the next six years and would play a significant role in obstructing the passage of employer sanctions.

This newly unified opposition from the Latino lobby, the "strange bedfellows" opposition of MALDEF, MAPA, UFW, and the Chamber of Commerce, along with the Carter administration's failure to engage key constituencies and members of Congress worked to weaken the Carter proposal enough that the administration was unable to capitalize on the window created by Eastland's retirement in 1978. The Carter administration had run headfirst into the tough wall of the fragmented structure of federal policymaking and the unique world of Washington policymaking.

With Carter's proposal dead in Congress, the White House decided to support the development of a bipartisan commission to study immigration policy. The idea for the commission had been proposed by Congressman Eilberg and Senator Kennedy, which allowed Kennedy, as he weighed a 1980 presidential run, to distance himself from his earlier employer sanctions proposals that split the key Democratic constituencies of organized labor and ethnic lobbies.[93] With President Carter's support, in 1978 Congress created the Select Commission on Immigration and Refugee Policy (SCIRP), which provided an outlet for both policy development and the political focus needed for broader consensus support.[94]

The establishment of the SCIRP signaled the end of legislative action on immigration policy during the Carter administration. Throughout the decade, the liberal coalition had broken apart significantly, posing challenges to forming a liberal immigration policy. At the same time, conservative restrictionist sentiment toward immigration had gained a strong following, not just in public discourse, but also within the Washington beltway on both sides of the aisle. While all of these changes should have spelled success for the growing restrictionist movement, a strong counterweight to restrictionist efforts had also emerged, namely a unified Latino opposition that supported a pro-immigration agenda. The viscous, fragmented American governing system and the unusual pairings of opposition ensured that no action was taken on federal immigration policy. In the next decade, and with a new administration in the White House, the broader issues at play would continue to be pulled between these oppositional forces.

4

"A Riverboat Gamble"

THE PASSAGE OF EMPLOYER SANCTIONS

ELECTION NIGHT 1980 ushered in a new era in Washington. Ronald Reagan won the presidency handily, surpassing expectations by winning 50.7 percent of the popular vote to Carter's 41 percent. While the popular vote was not a landslide, the Electoral College was. Reagan took forty-four states to Carter's six, winning the Electoral College 489–49. While the Democrats still controlled the House of Representatives, the GOP picked up thirty-five seats which, when combined with the strength of southern conservative Democrats, gave new potency to the conservative coalition. In the Senate, the GOP gained twelve seats, taking control of the chamber for the first time since 1954.[1]

This landslide victory would not only distinctly shape Washington but would also have a tangible impact on immigration politics. From the early days of the Reagan administration, the White House began developing an immigration strategy that both placated its traditional base of Republicans who supported expansive immigration to fulfill labor needs and opposed market regulations and also placated the rising popular call for restriction from those who viewed immigrants as a threat to the culture of the nation and a drain on government services. For the next five years, the White House would continue to try to find this balance to satisfy its split constituency. Nonetheless, the Reagan administration actually accomplished little on immigration because the balancing act was so difficult, and the administration often preferred to let Congress act first.

Congress took the lead on immigration reform during these years. Restrictionist Republicans, in particular, repeatedly proposed bills that included employer sanctions. Democrats and moderate Republicans alike sought to gain the support of the emerging Latino voting bloc without alienating other key members of their constituencies who were put off by the specter of unauthorized immigration. The difficulty of holding together a coalition for reform combined with the impending 1984 election and party politics repeatedly led to defeat of the immigration reform bills.

By the middle of the 1980s, opposition to immigration reform began to weaken, brought on by a confluence of forces: diminished opposition from Latino groups, more closed legislative processes, and general frustration with the lack of legislative action to address what the public viewed as an issue of critical importance. Congress shut out lobbyists from the negotiation process and the legislative process moved forward with surprising speed. In 1986, Congress passed the Immigration Reform and Control Act (IRCA). The new law included employer sanctions, anti-discrimination rights provisions that prohibited employers from discriminating based on national original or alienage status, a guest worker program, and a large-scale legalization program.

In the White House, vigorous debate ensued about the expansiveness of the rights provisions in the bill, leading Reagan to issue a signing statement limiting their scope. Overall, he refused to put the weight of the presidency behind any substantive restrictionist reform. Buffeted by growing public support for immigration restriction, the administration decided against punitive action toward employers of unauthorized workers. In doing so, Reagan doubled down on his commitment to a free market, deregulatory stance. In the end, debates in the 1980s over immigration restriction, surprisingly, led to relatively liberal legislation. These policies emerged not out of clear, ideologically coherent policy positions, but instead through tangled political compromises, sometimes crafted to address complex policy questions and, at other times, merely for the sake of incremental political gains.

Restrictionist activists had begun the decade with hope for aggressive action to close the border and end unauthorized immigrants' access to employment in the United States. What they got was the IRCA bill, which contained far more liberal provisions. By the end of the decade, frustrated and disappointed with the ineffectiveness of employer sanctions, the fractured federal legislative process and the federal government as a whole, they would turn toward state legislatures in the 1990s, where they believed they could more efficiently implement their agenda.

Reagan's Reluctant Start

Reagan initially hesitated to address immigration policy. During the 1980 campaign, then-Governor Reagan had promised to admit Mexican workers "for whatever length of time they want to stay." Long a supporter of free market economic policies, Reagan embraced the idea of a free trade zone between Mexico, Canada, and the United States where workers, goods, and services would freely flow, and supported the removal of any trade barriers that might hamper this ideal.[2] Reagan was not interested in engaging deeply on overhauling the nation's immigration system, but growing public concern with illegal immigration made immigration policy impossible to avoid.

Public concern over illegal immigration was growing and by June 1980, 91 percent of respondents to a Roper poll reported that they "wanted the federal government to make an all-out effort against illegal entry into the U.S." Furthermore, public favor for employer sanctions remained high, with a Gallup poll that year finding that 66 percent of Americans supported making it illegal to employ an unauthorized immigrant.[3] Recognizing these trends, White House Chief of Staff James Baker and Counselor Ed Meese made a strong argument for the administration engaging on the issue, telling the president that Americans viewed illegal immigration as "a major national problem." In a memo to Reagan, Baker and Meese argued that this national focus was rooted in two main elements. The first was a fear of racial change, which "while not representing America's best instincts, these are political facts that cannot be ignored." Second, they felt the changing economy was making immigration a major national focus. As unauthorized immigrants moved out of agricultural jobs and into blue-collar and service occupations, unauthorized immigrants were viewed as a greater threat to American job displacement.[4] Baker and Meese more urgently pressed Reagan to get ahead of the issue as the SCRIP prepared to present its report to the president. While the SCRIP had served as a means for the Carter administration to push any resolution of the immigration issue further down the road, the finished report was delivered to the new president soon after he came into office. The White House preemptively sought to disassociate itself from the commission and its recommendations, calling the report generally sound but with "controversial recommendations."[5]

While not enthusiastic, but viewing addressing immigration as necessary, both the political and the policy arms of the Reagan White House moved to consider what immigration policy options might be available. Beginning with the political implications, the administration turned to Reagan pollster Dick Wirthlin for his opinion, who argued that while there was broad support for stricter admissions measures, it was not without risk, as illegal immigration "contains both an opportunity and danger for us."

In particular, Wirthlin focused on the potential impact of the measures on Latinos. Reminding White House advisors that Latinos represented a new source of support for Reagan in 1980, he warned of a recent decline in Latino support for Reagan because the administration had been considering new immigration regulations. But he also argued that the issue could be an opportunity, if handled well, to solidify Latino support and "to demonstrate compassion and outreach."[6] Turning to the president's base of "blue collar ethnics-lower middle income voters," Wirthlin noted that they envisioned the continent as one where people and commerce moved through the United States, Canada, and Mexico more freely than current policy allowed so they would therefore be open to immigration reform. Wirthlin closed his memo urging balance, as this was a great political opportunity on immigration policy, but also advising to tread carefully due to the variety of opinions among traditional Republicans.

While the political strategists grappled with Wirthlin's advice, the policy side assessed the administration's policy options through an internal administration task force to look at both legal and illegal immigration.[7] After a few meetings, a divide emerged within the administration: those who favored a temporary worker program and those who pushed back with support for employer sanctions. Building on this divide, two camps emerged in the administration: one in favor of a legislative proposal with a large guest worker program, no legalization component, and no employer sanctions, and the other in support of a proposal of a more moderate guest worker program, a legalization program, and employer sanctions.[8]

Supporters of employer sanctions in the White House realized that they were not going to be an effective policy solution to reducing illegal immigration, but they felt sanctions were useful as a tool to provide the administration a restrictionist cover for pushing a larger guest worker program that fit with the administration's larger economic ideals. Joe Ghougassian, a staffer in the Office of Policy Development, noted, "while the concept of a guest worker is sound, in practicality, given the U.S. public and domestic labor and political forces, the *idea is a loser.*" Given the rising unemployment and the proposed Reagan budget cuts, Ghougassian felt that introducing a guest worker program alone without wrapping it in the restrictionist wrapper of employer sanctions would be "political suicide."[9] Further up the hierarchy, Deputy Chief of Staff Frank Hodsoll made a similar argument to Baker. "Even the strongest employer sanctions are not likely to solve the problem," but "politics in this country will not permit any kind of temporary workers program without a real demonstration of intent to enforce Immigration laws."[10] Hodsoll urged supporting employer sanctions as a restrictionist shell to pass a temporary worker program. With the political arm pushing to move on immigration policy and the White House coalescing around the idea that employer sanctions were necessary for political cover, they agreed to a plan with a legalization program, employer sanctions with a national identification card, and a guest worker program.

Given the sensitivity of the debate, the White House again turned to pollster Wirthlin, tasking him with polling the specific elements of their proposal. Wirthlin found widespread support to "put the onus on business" through employer sanctions but discovered strong opposition to a national identification system that involved cards for employment verification.[11] He warned that a national identification card system could be "disastrous" by uniting both ends of the ideological spectrum, with liberals opposing it as an "abridgement of civil liberties" while conservatives would go against it as "yet another intrusion by 'big brother' government."[12]

With Wirthlin gathering public opinions, a draft plan was circulated to the members of the cabinet for their feedback. The voices of deregulation and free enterprise in the White House reacted vehemently against the employer sanctions proposal. William Niskanen, a member of the Council of Economic Advisers, argued that employer sanctions were not only ineffective, but they would also run "counter to our basic policy of lessening regulation."[13] Lyn Nofziger, Assistant to the President for Political Affairs, argued, "We came here to get government off of our back and to reduce the size of bureaucracy and to cut back on the number of regulations. This proposal does just the opposite."[14] However, the strongest objections to the proposal in the White House were to the national identification card for employers to verify employment status. Secretary of Education Terrel Bell called the proposal "too Orwellian," warning it would result in "huge political . . . problems."[15] Martin Anderson, Reagan's domestic policy advisor, compared the idea to the use of tattoos on victims of the Holocaust, telling the president that the card could be "the first step to a police state."[16]

Given the cabinet opposition and its unpopularity in the polling data, the White House dropped the national identification card proposal from the Reagan package in July. Looking for alternative ways to verify an employee's eligibility, Baker and others came back to trust in the intentions of business owners. Pushing this view, they crafted the administration's position that employers need only demonstrate that they had made a good-faith effort to determine their workers' eligibility. By adopting a policy that employers would only need to make a good-faith defense to employer sanctions, the Reagan administration essentially guaranteed that employer sanctions would not be enforced and cemented its commitment to deregulation and free enterprise.[17]

As the White House continued to finalize its immigration plan, Reagan staffers began to reach out to key constituencies by holding a series of small meetings to brief them on the contents of the plan, doing the critical outreach that Carter had failed to do. Opinion within the Republican Party leadership and among Republican politicians from border states split. Some viewed sanctions as "a critical ingredient" in their calculus, while others feared that sanctions "would make farmers and ranchers 'law breakers and criminals.'" They were also concerned with the increasing bureaucracy and red tape that would be created by any enforcement of sanctions.[18] Latino organizations expressed strong objections to the employer sanctions proposal, raising concerns about the potential for employment discrimination if legislation imposed widespread sanctions.[19]

After taking into consideration the political implications of their policy proposal, the White House released its immigration proposal on July 30, 1981, which sought to ameliorate multiple constituencies by finding a middle ground between those calling for restriction and those committed to free enterprise. It was a product not of cogent ideology but of political strategy. Immediate press reactions varied on the specific policies but united in their recognition of the larger political game that the administration was playing. They recognized that Reagan sought to satisfy "growing public clamor for a clampdown," while simultaneously ensuring that the administration's key business supporters still had access to cheap Mexican labor.[20]

In hearings before the House and Senate over the subsequent weeks and months, administration officials, members of Congress, labor, business, and minority group representatives, as well as scholars, weighed in on the Reagan proposal. Much of the response was critical, and the criticism came from both sides of the ideological spectrum.

Latino organizations and business interests, each for reasons of their own, joined in publicly questioning sanctions in testimony before Congress. MALDEF and LULAC testified that the anti-discrimination provisions added to prevent racial profiling were not strong enough.[21] The National Council of Agricultural Employers (NCAE) testified, urging that if employer sanctions were imposed, there had to be significant concessions for employers' defense, and warned that sanctions would lead to a labor supply shortfall. The Chamber of Commerce focused on the burden that sanctions placed on employers and the lack of secure means of identifying an employee's work eligibility status.[22]

By and large, border state governors were unanimous in their opposition to the Reagan proposal. Most damaging to the Reagan administration was the surprise opposition from Governor Clements of Texas, who was the only Republican governor along the border, and who had been a key ally of Reagan's during his successful drive in Texas in the 1980 election. Clements, who had been actively courting Mexican American support in Texas, attacked the administration's plan, saying its amnesty was inadequate as it would still allow "the illegal sub-class to continue to exist . . . and this is wrong." Clements also argued the plan would make employers "law-breakers" and was "totally out of line," as well as being "unrealistic" and "doomed to failure."[23] The Reagan administration sought to downplay the differences with Clements and worked quietly to earn his support. Ultimately, the administration was successful at convincing Clements to back its plan by agreeing to support the state of Texas with a brief in the *Plyler* case.[24]

There were also those who criticized the administration's plan as too lenient toward businesses. Leaders from both the AFL-CIO and UFW testified that the administration's proposals did not go far enough, and advocated higher penalties.[25] Maudine Cooper of the National Urban League also testified in support of employer sanctions, citing the high rate of black youth unemployment as evidence for the need to crack down on the employment of unauthorized immigrants, asking "how much of the world's poor this country can absorb while its own poor become poorer."[26]

While the White House was interested in reactions to the immigration proposal from within political circles, Reagan staffers also closely watched national polling. In August, an NBC national poll showed that the issue of immigration was of growing importance, with 87 percent of Americans viewing immigration as either very or somewhat important, up from 74 percent four years earlier. Other polls showed widespread support for restricting immigration into the United States.[27]

Having observed how their predecessors had mishandled the immigration question, the Reagan administration's development of a policy and its public release reflected an awareness of the importance of winning over both the Washington political class and the fractured and complicated American public. The growing power of the restrictionist movement in the policy process can be seen in the administration's willingness to embrace a somewhat restriction- ist agenda, even though it was counter to Reagan's campaign proposals and general economic philosophies. The administration's stripping of a national identification card requirement from the proposal as well as the inclusion of employer sanctions as political cover—even as the White House foresaw their likely ineffectiveness, reflects the ways in which the administration sought to balance politics and policy, and mitigate the consequences of a proposal they knew would prove to be divisive within their own party and the country.

Congress Pushes Right

While Regan tried to control the policy process to assuage his supporters on both sides of the issue, Congress soon took the lead by introducing its own measures. Following extensive hearings on the administration's bill during the fall of 1981, the chairmen of the Senate and House immigration subcommittees responded by introducing their own reform legislation in March 1982. The legislation, sponsored by Senator Alan Simpson of Wyoming in the Senate and Representative Roman Mazzoli of Kentucky in the House, incorporated most of the administration's proposals, but it took an even more restrictionist bent. The Simpson-Mazzoli legislation was more punitive than the White House proposal as it included criminal penalties and extended employer sanctions regulations to a greater number of employers than the administration's proposal had called for. It also created a new national identification program, a proposal that Reagan's advisors had explicitly rejected earlier.

Reagan took his cue from opinion polls as he evaluated the Simpson-Mazzoli plan. He noted the sustained widespread political support on the Hill and nationally for doing something harsh on immigration and shied away from coming out against Simpson-Mazzoli. Instead, Reagan went back on key aspects of his policy approach and supported the Simpson-Mazzoli bill as its own vehicle for reform on the Hill.[28] But while the administration conspicuously supported the bill in public, Reagan officials privately expressed concern that it created too many enforcement and compliance burdens. The White House began to wage a quiet campaign to push back on several elements of the bill.[29] It soon became apparent that the White House's efforts to weaken the bill were unnecessary, as the legislation ran into strong opposition once it reached the House floor.[30]

Hearings on the bill brought out opposition from both the left and the right. MALDEF, NCLR, and LULAC all testified in opposition to the employer sanctions and warned about civil rights and discriminatory concerns.[31] On the right, Libertarian conservatives spoke out against the proposed identification verification process as a threat to civil liberties. The *Wall Street Journal* captured this viewpoint in an editorial that argued that the proposal "conjures up images of Soviet and Nazi tyranny, of South African pass laws."[32] Business interests such as the US Chamber of Commerce also opposed the bill as being onerous on business. Against this wall of opposition, the House bill died during the lame duck session, and President Reagan was spared from publicly supporting and signing a bill with which he had serious concerns. Reagan had been spared the political damage of opposing congressional leadership in his own party by the unusual alliance of libertarians and civil rights organizations. Both the legislation introduced by congressional leadership and the response given by the Reagan administration to avoid publicly opposing it shows the growing strength of the restrictionist movement within the Republican Party and how the deeply muddled political process shaped policy development.

Choppy Waters

While the policy process and politics on the Hill were playing out, they were only one part of the White House's focus as the impact of Reagan's immigration proposals on electoral politics increasingly drew the administration's attention. White House officials began to worry that the administration's support among Latinos was eroding. In the 1980 campaign Reagan had won 37 percent of Hispanics nationwide and notably, he made significant inroads in Texas, garnering 30 percent of the Hispanic vote, the largest percentage of that vote ever obtained by a Republican presidential candidate. Reagan and his campaign hoped to expand on these successes as they headed into the 1982 midterms and 1984 presidential election. Yet, while demographic trends at the time predicted the Hispanic vote would play an increasingly significant role in elections throughout the Southwest and nationally as that segment's population continued to grow, there were still substantial barriers to overcome for Hispanic voters to play a larger role in the electoral process. In the 1980 election, while there was a 55 percent increase in voter eligibility among the Hispanic population since 1970, voter turnout among this swath of the nation stood at only 30 percent. At the time, about one-third of all Hispanics in the United States were thought by pollsters to be ineligible to vote because either they were not citizens or they were too young.

Republicans saw the potential to win over the Latino vote in several ways. They made a special concerted effort to win over middle-class Mexican

Americans through appeals based on "cultural imperatives" such as home, family, and religiosity. Some political strategists and observers saw Reagan's moves on immigration as a way to appeal to a broader group of Latinos. As one well-known political reporter commented, "If President Reagan is able to naturalize the millions of Mexicans who live here legally or illegally and institute a guest worker program that is acceptable to many Mexican Americans . . . the Republicans might even lock up a share of that vote themselves."[33] While Republicans publicly discussed how to make gains over the 1980 election showing, privately there were signs that the opposite was occurring.

In early 1982, Elizabeth Dole, the director of the White House Office of the Public Liaison (OPL), the main conduit for outreach to the Latino community, began receiving anecdotal reports of an erosion of Latino support for the president. At the same time, a public poll also highlighted growing disapproval for the president and decreasing Republican affiliation among Hispanic voters. This data was confirmed by a private Wirthlin poll that showed a net drop of 24 percent in the president's approval rating by Hispanics over the previous nine months.[34]

Dole raised her concerns to James Baker, noting that during the previous few months, "Hispanic interest" in political plans to address the flood of illegal immigration had "intensified measurably," calling the matter "an extremely sensitive area" politically for the White House as Mexican Americans now numbered in the millions. Dole felt the Simpson-Mazzoli bill "constituted a crisis of major proportions among Hispanics and business owners in the Southwest." The future US senator recommended that the White House direct careful attention to this constituency given "the potential for extensive political damage of each of these issues."[35]

Dole's warnings took on increased urgency following the midterm elections, where the Republican Party absorbed deep losses in Congress and at the gubernatorial level. After shedding twenty-six House seats and seven governorships, some Republicans began to reconsider the potential of the Latino vote, while several prominent officeholders criticized the Reagan administration over its handling of the issue. Governor Tom Kean of New Jersey noted that the GOP was "never going to be a majority party until we do reach out and show that we care." Governor James Thompson of Illinois argued that the party needed to appeal better to "blacks, Hispanics, minorities, women," acknowledging "we haven't done enough about that, and this election proves it."[36]

As 1982 drew to a close, the Reagan White House struggled on several fronts. The administration had not been able to influence the development and consideration of immigration legislation in Congress, but was saved from having to sign a highly restrictionist policy they did not completely support by the work of outside opposition groups which stymied the bill in Congress. The White House was also struggling to reconcile the Republican Party's various political constituencies, wading between business interests and the emerging restrictionist interest groups and trying to balance calls for comprehensive legislation with a desire to cultivate the budding Republican support from Latino voters which now appeared to be wavering. But the end of the year did not signal an end to the immigration fight, which would resume in the next Congress.

When Congress reconvened in January 1983, it returned to the stalled issue of reform. Undeterred by previous failures, Senator Simpson and Congressman Mazzoli introduced legislation in February that was largely identical to the bills that passed in the Senate and the House Judiciary Committees in the previous session. New hearings were held in both chambers and testimony was heard, with the administration again testifying to its general support of the intent of the bills, and MALDEF, NCLR, and others continuing to lodge their opposition to Simpson and Mazzoli's plans.[37] In a shift, the Chamber of Commerce decided to press for changes to the proposed sanctions rather than trying to eliminate them, as it felt their passage was likely.[38] The American Bar Association reversed its position on the bill and announced its opposition to employer sanctions because of discrimination concerns.[39]

While the Reagan administration continued to testify in support of the Simpson-Mazzoli legislation, in private, concerns with the legislation grew. Fiscal hawks like Office of Management and Budget Director David Stockman were increasingly disturbed by the potential large cost of the legalization aspects of the bill as they argued that health, welfare, and social services costs would rise as legal immigrants would use services previously denied to them due to their unauthorized status.[40] Stockman began to push for the administration to announce a shift in its posture toward the legislation.

Stockman and Attorney General William French Smith brought the matter to the president at a cabinet meeting on April 21, 1983. French Smith argued for maintaining the administration's support of the Simpson-Mazzoli legislation, whereas Stockman warned that leaving the matter for Congress to decide was dangerous, as the "Hill thinks we want a bill bad enough to pay almost any price."[41] Reagan agreed with Stockman's budget concerns, but decided against immediate action, suggesting instead that if a passed bill came in with too big a price tag, he would veto it.[42]

Over the summer and fall, the administration heard more and more concerns about the bill from their political allies.[43] The White House again reached out privately to congressional leaders regarding their reservation with the legislation and warning that the administration was considering publicly opposing the bill.[44] With little success in convincing Congress to alter the bill, the administration began to prepare a public announcement removing its support for the Simpson-Mazzoli legislation. Given growing public support calling for immigration restriction, the administration took great pains to frame its withdrawal of support in a way that made it appear more restrictionist for political gain while opposing the more hardline legislation. The administration began preparing documents to announce that it had only supported the bill's large legalization for "political reasons to ensure interest group support for enforcement" and now were withdrawing their support since legalization was too fiscally problematic to allow the bill to go through. Second, they were preparing to say that the employer sanctions had been too diluted by agricultural interests.[45]

Before the White House was forced to show its hand, White House aides were relieved when House Speaker Tip O'Neill suddenly announced that the immigration bill would not come to the floor. O'Neill argued he would not allow the House to pass a bill only to let Reagan veto it in order to curry Latino favor in 1984. "Do I think the President is political enough to veto a bill to grant votes for his party?" O'Neill asked. "The answer is yes."[46]

The White House reacted immediately to O'Neill's statements, denying his charges of playing politics with the legislation.[47] However, just over a month later, O'Neill announced that he would work to get the same bill passed in the next Congress. O'Neill's reversal was said by his aides to be a result of conversations with Senator Simpson in which he assured O'Neill that they would not send a bill to the president without promises from the White House that the president would sign it.[48] O'Neill was playing the same politics he had accused Reagan of, but regardless, the bill was dead in the current Congress.

Democrats and Republicans alike in the early 1980s struggled to navigate the tricky political waters of immigration policy. Both wrestled to address growing calls for restriction and also gain traction with the expanding Latino vote, while at the same time avoid unsettling their more traditional bases of support for the 1982 midterm elections as well as the upcoming 1984 presidential election. The difficulty of forging a cohesive coalition to pass reform remained elusive for now.

Playing Presidential Politics

While electoral politics played a strong but not definitive role in the consideration of immigration bills in 1982 and 1983, by 1984 it was the single most determining factor of immigration legislation, influencing content, timing, and potential passage. The presidential race heightened the stakes as leaders in both parties struggled to manage the bill in a way that would allow them to gain the support of their traditional allies as well as gain new sources of support.

Early in May, the Senate passed Simpson's bill that was substantially the same as the Senate-passed bill of 1982. But action on the legislation was again bottled up in the House. It was increasingly apparent that immigration and the pending Simpson-Mazzoli legislation had opened significant rifts within the Democratic Party, and had the potential to "tear up the party" according to Ann Lewis, the political director of the Democratic National Committee. Peter Delly, chairman of the California Democratic Party, warned that if the Simpson-Mazzoli bill passed, "It would be a slap in the face to one of our biggest voting blocks, Hispanic Americans, and it would give Hispanic voters a strong reason to stay home or vote for President Reagan."[49]

Pressure to delay working on the legislation grew in advance of the May 5 Texas caucus and the June 5 California primary. In Texas, immigration became a hot topic not only in the presidential contest, in which Walter Mondale, Gary Hart, and the Reverend Jesse Jackson all campaigned against Simpson-Mazzoli, but also in the Senate primary race between conservative Representative Kent Hance and State Senator Lloyd Doggett which led to an eventual runoff between the two in early June.[50] In early May, responding to pleas made by the California Democrats and by Mondale, O'Neill agreed to delay action on the immigration bill until after the California Democratic primary.

While some Democrats sought to delay the bill, others in the Democratic caucus urged action on the bill, fearing that the delay would become a fall campaign issue and that President Reagan would use it to portray the party as soft on unauthorized immigrants and uninterested in protecting American jobs. In addition, agricultural interests with influence among many Southern and Midwestern members wanted an expanded guest worker program, so they exerted considerable extra pressure on the membership to give floor consideration to Simpson-Mazzoli. Ultimately these forces were successful, as the bill made it out of committee and to the floor.[51]

Floor consideration began in June and debate over the legislation and amendments was often highly charged.[52] One strong critic of the legislation, Congressman Barney Frank, a Massachusetts Democrat, warned that the bill as it was constituted would create a group of "unemployed across the border able to come in here, not as citizens, not as fellow human beings with full rights, but just as that group of domestics that come and go."[53] He offered an amendment that would prohibit employers from discriminating against legal immigrants in hiring or recruiting workers, make it an "unfair immigration-related employment practice" to discriminate on the basis of national origin or alienage and create an entity within the Justice Department to investigate complaints of job discrimination based on national origin or alienage. Frank's amendment passed the chamber overwhelmingly, 404 to 9. The language of the Frank amendment spoke directly to the Supreme Court's 1973 decision in *Espinoza v. Farah Mfg. Co*, by making discrimination on the basis of both national origin and citizenship status illegal. As seen by the broad support that it gained and its easy passage, the Frank amendment was not a very powerful anti-discrimination amendment. As MALDEF wryly noted in an internal memo, the passage of the tool "sealed the fate of any attempt to eliminate employer sanctions" as it "assuaged liberal guilt over the discrimination issue."[54] While MALDEF felt it was too weak, the Reagan administration was concerned by the amendment and the National Association of Manufacturers' (NAM) went on a public campaign against it, writing in the *Washington Post* that the amendment created "a new form of discrimination" and redundant "bureaucratic boards."[55] Several other developments occurred during the debate and importantly growers, relying on the lobbying prowess of well-known Washington attorney and former DNC Chairman Bob Strauss, secured a coup with the passage of an amendment creating a guest worker program. This spurred the AFL-CIO to abandon its support for the bill, but the effect was minimal and the bill passed by a narrow 216 to 211 vote.[56]

With the passage of the bill in the House, many in the Latino lobby were furious at the Democratic establishment by the summer of 1984. As Helen Gonzales of MALDEF said, "What it [passage] shows is the Republicans don't care about Hispanics and Democrats continue to take us for granted."[57] Latino discontent with the Mondale campaign, which had been growing for some time, worsened. In early primaries, Mondale announced a blanket opposition to Simpson-Mazzoli, but without taking a firm stance on many of the specific provisions.[58] During the Texas primary some within the Latino community, including Sylvia Rodriguez, a Democratic National Committeewoman from Houston, felt Democratic Latinos had given up too much of their political capital too early with the Mondale campaign and as a result felt the Mondale campaign was taking their support for granted and not addressing their concerns with the Simpson-Mazzoli bill. She urged, "now we have to build leverage between now and the convention."[59] Tensions rose further when Mondale did not attend the LULAC annual conference in June, leading LULAC President Mario Obledo to ask Latino delegates to withhold their first-ballot presidential votes at the convention to voice their displeasure over the immigration legislation.[60]

Latinos' simmering disappointment boiled over during the Democratic National Convention in San Francisco. Latino delegates, already angry at what they perceived as the party's lack of vigor in defeating Simpson-Mazzoli, felt the party platform should specifically reject the legislation. Several warned that it would be hard to mobilize the Latino vote if Simpson-Mazzoli was passed with Democratic support and Mondale also was the nominee.[61] Obledo issued an ultimatum to party leaders: "guarantee" a defeat of the immigration bill, or face a Latino delegate vote boycott of the first ballot.[62]

Mondale's team worked to try to mollify those Latino activists that one staffer noted were "soured by a sense of having been dealt out of the action." Mondale's son William went to the Hispanic caucus meeting at the convention to try to win over the delegates and was booed. Leaders of organized labor and other key leaders convened in a meeting orchestrated by AFL-CIO President Lane Kirkland and San Antonio Mayor Henry Cisneros to try to reach an agreement on a party position on the immigration bill. Latino leaders hoped to convince organized labor to join with them in defeating the legislation, but this effort failed.[63] Congressman Bill Richardson from New Mexico, Mondale's chief emissary to the Latino community, worried that the anger of Latino leaders might turn into "an incipient revolt" before the election.

Despite these efforts to unite the party, the split among Latino delegates and leadership remained, as grassroots delegates and outside activists like Obledo called for abstention from the first ballot, while others, mainly elected officials like Mayor Cisneros, New Mexico Governor Toney Anaya, and Congressman Roybal, pleaded for Democratic unity and urged delegates not to take up the Simpson-Mazzoli legislation at the convention.[64]

The showdown came at a two-hour meeting of the Hispanic caucus that was so charged, Chairwoman Polly Baca had to pound her shoe on the lectern to maintain order. Cisneros called for delegates to vote for Mondale rather than "harming the man who has the best chance to be the nominee . . . and helping Ronald Reagan," and was heckled with chants of "Hispanics first! Democrats later!"[65] While a threatened first-ballot boycott by Hispanic caucus members failed to materialize, many of the delegates did press Mondale and vice-presidential nominee Geraldine Ferraro to intensify their opposition to the immigration measure. Desperate to unite the party, Mondale promised to do whatever he could to kill Simpson-Mazzoli. Watching the process play out from Washington, Senator Simpson criticized the "partisan hysteria, hoopla and hype against this legislation that sprang from the Democratic convention."[66]

Viva '84?

Immigration was not only causing splits among Democrats in 1984, it was also continuing to fracture the Republican Party, leaving the Reagan administration in a tough position. Up until now, Reagan had "enjoyed the best of both worlds. He could show leadership by calling for the protection of U.S. borders while blaming O'Neill for blocking immigration reform," as one reporter noted.[67] Now, with O'Neill's shift of position, the White House knew it would be forced to publicly take a hard stance on the bill.

Politically, the White House feared that Reagan's support for the Simpson-Mazzoli legislation would undermine the work Republicans were doing to build on their 1980 showing with Latino voters by appealing to shared conservative values. Ed Rollins, Assistant to the President for Political Affairs and Director of the Office of Political Affairs, and Vice President Bush worked together on crafting messaging to address immigrants' political concerns, and the RNC was running "Viva '84," a campaign to raise and spend $1 million on Latino outreach.[68] Efforts were particularly focused in Texas and California, where just more than half of the nation's Latino population lived and together cast 28 percent of the total Electoral College votes.[69] Given this outreach operation, the administration waffled on what approach to take. As one Reagan advisor noted, the political impact of Simpson-Mazzoli was unclear, calling it "a real roll of the dice" for the Republican ticket.[70]

Looking for guidance, the White House and the reelection campaign turned again to Dick Wirthlin. A Wirthlin poll found overwhelming support for Simpson-Mazzoli's employer sanctions provisions, as 72 percent of adult Americans supported the policy. Looking at several battleground states with large Mexican American populations—California, New Mexico, and

Colorado—Wirthlin found that 80 percent of voters felt that current immigration laws needed overhauling and were generally supportive of the Simpson-Mazzoli bill, but there was "a sizable block who either don't feel the laws need revising or oppose the passage of the legislation."

While Wirthlin warned of the erosion of Latino support, he felt the bill's greatest danger came from its amnesty provisions, which would turn off core conservatives. "Although Americans still like to believe the words on the Statue of Liberty, a review of the appendix suggests that there may be latent anti-immigrant sentiment in the country," he noted about the Republicans' core constituency.[71] Consequently, Wirthlin advocated deadlocking the bill in conference to ensure the president wouldn't have to take a firm stance on it before the election.

While Wirthlin advocated deadlocking the bill until after the election, the administration decided to come out publicly against the bill, but couched its opposition in a way that sought to appeal to its supporters' deregulatory ideals as well as those supporting immigration restriction. The White House argued the bill was too costly because of the legalization and too liberal because of the Frank amendment's expansive notion of alienage rights. William Bradford Reynolds, the Assistant Attorney General for Civil Rights, characterized the Frank provisions as "chart[ing] an unprecedented course in civil rights law," noting that his office did not enforce existing statutes to prohibit discrimination on the basis of alienage.[72] Defending employers' rights to hire in such a way, Reynolds said that it was "understandable that some private employers might prefer to provide employment for United States citizens rather than for citizens of other countries who come here to work."[73] With this announcement, the administration forfeited an opportunity to court the Latino vote in order to solidify the president's standing with conservative restrictionists. This decision was criticized by some in the Republican Party, including Fernando Oaxaca, head of the Mexican American Republican Council, who called the administration's overconfidence in winning the Latino vote "mind blowing."[74]

Even though the White House sought to appeal to restrictionists with its opposition to the bill, their actions drew criticism from some Republicans who still felt the White House did not go far enough. One of the groups who was disappointed in Reagan was the self-styled "New Right," a group that had emerged as a force in the last decade by claiming that the Old Right was an "elitist establishment" and ignored the concerns of the common man. The New Right's support had been a key part of the coalition that elected Reagan.[75] At the Republican convention, leaders of the "New Right," including Richard

Viguerie, Howard Phillips, and Paul Weyerich, denounced Simpson-Mazzoli and expressed their concern over legalization, sanctions, and discrimination provisions, pledging to defeat it.[76] Arthur Laffer, whose supply-side economic policies held considerable sway in the party at this time, wrote an editorial in the *Los Angeles Times* decrying the bill as a discriminatory effort "to impose tyrannical misjudgment" that would allow "illegal aliens to take jobs away from Americans."[77]

As summer turned into fall, opposition to the bill and election concerns continued to block the convening of a conference and final passage of the bill. On the Democratic side, by threatening to withhold support from the Mondale-Ferraro ticket, Latino leaders succeeded in pushing congressional Democrats to block the bill at its final stage.[78] On the Republican side, Latino groups began to focus on emerging party leaders who voted against the bill before, like Jack Kemp, to lobby against the bill. They also leaned on Vice President Bush and Senator Howard Baker as "pressure points" given that they had ambitions for the presidency in 1988.[79] While a late deal appeared possible, it fell apart and the bill died at the end of the session.[80]

The political pressures of the presidential election had made it impossible for Simpson-Mazzoli to be passed. Electoral concerns shaped the bill's timing and House passage, but the divisions evident at both parties' conventions and within the greater electorate strengthened the opposition and altered the administration's position, dooming the bill. Fear of angering key constituencies in an election year led both Republicans and Democrats to view deadlock as the most politically attractive option, and the one both ultimately embraced.

Breaking the Dam

While the intensity of political infighting and gridlock in 1984 did not bode well for future action, over the subsequent two years, a growing sense of frustration from years of inaction, reports of increasing unauthorized immigration, and the fracturing of the opposition movement came together to produce immigration reform in a surprisingly quick fashion.

The final product, the Immigration Reform and Control Act of 1986, included a large legalization program, a guest worker program, and employer sanctions as well as anti-discrimination provisions that expanded the bounds of Title VII of the Civil Rights Act of 1964. The final product reflected the strong influence of politics on the policy process and exposed the ways in which the deregulatory, free market wing of the Republican Party that wanted to ensure sustained access to cheap labor continued to drive immigration policy. Employment status verification became voluntary, the mechanisms of employer sanctions enforcement were virtually nonexistent, and the expanded alienage discrimination provisions were limited in their enforcement by a signing statement that favored employers. It was a product of many political contingencies and tangled political compromises. The fractured and fragmented federal structure had made reform difficult to achieve, and when it did occur, it lacked an ideologically coherent policy position.

In the spring of 1985, reports of unauthorized immigration continued to pepper public discourse. The theme of invasion and questions of cultural change continued to be at the forefront of news reporting. The cover of *U.S. News and World Report* in August 1985 asked, "The Disappearing Border: Will the Mexican Migration Create a New Nation?" The accompanying article told of "the march of new conquistadors in the American Southwest . . . At the vanguard are those born here . . . Behind them comes an unstoppable mass . . . America's riches are pulling people all along the continent's Hispanic horn on a great migration to the place they call El Norte."[81] The contracting Mexican economy—shrinking 4 percent in 1985—spurred the drive to immigrate as the Mexican peso continued to fall against the US dollar, increasing the value of remittance payments workers could earn in the United States.[82] As Mexican migration continued, apprehension rates of unauthorized immigrants continued to grow year after year. In 1986, the INS reported just under a million apprehensions, a 39 percent increase over the previous year. INS Western Regional Director Harold Ezell inflamed public opinion by calling the borders "out of control" and describing Mexican immigration as "an invasion."[83] Polling showed that 49 percent of adult Americans wanted immigration decreased.[84]

While this support for action on immigration restriction was growing, the opposition movement began to fracture as members of the Congressional Hispanic Caucus began to shift their positions. In the spring of 1985, Roybal sponsored a surprise alternative immigration bill that included an employer sanctions provision.[85] Roybal's bill made no progress in the House, but its mere creation signaled some of the larger shifts that were occurring within the Hispanic caucus. Across the Congressional Hispanic Caucus, the consensus on immigration reform that had formed between the late 1970s and 1984 began to shift. Congressman Bill Richardson, the new chairman of the caucus, spoke increasingly of the need to compromise and "mainstream Chicano demands in order 'to break into the political infrastructure.'"[86] Other new, younger members from border states, like California's Representative Esteban Torres, felt pressure from more restrictionist constituencies to support employer sanctions.[87] Richardson and some of these newer members reached out to Judiciary Committee Chairs Rodino and Mazzoli and offered the caucus's support for the legislation in exchange for some minor revisions.[88] These actions divided the caucus.

But the fracturing went well beyond just the Congressional Hispanic Caucus, as the Latino interest group lobby also began to fracture in 1985. While some scholars have noted the unification of the Latino lobby on immigration policy as a triumphant moment of the 1970s and 1980s, it was actually short-lived, only lasting through 1984.[89] Under pressure, as they felt even their allies on the Hill were restless to get a bill passed and nervous about the closed-door nature of the negotiations, many within the Latino lobby began to shift strategies, leaving MALDEF as one of the few groups opposing the bill.[90] Unity among the groups fell apart when NCLR, seeing passage of some bill as inevitable, returned to its more moderate roots by announcing that it no longer opposed the bill. Making what it viewed as a necessary concession on employer sanctions, NCLR instead lobbied for additional inclusion of anti-discrimination provisions.[91]

LULAC's leadership underwent significant changes during the early months of 1985, and those changes resulted in the organization shifting its strategy in Washington. Arnold Torres, the group's executive director, left after disagreements with the board, who did not approve of either how closely he worked with other groups, which they felt compromised LULAC's leadership, or his obstructionist stance on immigration policy development, which they felt had cost the group credibility in Congress. They wanted the group to reestablish a working relationship with the Reagan White House. With Torres ousted, Joseph Trevino was given control over the operation and took a much more conciliatory approach on immigration policy and employer sanctions with the Hill and the White House.[92]

With the opposition experiencing internal dissention and fracturing, early in 1985, Simpson once again introduced an immigration reform bill, but it differed in several pro-employer ways from his earlier versions. It made employer verification of worker eligibility voluntary, a move advocated by the Chamber of Commerce, and eliminated criminal penalties, even for repeated employer violations. Rather than oppose the bill, the farm lobby chose to lobby instead for provisions beneficial to their interests, an approach they had also taken in 1984. Significantly, as a result of lobbying by the National Council of Agricultural Employers, the Farm Bureau Federation, and other groups, an amendment was included in the legislation that created a large agricultural guest worker program.

In the House, Rodino and Mazzoli introduced a bill that was vastly different from Simpson's and included a sunset provision on employer sanctions, and Frank's anti-discrimination provision was offered as an amendment. Working with Congressman Howard Berman, a farmworker advocate, and Congressman Leon Panetta, who had close ties to growers, Congressman Charles Schumer brokered a compromise bill to create a farmworker program that was approved by both growers and organized labor, including the UFW, removing one of the largest hurdles to passage. With the major opposition cleared, both the Simpson and the Rodino-Mazzoli bills passed their respective chambers early in the fall.

Since the bills were not identical, many compromises had to be made in conference. The White House decided to work quietly with the sponsors and the congressional leadership to get its priorities addressed but would remain publicly silent regarding the conference committee negotiations.[93] The 1986 conference was much less contentious than the one in 1984. The scars from many earlier battles, and fatigue from earlier near-misses, added a sense of urgency for many of the members. As Congressman John Bryant from Texas put it, "Everybody had been through this. There was not a need to posture." Schumer said conferees decided, "we don't want to do this again."[94] Significantly, conferees also made an effort to prevent outside influences from weighing in at this final stage. As the Chamber of Commerce's lobbyist Virginia Thomas noted, "They were closing off all the doors and windows to outside groups. . . . There was no access."[95]

In conference, a proposal requiring the Government Accountability Office (GAO) and Congress to evaluate the impact of employer sanctions on employment discrimination in three years was accepted in lieu of a sunset provision for employer sanctions. Importantly, IRCA also spoke directly to the state actions of the 1970s, expressly forbidding any state or local law from "imposing civil or criminal sanctions (other than licensing and similar laws) upon those who employ . . . unauthorized persons."[96] At the same time, Simpson accepted the Frank amendment's anti-discrimination provisions. The final sticking point was the Panetta and Berman compromise farmworker package, which was eventually adopted and eased final passage of the bill. Many who had worked on the bill were resigned to its imperfections. Representative Dan Lungren noted, "It isn't the Sistine Chapel, but it's not a bad paint job."[97] Schumer praised the final product while acknowledging its limits, saying, "[t]he bill is a gamble, a riverboat gamble. There is no guarantee that employer sanctions will work or that amnesty will work. We are headed into uncharted waters."[98]

Once the conference report was passed in the House and the Senate, the White House was forced to decide whether the president should sign the bill. For Reagan, the Frank amendment was the main area of concern. DOJ lobbied the White House to veto the bill, arguing the Frank provision's alienage clause would create a "new concept of civil rights," with Reynolds saying it "would devastate civil rights."[99] President Reagan agreed to sign the bill only after Simpson and Rodino made floor statements clarifying the provisions that would limit the scope of the Frank amendment.

But those floor statements were not enough to address the administration's concerns. Fearing too much in the bill was left to judicial and prosecutorial discretion, the White House drafted a signing statement in order to reduce ways in which the bill could be interpreted.[100] Putting it bluntly, Associate White House Counsel Charles Raul argued the signing statement was critical to weaken the Frank provision as it posed "the most serious attack to date on the value of citizenship and on the idea that citizenship should matter . . . The Amendment would provide an unprecedented kind of 'civil right' in that neither the majority nor any minority of American citizens would be the beneficiary."[101]

When Reagan signed the bill on November 6, 1986, his signing statement noted that a noncitizen who asserted that he had been unfairly denied a job could prevail in a lawsuit only if he could prove an employer acted with "discriminatory intent." This shift of the burden of proof to the employee to prove intent would make it significantly harder for an employee to successfully sue on the basis of discrimination. The announcement of the signing statement infuriated liberals. Congressman Frank called it "intellectually dishonest."[102] The ACLU's Wade Henderson charged that Reagan's move was "nothing more than a political thrust by the President to shape the provision to his liking."[103] But there was little they could do in response.

After fifteen years of legislative battles, the fact that any sort of immigration reform was passed at the federal level reflected the growing strength of restrictionist sentiment both in Washington and in the nation as a whole. However, the final version of IRCA lacked any of the significant employer sanctions enforcement mechanisms and included a guest worker program, neither of which were present in the restrictionist legislation that had been proposed in the 1970s, demonstrating the resilient muscle of both business and agricultural interests, as well as the declining strength of organized labor during the period. The inclusion of the Frank amendment and the large legalization provision spoke to the continued strength of liberalism and the legacy of the civil rights movement among many political and social leaders, while the presidential signing statement signaled the slowly rising influence of conservative philosophies that opposed the expansion of rights for immigrants.

The legislative fight over the passage of employer sanctions also provides a window into the dynamic political forces circulating at this moment in American politics. The new economy had fractured the liberal coalition of the postwar era, and conservative immigration restrictionist Democrats began to hold increasingly more influence within the party. At the same time, Latino lobbying organizations had emerged to play a strong role in Washington. Republican politicians were also negotiating with the strength of this new restrictionist movement and the growing Latino vote, but ultimately the Reagan administration prioritized its free market base over both the growing restrictionist sentiment and cementing Latino outreach efforts.

The restrictionist movement grew significantly during this period in large part due to its appeal to those experiencing neoliberal economic restructuring who saw the growth of Latino and unauthorized populations as the most visible symptom of the new economy. Throughout the next few years, when employer sanctions would emerge as an ineffective policy proscription for reducing unauthorized immigration, the restrictionist movement, which had fought so hard for these measures in the 1970s and 1980s, by the 1990s would become frustrated both by their failure to curb immigration and with the federal government as a whole. Disappointed, they would turn their attention to state governments in the 1990s in order to implement their agendas.

5

"To Reward the Wrong Way Is Not the American Way"

WELFARE AND THE BATTLE OVER IMMIGRANTS' BENEFITS

IN AUGUST 1993, approximately seventy people gathered in a community room at an Orange County shopping mall for a meeting of the newly formed California Coalition for Immigration Reform (CCIR), a grassroots organization that sought to reduce immigrants' access to social welfare. Participants told stories of their grievances with unauthorized immigrants and complained of the financial burden that immigration imposed. One activist—telling of an acquaintance dying of cancer who was unable to get the proper treatment because of the cost—charged that, at the same time, "millions of dollars . . . have been spent on heart transplants and operations for illegal immigrants." In short, the group's grievances were clear: immigrants' use of social welfare programs burdened the American economy and allowing access to these assistance programs increased immigration to the United States. For many in the room, the battle over benefits was one manifestation of a larger war that they were losing for the heart of the nation. As one attendee remarked, "We've lost our country without ever firing a shot."[1]

While born in shopping malls, meeting rooms, and sleepy suburban communities, the CCIR movement quickly grew beyond Southern California. Its influence ultimately extended all the way to Washington. CCIR, joining with like-minded organizations from across the country, played a pivotal role in the passage of the 1996 Personal Responsibility and Work Opportunity Reconciliation Act (PRWORA), which removed most lawful permanent residents from welfare eligibility. During the 1990s, relying on both welfare and immigration reform measures, the federal government initiated a full-scale effort to transform putative insiders into outsiders; to transform rights-bearing legal residents into immigrants without rights. For all the many studies done of the PRWORA since its passage—analyses of its work requirements and job training, its outcomes for families and individuals or of the political circumstances that led to its passage—scholars have not adequately engaged the role that the politics of immigration played in its passage.[2] The stripping of welfare eligibility for lawful permanent residents in 1996 shows how the rights of immigrants in the United States now depended on citizenship status rather than whether their immigration to the United States was legally authorized.[3]

The battle over authorized immigrants' benefits in the 1990s was a fundamental turning point in the politics of immigration. While anti-immigrant activism had grown over the previous two decades, it emerged with new strength during the nineties, driving both political parties and their policies rightward.[4] For Democrats, as Clinton's 1996 reelection campaign loomed large, strategists concerned with winning California and competing for White, middle-class voters pushed the administration away from the liberalism that seemed to define the president's first years in office toward an embrace of triangulation in immigration policy formation. Within the GOP, emerging new conservative forces of the Republican revolution spearheaded by Speaker of the House Newt Gingrich and reflected in the "Contract with America" pushed the Republican Party toward restriction on immigration policy. The free market deregulatory wing of the party, which had continued to play a large role in policymaking during the debate over employer sanctions, lost out to the restrictionist deficit hawks in the 1990s. This takeover of the party by those who supported neither expansive admissions policies nor expansive alienage rights was a significant departure from the 1980s when Reagan and other free market expansionists controlled the party's policy position.[5]

The 1990s was a turning point not only for immigration politics, but also for the role of states in forging immigration policy.[6] Anti-immigrant activists, in the wake of what they viewed as the federal failure of IRCA and federal inaction, increasingly focused their efforts at the state level. In turn, states and localities implemented their own policies, which pressured the federal government either to delegate authority to the states or to change federal immigration policy to accommodate state pressures. The changes that occurred in the politics of immigration and in immigration federalism during the 1990s would shape policymaking in the decades to come in arenas far from welfare benefits.[7]

Roots of Alienage Restriction

Social welfare programs, from their establishment during the New Deal, had few de jure alienage restrictions. That is, immigrants had access to most programs, regardless of their immigration status.[8] With the passage of the Hart-Celler Act in 1965 and the corresponding shifts in immigration patterns, efforts to restrict immigrants' access to social welfare programs began to solidify during the 1970s.

Broadly, the welfare system was under attack during this period. The percentage of Americans on welfare began to rise, and aggregate spending on welfare also rose.[9] Minorities were increasingly portrayed as sources of poverty and dependent on welfare benefits, and African American women were targeted with the rise of the "welfare queen" stereotype.[10] Seemingly contradictory, during the 1970s, immigrants were increasingly portrayed not only as a threat to citizens' employment opportunities but also to the state's social welfare and health resources through their abuse of the welfare system. A *U.S. News and World Report* cover article from 1977 asked if unauthorized immigrants were "out of control?" and claimed that Mexican immigrants' use of welfare and medical services were "out of control" behaviors.[11] A Gallup poll in 1976 showed that 57 percent of Americans felt that "'illegal immigrants' receiving 'unemployment payments or welfare' were a 'serious problem' as they were 'a drain on the taxpayer.'"[12] As one reader of the *Denver Post* wrote to the editors, "citizens of this country are deeply concerned about the 13 million illegal aliens . . . millions of these aliens are collecting government benefits, at the expense of the taxpayers."[13] News reports at the time portrayed immigrants as a particular drain on welfare because of their supposed excessive fertility. The *Los Angeles Times* told the story of a thirty-two-year-old Mexican woman, Hilda Tovoar, living unauthorized in the United States, who had eight children and received welfare, housing, and food support. The newspaper "presented her as promiscuous for her 'overt' fertility."[14] In addition, women were increasingly portrayed as crossing the border in order to have children with US citizenship and access to benefits.[15] The rise in anti-immigrant activism targeting immigrants' reproduction and use of welfare seen in this era would continue to play a significant role in policy debates in the decades to follow.

Coupled with these rising concerns over immigrants' use of welfare and health benefits came the first serious legislative efforts to restrict immigrants' access to social welfare programs. As part of a larger effort of welfare retrenchment during this period, states began to pass legislation that restricted eligibility for state welfare benefits based on immigration status or residency requirements.[16]

In a manner similar to the *Plyler* case, immigrants, with the assistance of young legal aid lawyers, challenged several restrictive state laws. In one case, Carmen Richardson, an authorized immigrant from Mexico who had become disabled thirteen years after she arrived in Arizona, was rejected for public assistance because of the state's fifteen-year residency requirement for noncitizens.[17] In another case, Elsie Leger had legally come to the United States from Scotland at age sixty-five, but when she had to stop working four years later due to illness, Arizona deemed her ineligible for the state assistance program because she was not a citizen.[18] The Supreme Court consolidated the two cases into *Graham v. Richardson* (1971) and ruled that state alienage–based residency restrictions violated the Equal Protection provision of the Fourteenth Amendment and infringed on the federal government's exclusive control of immigration.

While officials at the Department of Health, Education, and Welfare (HEW) initially planned to interpret the *Graham* ruling in an expansive way to prohibit states from blocking federal aid to all immigrants, the Nixon administration reversed course. Under pressure from the Texas and California congressional delegations, which were concerned about an increased fiscal burden that resulted from providing benefits to unauthorized immigrants, the Nixon administration prohibited states from providing federal welfare support and Medicaid to unauthorized immigrants. Over time, this move paved the way for barring unauthorized immigrants from most federally funded programs.[19] By 1976, unauthorized immigrants were prohibited from receiving Social Security numbers, Food Stamps, Aid to Families with Dependent Children benefits (AFDC), and unemployment insurance.[20]

In its final footnote in the *Graham* decision, the Court noted that while it had ruled against state alienage restrictions, it was not making a pronouncement on federal alienage restrictions, leaving the door open for further litigation.[21] Five years later, in *Mathews v. Diaz* (1976), the Court affirmed the federal government's right to deny welfare benefits to some immigrants. In that case, the justices unanimously upheld a five-year residency requirement for immigrants to become eligible for Medicare. "[T]he fact that Congress has provided some welfare benefits for citizens does not require it to provide like benefits for all aliens," Justice John Paul Stevens wrote for the Court. Stevens distinguished the holding from that in *Graham*, noting that the federal government, not the states, had the primary responsibility for immigration policy.[22] These cases and regulation changes at HEW under the Nixon administration in the 1970s were the first significant moves in the expansion of welfare restrictions and led to many of the subsequent restrictions.

In the decades that followed *Graham*, alienage-based welfare restriction would move from an issue debated in legal decisions to a contested issue of national partisan politics. The anti-immigrant activism that peddled immigrants as a burden on the welfare system and immigrant women's reproduction as uncontrolled would expand from targeting unauthorized immigrants during the 1970s to targeting authorized immigrants by the mid-1990s. *Graham* and the changes at HEW under Nixon were undoubtedly important steps in the evolution of immigrants' rights. Still, the removal of authorized immigrants from welfare is significant as it highlights the hardening of citizenship as the essential element in determining the relationship between the individual and the welfare state. When authorized immigrants lost many of their claims upon the welfare state, it created newly sharpened distinctions between people who had full citizenship status and rights and those who did not.

By the early 1990s, unauthorized immigrants could only receive Women, Infants and Children (WIC) benefits and Head Start (early childhood education services), along with emergency medical services, but authorized immigrants remained eligible for most benefits of the welfare state. Authorized immigrants and other noncitizens had access to the major public assistance programs such as Aid to Families with Dependent Children (AFDC), Supplemental Security Income (SSI or disability), Food Stamps, and Medicaid on the same basis as citizens. There were some restrictions, for example, for those who entered as "sponsored aliens" by family members, there was a three-year waiting period in which their eligibility for benefits was deemed by the income of their sponsor.[23] Immigrants who were newly legalized under the IRCA were prohibited from receiving public benefits for five years. But in 1990, by and large, authorized immigrants still had access to the major public assistance programs. This all changed in 1996, when Congress and the president, after several years of political debate, stripped welfare eligibility for most noncitizens.

Rising Tide of Restriction

To a casual Washington observer in 1990, it would have appeared unlikely that Congress would turn its focus to immigration policy, particularly restrictive immigration policy. Under President George H. W. Bush, the decade began with the signing of the Immigration Act of 1990, which increased the quotas for legal immigration. Bush, recognizing the "fundamental importance of immigrants to our country," praised the bill as a blending of the nation's commitment to "family as the essential unit of society" and admitting those with skills needed by the nation.[24] The act—building on a long tradition of establishing commissions to avoid tackling the difficult issue of immigration in any forthright or decisive way—also established the Commission on Immigration Reform, led by former Congresswoman Barbara Jordan. Over the next seven years, the bipartisan body, made up of a mix of expansionist and restrictionist members appointed by Congress and the White House, examined and made recommendations on virtually every aspect of the immigration system; the commission issued four reports between 1994 and 1997.

Neither Bush nor Clinton spoke extensively on immigration during the 1992 presidential campaign, and both largely made broad statements of support for the 1990 Immigration Act, coupled with calls for increasing border enforcement. Clinton called immigration "a source of strength" for the nation.[25] The only immigration issue that appeared divisive between the candidates was how to address the growing number of refugees fleeing Haiti for South Florida after the coup which overthrew Jean-Bertand Aristide in September 1991.[26] Clinton initially criticized the Bush administration approach of forcibly returning refugees and instead advocated for asylum hearings and temporary asylum status. However, before his inauguration he reversed his campaign promises for hearings by calling for a continuation of the Bush policy.[27]

While not a central issue in Washington or on the campaign trail at this time, across the nation, and most clearly in California, the question of immigration, and particularly unauthorized immigration, began to gain new prominence. Immigration permeated the public discourse. *Time* magazine's April 1990 cover asked "What Will the U.S. Be Like When Whites Are No Longer the Majority?" and was accompanied by a graphic of an American flag where the white stripes were replaced with black, brown, and yellow stripes.[28] In high schools across the country, students debated the future of immigration policy when it was named the national high school debate topic for 1994–1995.

In the 1990s, anti-immigrant sentiment thrived and took on aggressively restrictionist tones. As one reporter noted at the time, "Americans have felt freer to voice a rude inhospitality that at other times they might have

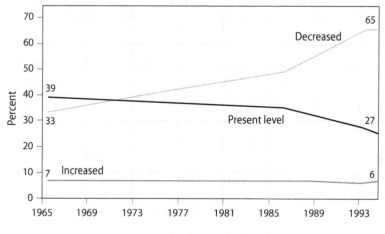

FIGURE 5.1. Gallup historical polling data

considered racist or at least xenophobic."[29] Polling demonstrated that support for an outright reduction of immigration grew to an unprecedented 54 percent in 1992, to 61 percent in 1993, and 65 percent in 1994.[30]

The growing concern over immigration was the result of a confluence of factors, including increasing immigration levels, emerging terrorism concerns, a faltering economy, and the fight over rising entitlement spending.

Public concern over immigration grew in response to increasing immigration from Mexico. The signing of the North American Free Trade Agreement (NAFTA) in December 1993 required Mexico to remove its protectionist agricultural policies, hurting struggling subsistence farmers, and in turn pushing many of them to abandon their farms to seek work in the United States. Between 1990 and 2000, the foreign-born population in the United States increased by 11.3 million people, representing a 57.4 percent increase.[31] By the mid-1990s, about 5 percent of the US population was of Mexican origin, but in California it was almost four times that.[32] Areas like Orange County were undergoing intense demographic shifts. Whereas in 1980, Orange County had been a middle-class conservative community of 1.9 million people that was 87 percent white, by 1990, immigrants made up almost a quarter of the 2.4 million people living there, and more than half of the immigrants had lived in the United States for less than ten years.[33]

In addition, while traditionally settling in the border states of California and Texas, by the 1990s nearly one-third of newcomers were settling in other states.[34] In the wake of the large legalization passed as part of the 1986 IRCA, newly authorized immigrants, who had previously avoided mobility to minimize the risk of detection, exercised their freedom to move, especially to escape a growing economic downturn in California. This movement inflamed tensions in many communities, as Americans increasingly called the northern migration an "invasion." These broader fears were exacerbated after foreign-born men committed several domestic terrorism acts in the early 1990s. In January 1993, a Pakistani gunman who had entered the United States on a temporary business visa and later filed for asylum attacked the CIA headquarters. Less than a month later, a bomb placed by six men of Middle Eastern descent was detonated in the basement of the World Trade Center.[35]

The economy was another factor in the mounting public concern with immigration. In 1990, the United States again entered a recession. The recession hit California particularly hard as a result of cuts in the defense industries with the end of the Cold War. Two-thirds of all jobs lost in the United States between 1990 and 1993 were in California, and the state unemployment rate climbed to 9.2 percent, the second highest in the nation.[36] It was the longest and deepest period of economic difficulty California had experienced since the Great Depression. Seizing on public frustration, anti-immigration activists argued that immigrants were taking jobs from native-born workers and were depressing wages. A 1993 CBS News/New York Times poll found that 60 percent of Americans felt the nation could not welcome new immigrants because of existing economic conditions.[37]

Concurrently, the national political debate focused on the growth of entitlement spending. Several of the key programs were growing rapidly; for example, AFDC served 14.4 million parents and children in early 1994, up from 10.9 million five years earlier. As seen in figure 5.2, it was not just AFDC that was growing, but across the board, programs that supported low-income individuals and children were expanding.

The bleak economic outlook in the United States, coupled with the surge in immigration from Mexico and increased spending on social welfare programs at both the state and federal levels, led many Americans to question the cost of immigration.[38] A strain of rhetoric arose in both in the media, government, and popular discourse that labeled immigrants a burden on the American economy.[39] Various periods of regional and national economic downturn throughout American history have seen a spike in nativist rhetoric claiming immigrants were a tax burden, including during the 1970s and 1980s as discussed previously in this work, but this strain of negative ideology gained national salience in the early 1990s, metastasized by growing concerns over

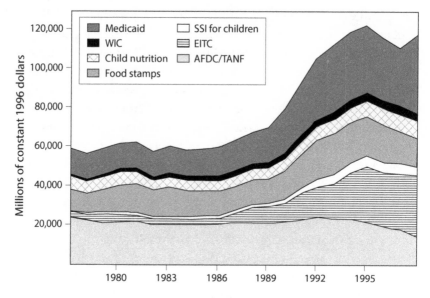

FIGURE 5.2. Combined federal and state spending on major programs for low-income families with children, 1977–1988. From Weaver, R. Kent. *Ending Welfare as We Know It* (Washington, DC: Brookings Institution Press, 2000)

the expansive nature of the welfare state and the role that immigrants and their children played in that growth.[40]

Indeed, noncitizen participation in social welfare programs had begun to rise, as noncitizens made up 9.3 percent of AFDC recipients in 1993, up from 5.5 percent in 1983. A GAO report in 1993 estimated that the cost of providing AFDC benefits to citizen children of unauthorized immigrants was $479 million for fiscal year 1992, but they only made up 2 percent of total AFDC benefit costs. In other programs, noncitizen immigrants comprised a more sizable population. In 1994, noncitizens made up 30 percent of the aged national SSI caseload, constituting an even higher percentage in California.[41] State revenue was paying the large part of these benefits, covering 81 percent of the $2.9 billion in benefits that were being paid to unauthorized immigrants per year.[42] Adding to this chorus of concern over rising welfare spending was the increasingly prominent notion that immigrant women were reproducing at above average levels. This focus on immigrant women's fecundity was closely linked with the notion that immigrant women were coming to the United States to give birth to children who would be citizens by birthright, and thus provide a path for their mothers to acquire citizenship. This view gained newfound prominence in the 1990s with the vitriolic trope of the "anchor baby."[43]

A corresponding line of discourse among conservative intellectuals enhanced this growing public concern with welfare spending on immigrant populations. While the majority of studies have long found that immigrants pay more in taxes than they receive in public benefits and entitlements, during the early 1990s, several prominent conservative intellectuals began to argue that immigrants were a drain on the national economy because of their use of benefits. Peter Skerry, a professor at UCLA, wrote an article in the *National Review* arguing that immigrants created "enormous burdens" on state and local governments that received wide circulation.[44] Most notably, Donald Huddle of Rice University authored a study that claimed that post-1970 immigrants cost the United States $42 billion annually in services. Huddle's study was then quoted prominently in major media outlets such as the *Washington Post*, the *Los Angeles Times*, and the *New York Times*. The support for Huddle's work came from familiar sources. Huddle's study was funded by the Carrying Capacity Network (CCN), a Washington-based group that employed environmental arguments about overpopulation as a rationale for supporting immigration restriction. Like FAIR, CCN had emerged in reaction to Zero Population Growth and the Sierra Club's refusals to address immigration, as discussed in the first chapter.[45]

Prominent right-leaning think tanks as well as several municipalities in California including Los Angeles, San Diego, and Orange County all commissioned studies to explore the cost of new and unauthorized immigrants. In Orange County, the study was a result of pressure from the local Chamber of Commerce.[46] The Los Angeles County study found that immigrants, both authorized residents and unauthorized, paid $139 million in taxes to Los Angeles County, but it estimated that the county spent $947 million on services for the same population, leaving a deficit to the county of $808 million per year. The study also found that only 3.2 percent of the taxes paid by this population subset went to the county, with the federal and state governments receiving virtually all the rest.[47] Regardless of the validity of the studies, the belief that immigration was a drain on the nation was gaining increasing validity in the public realm and at various high levels of government.

As a result of these economic, demographic, and ideological influences, restrictionist sentiment grew nationwide. Legislators and local officials followed this trend. In the Northeast, the New Jersey legislature moved to remove access to public benefits for unauthorized immigrants, and in New York, a local school authority on Long Island began to report unauthorized immigrant students, acting in direct opposition to the *Plyler* decision.[48] In

California, illegal immigration became a major campaign issue in races across the state, including the 1992 Republican primary for the 45th congressional district, as well as the LA County Supervisors' race and the 1993 LA mayoral primary, with candidates blaming the region's fiscal woes on increasing unauthorized immigration.[49]

Clinton Struggles to Respond

By May 1993, the Clinton White House was well aware of the potential political firestorm brewing in California over immigration. Immigration had not been a focus of Clinton's governorship or his campaign, but shortly after taking office, an immigration issue caused one of President Clinton's first missteps. President Clinton had to withdraw his nomination of Zoe Baird as attorney general on January 22 when it became public that she had hired unauthorized workers as her nanny and chauffer and had not paid their Social Security taxes. On the immigration policy front, Clinton initially took a measured position. He ordered Vice President Al Gore to conduct an immigration policy review, he appointed Doris Meissner, an immigration expert who had worked in INS in the 1980s, as INS commissioner, and he made the presidential appointments to the Jordan Commission.

However, growing concern over immigration in California pushed the issue to an even more prominent position in the Clinton White House. California had been a critical component of President Clinton's winning electoral coalition in 1992, the first time it had voted for a Democratic presidential nominee since 1964. Clinton had won the state by espousing a centrist approach that drew White middle-class voters who had left the Democratic Party during the late 1970s and 1980s. He did so by embracing many of the policies advocated by the centrist Democratic Leadership Council (DLC), including welfare reform, deficit reduction, and free trade. Clinton had been chair of the DLC, an organization founded in 1985 by Al From.

Tom Epstein, Special Assistant to the President for Political Affairs, wrote to Rahm Emanuel, a senior advisor, outlining the political situation in California. California Governor Pete Wilson—a former mayor of San Diego and US Senator who was considered a likely Republican presidential candidate in 1996—faced a tough 1994 reelection battle in the wake of the state's fiscal woes. Looking for a scapegoat, Wilson blamed California's economic problems on the influx of unauthorized immigrants. He claimed California spent $2 billion a year on education, emergency health care, prisons, and other outlays for unauthorized immigrants, and he argued that the federal government should pay for those costs.[50] It was not just Wilson who was pushing immigration to the forefront of the state's political debate; other legislators in Sacramento had begun to introduce a series of punitive anti-immigrant bills.

As a result, Epstein warned, "Immigration is emerging as the most powerful political issue in California, and the Administration must begin to deal with it." Epstein wrote that while immigration was "largely a California issue," it could have "significant ramifications" in other states dealing with similar problems. While he conceded that any action the White House undertook would be controversial, "the penalty for inaction is far greater. Middle class swing and Democratic voters are angry and want something done. It's time for a New Democrat solution."[51]

Growing anti-immigrant sentiment in California, combined with Governor Wilson's moves to capitalize on it politically, became even more pressing to the White House when in early August, Wilson sent an open letter to Clinton and had it printed as an ad in the West Coast editions of the New York Times, USA Today, and Washington Times. In the letter, Wilson called on the Clinton administration to amend the Constitution to abolish birthright citizenship, to deny education and other social services to unauthorized immigrants, and to institute a nationwide identification card that included immigration status.[52]

By the end of the summer, media coverage of rising national anti-immigrant anger was on President Clinton's "radar screen big-time," in the words of his chief of staff, and he was routinely sending his staff news articles, including a USA Today/Gallup poll indicating that anti-immigrant feelings were strongest "among whites, Southerners and those with lower incomes, less education and conservative views."[53] Reading the clippings, the president urged his staff to "move on immigration."[54] President Clinton felt the administration could no longer afford to be passively engaged through Gore's policy review and the Jordan Commission's work, he felt it needed to be seen as taking action.

The entire White House staff watched the issue closely, not just the political hands, as Clinton aides began to consider ways to address the groundswell. As Christopher Edley, who served as associate director at OMB, noted, "In mid-'93 there was what felt from the White House perspective like a crisis. . . . There were some people who were single-mindedly focused on: How do we make sure that the President has a good shot of getting reelected and so he's got to carry California, therefore he must be seen as being vigorously engaged in trying to do something about, quote, the problem, close quote, in California." On the other side, Edley noted that there was also an administration segment that sought to "fend off" the rising anti-immigrant restrictionist sentiment nationally and supported expansive rights and benefits for immigrants.[55]

Understanding the electoral tightrope he had to navigate, and in order to balance the two competing factions while at the same time be seen as taking action, President Clinton announced a proposal of legislative reforms that contained some liberal provisions, including expedited asylum hearings for refugees, but also called for a dramatic increase in funding for Border Patrol in order to placate restrictionists. Nowhere in the package was there any mention of immigrants' access to social welfare programs. According to one journalist, the Clinton proposal "walked a careful middle road and did not overly offend—or please—anyone."[56]

Indeed, while the Clinton White House deftly balanced competing views and passions, the proposal did not address the issue of social welfare benefits, an omission that Republicans at the state and then federal level quickly used to attack the president. While state-level conservative groups focused on cutting benefits to unauthorized immigrants, congressional Republicans began to develop policies that would eventually push the Clinton administration toward restricting social welfare programs for authorized immigrants.

Hill Moves

In the spring of 1993, initial plans for restricting authorized immigrants' access to social welfare programs were floated by Republican leaders in Washington. Staffers on the tax-writing House Ways and Means Committee had long been eyeing immigrants' benefits as a possible source of cost savings, as many Republicans believed that immigrants using welfare benefits went against the notion of coming to America to work and for opportunity. For many staffers, the ideological reasons for opposing immigrants' access to welfare were more motivating than the possible cost savings.[57] This ideological argument would be revisited time and again at both the staff level and more publicly. Later that year, the House Republican Welfare Reform Working Group, a caucus of several conservative Republicans, as well as members of the Ways and Means Committee, introduced a bill to substantially overhaul the federal welfare program. It included a provision that removed all SSI benefits for noncitizens in order to save $15 billion over five years.[58]

Representative Rick Santorum of Pennsylvania, co-chair of the Welfare Reform Working Group and a lead architect of the bill, spoke at a press conference announcing the legislation. In defending the purpose of the legislation, Santorum echoed the ideological argument for restricting benefits. He contended that "immigrants should . . . come to America for opportunity, not welfare. We offer immigrants a straightforward deal: Come to America and enjoy immense personal freedom and gain access to the world's most productive economy. However, until you become a citizen, you must support yourself or be supported by a sponsor."[59]

Despite the partisan fervor swirling around harsh immigration reform, it wasn't just Republicans on the Hill targeting immigrants' benefits, as many Democrats also supported significant welfare reform. Democrats associated with the DLC, including President Clinton, had supported the notion of a more restrained role for the federal government in providing services. Following that vein, they supported overhauling the welfare system to include more work requirements for welfare recipients, a greater emphasis on job placement over training, and an increase in the tax credits for low-income Americans.[60] Building on this policy framework, the Mainstream Forum, a group of ninety moderate and conservative House Democrats associated with the DLC, introduced a welfare reform bill that included the policy shifts mentioned above as well as cuts in benefits for immigrants.

While uniformly committed to cutting welfare, there was division among Democrats over just how far any cuts should go and in particular about the reduction of immigrants' benefits. Some, like Representative Jim Slattery of Kansas, a member of the Mainstream Forum who had helped draft the proposal, ultimately refused to co-sponsor the bill, disagreeing with its cuts to immigrant legal assistance.[61] Other Democrats remained firmly committed to cutting immigrants' access. In the vote on the Santorum amendment to deny SSI and Medicaid to authorized immigrants, the Democrat-controlled Ways and Means Committee voted down the amendment, but the margin was very close, 20 to 16, with the measure garnering a good deal of support among Democrats.[62]

Politics Meets Policy

With Republicans continuing to push welfare reform, and growing unrest among conservative Democrats on the issue, the Clinton administration scrambled to formulate a position. The White House Domestic Policy Council (DPC) staff had initially planned to push an overhaul of the healthcare system before addressing welfare reform, believing that providing healthcare coverage was an important step in getting people off welfare, but others in the White House pressed for action, arguing that the administration could not ignore the Republican proposal and thereby give the opposition control over the welfare narrative.[63] As Health and Human Services Secretary Donna Shalala reminded the president, momentum was building, and reforming welfare was a campaign promise.[64] Heeding the advice of Shalala and other aides, in an early January meeting, the president and Mrs. Clinton asked DPC aide Carol Roscoe to develop a welfare reform plan.

In earlier conversations about drafting a welfare reform proposal, the Clinton White House had not focused on reducing immigrant benefits as a potential cost savings and thus a revenue source. The initial draft circulated within the administration in the fall of 1993 by the welfare reform working group had identified increased child support collections and reductions in caseload, along with entitlement savings through fraud reduction as possible revenue sources, and only as an afterthought mentioned possibly "tightening the rules regarding non-citizens seeking to collect public assistance."[65] Political pressure, both at the state level and from Congress, shifted the terrain beneath the administration, forcing the president to reckon with public demands to reduce immigrants' access to social welfare spending.

The White House weighed its options before formally introducing its plan. One option floated was to require families who sponsor immigrants to take responsibility for them for five years or until they became citizens. Given that it was similar to the Republican plans for immigrant benefits, staffers wondered, "Is there any way to persuade anyone that our proposal is more reasonable and theirs [Republicans] is harsh and draconian?" Other options included cuts to some Social Security benefits, raising new revenue, or finding some expenditure to the wealthy to cut.[66]

Just as the Reagan White House engaged Dick Wirthlin to poll its standing vis-à-vis immigration, the Clinton White House turned to Stan Greenberg, President Clinton's pollster, to survey the popularity of the various options for funding welfare reform. Greenberg found that funding welfare reform by cutting benefits to authorized immigrants had "popular, but not overpowering" support, favored by 64 percent of those polled. Denying benefits to new immigrants until they became citizens was favored by 73 percent. Importantly, eliminating benefits for authorized immigrants was attractive to swing voters, as 71 percent of independents favored it.

In summarizing his findings, Greenberg noted though that other possible alternatives proposed by Democrats, including cuts in welfare for the wealthy, "making work pay" by increasing the Earned Income Tax Credit, and enforcing child support payments from "deadbeat dads" were even more popular. There was a definite attraction to the Republican proposal to restrict immigrants' access to welfare, but Greenberg felt "most voters are looking for reforms that will reduce the welfare caseload without creating new hungry, homeless and sick people on the streets."[67]

Echoing the support for some restrained cuts to immigrants' benefits seen in the polling data, the Clinton proposal unveiled in June 1994 did not directly bar all authorized immigrants from receiving benefits, but it did take a more conservative position increasing the period during which some immigrants were ineligible for benefits. As the existing law stood, immigrants were the responsibility of their sponsor for a period of three years, during which time no Food Stamps, Social Security insurance, Medicaid, or funds through AFDC were available unless their combined family income was lower than the national poverty level. Under the Clinton proposal, sponsors would be deemed financially responsible for sponsored immigrants for five years, and the period would be longer if the sponsor's annual income was above the US median family income. The savings from these proposed restrictions would fund approximately 40 percent of the Clinton welfare reform plan, or approximately $3.7 billion.[68] In order to sell its proposal, the administration highlighted the sharp increase in the number of authorized immigrants collecting SSI in national news reports. According to the Clinton administration, "Immigrants rose from 5 percent of the S.S.I. aged caseload in 1982 to over 25 percent of the caseload in 1992 . . . Since 1982, applications for S.S.I. from immigrants have tripled, while immigration rose by only about 50 percent over the period."[69] The Clinton proposal reflected a centrist approach favored by the DLC. The more stringent Republican proposal gave the Clinton administration political cover to seek cuts to the program while at the same time arguing that the Clinton proposals were more humane.

On the Hill, centrist DLC members praised the bill, but Republicans opposed it, claiming it was not aggressive enough in its programmatic cuts.[70] While less punitive than the Republicans' bill, the Clinton proposal still drew ire from the left. Liberal Democrats attacked the plan for being too punitive toward low-income welfare recipients. Immigrants' rights groups emphasized that authorized immigrants also paid taxes that supported the programs in question. Catholic Charities from across the nation, from Philadelphia and Miami to Missouri and Georgia, reached out to the White House to express their opposition to the president's proposal to restrict immigrants' access to welfare programs. Many state and local governments opposed the measure. The National Conference of State Legislatures contended that the proposal put an undue burden on states, because while the federal government could exclude immigrants from their welfare programs, the states could not because of the 1971 *Graham v. Richardson* decision, which held that state alienage–based welfare restrictions were unconstitutional.[71]

California's Grassroots

While the discussion in Washington over welfare reform focused on authorized immigrants' access to programs, in California the debate over unauthorized immigration continued to gather steam as activists became much more organized. A congregation of political beginners and experienced operatives came together on October 5, 1993 at the Center Club in Costa Mesa for a first significant meeting, united by a desire to address the increasing rise of unauthorized immigration. Robert Kiely, a forty-six-year-old Republican political consultant and former chair of the Orange County Republican Party and his wife Barbara Kiely, the mayor of Yorba Linda, organized the meeting. Other seasoned political activists at the meeting included Alan Nelson and Harold Ezell, two high-ranking INS officials from the Reagan administration. Also present was Richard Mountjoy, a Republican assemblyman from Monrovia, a suburb of Los Angeles, who would emerge as a key backer of the Proposition 187 initiative in the State Assembly.

The seasoned political activists at the Cosa Mesa meeting were joined by two more local anti-immigrant activists, Ronald Prince and Barbara Coe. Prince was an accountant in his mid-forties who claimed he had been cheated out of half a million dollars on a construction project by an unauthorized Canadian immigrant. Coe, who newspapers described as a sixty-year-old "diminutive, chain-smoking woman with an apocalyptic vision of the world," was a former municipal worker who became incensed about immigration when she went to an Orange County social services office several years earlier and claimed that she noticed there were open windows for Spanish- and Vietnamese-speaking clients but not a single one open for English-speaking applicants. Coe had formed a group called Citizens for Action Now with a former INS agent, Bill King.[72] By 1993, Citizens for Action Now became part of the larger statewide umbrella organization, the California Coalition for Immigration Reform discussed in the opening of this chapter. CCIR focused on the economic as well as social and cultural aspects of immigration and claimed a statewide mailing list of more than 10,000 people.[73] CCIR members testified at public hearings before the state and local governments, protested at events of public officials such as Senator Barbara Boxer, and organized picketing of job centers where immigrants sought work.[74] While CCIR was a new group, several aspects of CCIR were anything but. The language used by CCIR in their literature echoed the language that emerged in the previous two decades. CCIR claimed that immigration was an "invasion" that was destroying the cultural fabric of the nation and that unauthorized immigration was a crippling problem for the state. CCIR's literature noted "illegal aliens . . . [brought] their values and culture into our midst, are major contributors to our mounting financial burdens and moral and social degradation."[75] One member of Citizens for Action Now put it more bluntly, saying that his recent visit to downtown Los Angeles was like visiting another country, as "Hispanic immigrants were having a paseo, walking on the sidewalk, eyeing each other, playing loud music. I felt displaced and alienated. They are on the attack."[76] Not only was the language not new, their financial support wasn't either. CCIR drew significant funding from the group US Inc which had been founded by John Tanton and was funded by Cordelia May Scaife.[77]

While there are differing accounts of the details of that first meeting at the Center Club, what emerged was a group called the Save Our State Committee (SOS), dedicated to addressing illegal immigration in California. They left the meeting planning a ballot initiative which would prohibit unauthorized immigrants from using non-emergency health care, public education, and other services and would compel any "public entity" to report to the INS and the California Attorney General's office any person that it "reasonably suspected" of being an unauthorized immigrant.

Assemblyman Mountjoy helped shepherd the ballot initiative's drafting by legislative counsel and it was given a title by the state attorney general in January 1994. The measure's proponents then had 150 days to collect 385,000 signatures in order to get the initiative on the ballot in November. During the first three months, grassroots activists who were members of the CCIR, Ross Perot's United We Stand America Party, and the California state Republican Party, gathered most of the signatures.[78]

When the ballot initiative organizers were still about 60,000 signatures short before the filing deadline, they hired a professional firm to collect signatures. Funding for this effort and other campaign efforts came from $136,482 raised by the proposition's organizers. The state Republican Party and California State Senator Don Rogers made the largest cash donations.

Looking to support the grassroots mobilization, Nelson and Ezell established Americans Against Illegal Immigration (AAII) using seed money from an organization called the Howard Jarvis Taxpayers Association, named after Howard Jarvis, a co-author of Proposition 13, and from Butcher, Forde and Mollrich, the political consulting firm that ran the Proposition 13 campaign.[79] Turning to familiar tactics, AAII launched a direct mail campaign supporting the ballot initiative. Private citizens were also a source of great fiscal support for Prop. 187, with more than 58 percent of individual donations coming from retirees.[80] Retirees supported the measure because they believed that unauthorized immigrants' use of services was draining the available benefits for the elderly and driving up the tax burden on the elderly.

The Opposition Organizes

In the first few months of 1994, there was scarce structured opposition against the ballot initiative. Later, some argued the civil rights organizations had not publicized their opposition because they feared that giving any attention to the initiative would bring it the support it needed to get on the ballot. Others suggested that the initial lack of opposition was because potential opponents did not think it had a good chance of qualifying for the ballot in November.[81] Nevertheless, by April opponents became more organized with the founding of a fund-raising committee, "No on SOS." The group drew support from a wide range of sources, including civil rights organizations, teachers' unions, public health advocates, and labor unions, as well as from organizations including MALDEF, the California Parents and Teachers Association, the American College of Emergency Physicians, California School Boards Association, the California Teachers Association, the California Medical Association, and the Roman Catholic Church.[82] The education groups who spoke out against the proposition argued that it would lead to more dropouts and kids on the streets. Public health officials warned it would lead to major health problems as immigrants were denied access to basic medical care and immunizations.[83] Cardinal Mahoney, the highest-ranking Catholic cleric in California, called the measure "punitive . . . [and] a devastating assault on human dignity."[84]

In July, this coalition hired Woodward & McDowell, a Burlingame-based professional political consulting firm known for successfully defeating ballot initiatives.[85] Based on polling and focus group data, the firm advised the coalition that it would be fruitless to engage the argument that unauthorized immigration was a problem given the widespread restrictionist sentiment in the state. Instead, the firm advocated that the coalition adopt a message that acknowledged that unauthorized immigration was an important and growing problem in California, but argued that the proposition was not the correct way to address it.[86] The firm believed that identifying fiscal concerns as a way of persuading voters on various policy issues, including immigration, seemed like a logical political approach, given California's history in the postwar years. Embracing that approach, Woodward & McDowell established a group called Taxpayers Against 187, to undertake the campaign for the initial "No on SOS" coalition.

As Taxpayers Against 187 began to undertake the opposition campaign, the group emphasized that the initiative was not the right way to address unauthorized immigration as it would end up costing the state more. They argued that if the ballot initiative was approved and found to violate the rights of individuals, it would lead Washington to cut off $15 billion a year in federal health and education money.[87] Not only was this concern the most politically viable according to the political consultants, it also played a large role in drawing large donors to the opposition movement. The top donor to Taxpayers Against 187 was a group likely be hit hard by potential federal cuts, the California Teachers Association's PAC. Other key funders included the California State Council of Service Employees; and $100,000 from Univision Television Group Inc.[88]

In addition to Taxpayers Against 187, the campaign against Proposition 187 drew significant support from another newly formed group, Californians United Against Proposition 187, which was a coalition of grassroots civil rights organizations, including the Chinese American Citizens Alliance and many student-led organizing groups. Other opponents included many in the law enforcement community, including Willie Williams, the Chief of the Los Angeles Police Department, the Los Angeles Police Commissioner, and the Los Angeles County District Attorney Gil Garcetti, who felt the proposition was divisive and counterproductive to their public safety mission. Many religious groups opposed the measure as well, including the Episcopalian General Conference, the Evangelical Lutheran Church of America, and the Board of Rabbis of Southern California.[89]

By the summer, consideration of Proposition 187 dominated the state political landscape. The state Republican Party endorsed the measure early in the year at their February convention, but the initiative put Democratic politicians in the state in a difficult position. Opinion polling showed that a majority of

Californians viewed unauthorized immigration as a serious problem, but many Democrats believed that coming out too strongly for the proposition would risk alienating key Latino constituencies. As a result, while Democratic elected officials announced their opposition, many couched their views with acknowledgments that unauthorized immigration was problematic and called for other solutions that focused on border enforcement.[90] Waiting until September to avoid taking a stance on the divisive issue, the Democratic Party finally declared its opposition, saying the problems associated with "illegal immigration will not be solved by Pete Wilson's cowardly blame casting and finger-pointing . . . It will not be solved by an initiative which is funded by racist and white supremacist organizations."[91]

Immigration became a central issue in the contested gubernatorial race between Governor Wilson and State Treasurer Kathleen Brown as well as in the Senate race between incumbent Democratic Senator Diane Feinstein and Republican Congressman Michael Huffington. In their contest, both Feinstein and Huffington adopted sharp restrictionist tones in their campaigns, calling for beefed up border enforcement. Feinstein toured the border with the press and ran ads that showed images of unauthorized immigrants crossing the border into the United States while airing an ominous voiceover. However, both candidates waited until October to announce their positions on 187. Huffington backed the measure, saying "Proposition 187 would send a message to illegal immigrants as well as to leaders in Washington that Californians have had enough."[92] Conversely, when Feinstein finally came out against the Proposition, she alleged it was unconstitutional and would do nothing to reduce illegal immigration. Trying to play to the political popularity of fiscal conservatism and reducing taxes, rather than frame her opposition to the initiative because of its discriminatory effects, Feinstein echoed the argument made by Taxpayers Against 187. She warned that if Proposition 187 passed, a $15 billion bill would be transferred to California taxpayers due to the loss of federal funding.[93]

In the gubernatorial race, Governor Pete Wilson highlighted his support of the measure, making it a centerpiece of his campaign and calling it vital to get the federal government to live up to its responsibility to pay the costs of illegal immigration.[94] Wilson's support for the measure marked a strong change in his approach to immigration. During the 1980s when he was a US Senator, Wilson had not championed reducing immigration levels or benefits to immigrants, and had instead advocated for increasing access to migrant labor for agribusiness, an industry composed of some of his biggest political donors.[95] But as the economy in California began to falter, Wilson identified immigrants as a driving cause of the state's fiscal woes. After a contentious budget stalemate, Wilson's approval rating fell, and since he was up for reelection in 1994, he turned to unauthorized immigration to mobilize his base of White, middle- class voters.

Wilson ran a series of campaign ads on television that showed film footage of migrant workers running from US Border Patrol agents across the San Diego border crossing, which warned, "There is a right way and a wrong way . . . to reward the wrong way is not the American way . . . American citizenship is a treasure beyond measure," and urged voters to send "a strong message to Congress and to the Courts to stop illegal immigration."[96] While Wilson had trailed by more than twenty points earlier in the year, he surged to a lead of more than ten points by October 1994 in large part because of his focus on unauthorized immigration.[97] His opponent, state Treasurer Kathleen Brown, openly opposed Proposition 187. She contrasted Wilson's support for a guest worker program and opposition to employer sanctions in the 1980s against his pivot toward more hardline immigration views, blasting the governor for hypocrisy and a lack of political courage.

Grassroots Goes National

Even before November, Proposition 187 attracted national attention and influenced policy in both the Republican and Democratic parties. Pat Buchanan, who ran for the Republican nomination for president in 1992 and again in 1996, noted that if Proposition 187 was successful, "the issue of illegal aliens will vault to the top of the national agenda."[98]

At the White House, Clinton aides worried about the increasing strength of the anti-immigrant movement and feared Republicans could use the issue to make gains in the midterm elections. Concerned that the administration and the Democratic Party could lose the support of the centrist vote that had put Bill Clinton in the White House, staffers Rahm Emanuel and Ron Klain urged the president to take swift action publicly to address immigration. "In both the short and long term, the Administration's objective with regard to immigration should be to strike an aggressive posture," they wrote the president. "We must be seen as taking proper, forceful steps to seriously address the immigration problem without alienating the Hispanic and civil rights constituencies. Our goal is not to out-do the Republicans, rather to use our achievements and proposals to prevent them from using this as a wedge issue against us."[99] They feared Republicans would use immigration as an issue to split the Democratic Party between those supporting restriction and those supporting a liberal immigration policy. The White House subsequently undertook a communications strategy highlighting actions such as the release of a report on immigration and the commencement of Operation Gatekeeper, an INS and Border Patrol effort which included the installation of an eight-foot-high steel fence and high-intensity floodlights along a fourteen-mile stretch of the border near San Diego, notably the same stretch featured in Wilson's "treasure beyond measure" ads.

In response to the growing firestorm, President Clinton traveled to California in the weeks before the election to campaign and ridiculed Proposition 187. Clinton argued that the immigration measure and the "Contract with America," the Newt Gingrich–written political platform congressional Republicans were invoking on the campaign trail, used similarly negative approaches of "be mad now; worry about the details later," and were not well conceived policy proposals.[100] Tony Coelho, senior advisor to the DNC and chief strategist for the 1994 midterms, noted that Clinton's aggressiveness on the campaign trail against Proposition 187 stemmed in part from the belief that opposition could spur Democratic turnout in the midterms.[101] Given the Democratic base's opposition to the measure, Coelho hoped that the ballot initiative would spur the base to turn out more than would be expected for a normal midterm election.

Despite the president's involvement against the measure, on November 8, 1994, California voters approved Proposition 187 by a wide 59 to 41 margin. The next day, several civil rights groups led by attorney Peter Schey, who earlier had been counsel in a case that had been consolidated in *Plyler*, filed suit in federal court to block it from going into effect, and a judge granted the request by issuing an injunction blocking Proposition 187's enforcement in schools. Soon after, a temporary restraining order was issued halting enforcement of the healthcare provisions as well.

Yet, while temporarily stopped from being enforced, Proposition 187 nevertheless had a large impact at both the state and federal levels on campaigns and policymaking. While the constitutionality of Proposition 187 would be litigated for some time and the proposition was eventually invalidated, in the court of public opinion California voters had made their position loud and clear, and in so doing drastically reshaped the political landscape across the nation.[102] After its passage, restrictionist activists were eager to replicate their victory in California through similar ballot initiatives in Arizona, Texas, and Florida.[103] Ezell noted that "like it or not, California is a national trendsetter . . . [a]nd the whole nation is focused on California right now over this issue." Coe, hoping to expand on her successes, was effusive in her optimism about possible Prop. 187 replication across the nation, saying "we felt initially this would have a ripple effect . . . but now are thinking it will be a tidal wave."[104]

The political implications went beyond immigration specifically. The success of Proposition 187 buoyed Republicans' hopes that California's 54 electoral votes would be up for grabs in the 1996 presidential election. While Clinton had been able to capture the eureka state, he had done so with only a 46 percent plurality. Ross Perot had won 20 percent of the vote, and without a viable third-party candidate in 1996, Clinton's hold on the state looked to be more tenuous. Indeed, Proposition 187's success seemed to reveal new electoral fault lines. The passage of the referendum suggested that state Republicans would have to push aside earlier pro-immigration positions adopted at the urging of agribusiness and moderate Republicans and unite behind a much more restrictionist agenda. At the same time, the lopsided result in favor of a hardline immigration solution forced Democrats to take the result into their political calculus, the party eager to avoid alienating their Latino base.

While the Carter administration had intervened in the *Plyler* case in the 1970s, even filing an amicus curiae brief supporting the rights of unauthorized students, the Clinton administration was silent on Proposition 187 litigation, with many leaders in the party urging the president to adopt a more restrictionist stance well before his reelection campaign.[105] Here in the 1990s, the federal government was growing more complicit in furthering the state-led efforts to restrict rights.

In the 1994 midterm elections, Republicans picked up fifty-four seats to gain a majority in the House chamber for the first time since 1952. The election had brought into power dozens of activist conservatives bent on reshaping American government and returning power to the states. Just as Barbara Coe had hoped, the House leadership looked to California as a blueprint, with Newt Gingrich, who was seen as an enormous hero and top leader in his party at the time, saying, "I think on the whole issue of immigration, California's going to be very positive about what we'll be doing." Gingrich's endorsement of the tough California immigration measures appeared to show the Republican Party embracing a more restrictionist stance in order to secure California's and other states' electoral votes in the 1996 election.[106]

A few days after the election, Governor Wilson traveled to Washington to meet with the GOP leadership to discuss unauthorized immigration and build support for his proposal of a national version of Proposition 187.[107] After the meeting, Gingrich noted to reporters that he believed that "the best response is to eliminate the mandates [to provide services] because the welfare magnet [is] drawing people into the United States."[108] Texas Congressman Lamar Smith, chair of the Judiciary Committee's Immigration Subcommittee, echoed Gingrich's view, saying that the essence of Proposition 187 was going to be seriously considered by Congress.[109]

In December, Gingrich established the Speaker's Task Force on Immigration Reform and appointed California Congressman Elton Gallegly as its chairman. Gingrich, as speaker, made an effort to shift the power from committee chairs to the party leadership, and the use of task forces was an important manifestation of this trend. The speaker appointed members to the task forces and aides of the chair generally staffed the task forces.[110] Demonstrating the importance of California's perspective to the national debate, nearly half of the Immigration Reform Task Force's fifty-four members were from California.[111] The Task Force was charged with developing proposals to end illegal immigration as "the federal government has failed in its efforts to enforce existing laws or adopt effective policies to prevent illegal immigration."[112] Operating for three months, the body delivered a report to Gingrich that proposed excluding unauthorized students from public education, denying unauthorized immigrants access to all federal welfare and health benefits except emergency care, mandating reporting from hospitals to the INS about patients' immigration status and other similar measures.[113] Congressman Gallegly also introduced a bill to exclude unauthorized students from public education and bar all unauthorized immigrants from receiving any federal welfare payments.

Gallegly was not the only member to introduce legislation inspired by Proposition 187 that spring, as congressmen from both sides of the aisle introduced bills and amendments that proposed restricting unauthorized immigrants' access to federal disaster aid, repealing birthright citizenship, reimbursing states for incarcerating unauthorized felons, and other similar efforts aimed at preventing unauthorized immigrants from receiving various forms of federal assistance.[114]

While Wilson, Gallegly, and others in the Republican Party were eager to capitalize nationally on the success of Proposition 187, there were many prominent Republicans who felt the party's embrace of the measure could do more harm than good. Governor-elect George W. Bush of Texas spoke out against the measure. Another critic was William Bennett, the former Secretary of Education and drug czar in the George H. W. Bush administration. Bennett accused Wilson of "scapegoating . . . stirring up nativist juices" and being "less than fully candid" about what was really causing budget issues in California. Instead, Bennett suggested that Wilson and other Republicans look at the welfare state more broadly, as well as teachers' unions.[115] Former Congressman and HUD Secretary Jack Kemp, who was considering a presidential run in 1996, was more outspoken in his opposition to the measure. Kemp warned that while he felt unauthorized immigrants ought not to be provided services, the political costs of passing sweeping measures on a national scale could harm the GOP for generations. Kemp linked the party's potential "big mistakes" on losing the immigrant vote to being on the wrong side of the civil rights debates of the 1950s and 1960s.[116]

Those voices urging moderation and a rejection of the California model did not have the same clout within the party as they had a decade earlier during the battles over employer sanctions. Then, centrist members of the Republican Party had managed to hold off restrictionist voices in order to ensure that employer sanctions were passed without any enforcement mechanism and admissions numbers remained high. However, following the success of Proposition 187 and the elevation of Gingrich to Speaker, restrictionist views were ascendant among the party's leaders and so were now driving the GOP's immigration policy agenda.

The seismic change of the Republican revolution impacted not only the direction of the Republican Party, but also the Democratic White House, which moved rightward after the election.[117] The administration's immigration proposal, planned for introduction that spring, was shelved. The Clinton White House watched that winter as restrictionist sentiment continued to grow and polling showed strong support for a national Proposition 187 type legislation. Clinton's internal polling found that three-quarters of those polled believed that unauthorized immigrants used more than their "fair share of government services" and contributed to economic problems.[118]

While the Clinton welfare plan included some steps to reduce immigrants' access to public benefits, the passing of Proposition 187 and the resultant national support for broad immigration restrictions changed the White House's approach. Several Clinton aides now wavered on whether to make their proposal more punitive or wait to see what congressional Republicans proposed.[119] As one internal strategy memo noted, "We are taking gratuitous hits on immigration; we need to begin to transform the debate . . . We should discuss how to help heal some of the wounds that are beginning to show already in Southern California." The memo outlined the possibility that the issue of immigration could create electoral problems in an even wider swath of states beyond California, and called for analysis of the "political considerations in each of the immigration states" of a broad reform plan.[120]

Early in January 1995, Carol Roscoe, the head of the DPC, presented President Clinton with several new immigration proposal options for responding to Proposition 187 and the increasing domestic unrest with unauthorized immigration. Roscoe told the president that while the administration had been able to remain unengaged for a time, that would soon change as Congress was going to introduce legislation to nationalize Proposition 187 and other states would seek to pass similar legislation, forcing the White House's hand and making it impossible not to commit itself.

Also creating pressure were several agencies who were eager to respond to the passage of Proposition 187. The Department of Education, for example, wanted to publicly make the case based on *Plyler* for allowing unauthorized students access to schools. Given that the administration had opposed the Proposition before the election, and not participated in the litigation challenging it, Roscoe told the president, "the primary issue now is strategic: how prominent should the administration now be in presenting its views on [Republican] efforts to expand Proposition 187 beyond California."

Roscoe presented Clinton with two options. First, avoid taking a public stance as long as Proposition 187 was enjoined in litigation. Intervention might backfire, as it would bring Clinton back into the fray and his critics' focus back to the administration's commitment to addressing unauthorized immigration that they had previously attacked. Second, take a more prominent role in opposing efforts to nationalize parts of Proposition 187. However, to continue appealing to the growing restrictionist sentiment, "we can support several items, such as the increase on penalties for use of fraudulent documents and the ban on postsecondary education benefits."[121]

Roscoe urged Clinton to adopt the second option, a more engaged stance. Remaining silent, she contended, would soon be impossible given inevitable congressional action on the issue. But Roscoe also suggested that the administration continue to remain uninvolved in the lawsuits involving Proposition 187.[122]

Clinton decided to take the more public stance that Roscoe had advocated, firing one of his first salvos in his 1995 State of the Union address. Yet, the president's message had a distinctly restrictionist tone, as he echoed some of the language of Proposition 187 supporters, saying that its proponents "are rightly disturbed by the large numbers of illegal aliens entering our country" and the "burdens [immigrants impose] on our taxpayers." Clinton then highlighted his administration's immigration proposal, which included plans for bolstering the nation's southern border, increasing deportation efforts, and barring welfare benefits to unauthorized immigrants. In closing his remarks on immigration, he noted that while the United States was a nation of immigrants, "we are also a nation of laws. It is wrong and ultimately self-defeating for a nation of immigrants to permit the kind of abuse of our immigration laws we have seen in recent years, and we must do more to stop it."[123] As administration officials noted, by making this argument in the State of the Union, President Clinton "hoped to beat Republicans to the punch" on an important issue for moderate voters who had deserted the Democrats in the midterm elections.[124]

Soon thereafter, the White House began to reveal its immigration policy intentions with the release of a presidential memorandum. As part of the rollout, staffers prepared possible answers to likely questions that the press would pose during a press conference. The suggested response to any questions about nationalizing Proposition 187 focused on taking a tough restrictionist stance but not endorsing Proposition 187, by saying "Proposition 187 is in court now, but the real answer to illegal immigration is a tough and meaningful strategy to deter and punish illegal immigration." It further advised supporting denying welfare benefits to unauthorized immigrants with a few exceptions, as well as all public services excepting emergency health care, K-12 education, individual disaster relief, and public health services that protect the whole community, such as immunizations.[125]

Benefits of the Welfare State?

As the White House calibrated its immigration position, on Capitol Hill the question of benefits for authorized immigrants became the centerpiece in the new GOP Congress. The House Republican leadership announced the Personal Responsibility Act as part of the new majority's "Contract with America."[126] Gingrich and other leaders in the GOP had been elected promising to "devolve" power in a host of areas from Washington to state and local governments. The welfare bill did so by moving control over many of the welfare programs to the state level. In addition, the bill sought to remove most authorized immigrants under the age of seventy-five from sixty federal programs including AFDC, SSI, non-emergency Medicaid, foster care, nutrition programs, and housing assistance. The proposal was also retroactive, removing those currently qualified after a one-year grace period.

Many conservatives embraced the proposal. The Cato Institute's Steve Moore applauded the Republicans' bill, saying, "Our belief is that nobody should get these programs, but if welfare is not going to be eliminated outright, then we argue that it should be for citizens only."[127] Conservative scholars at the Heritage Institute supported the bill as they warned that "America is becoming a deluxe retirement home" and the bill would help address the issue by removing elderly immigrants from benefits.[128] The SSI program, which provided cash benefits to elderly immigrants, had seen a 580 percent increase in resident immigrants receiving SSI aid between 1982 and 1994, fueling frustration with the program.

Still, while conservative think tanks joined a particular faction of the GOP in pushing hard to block immigrant access to social welfare programs, the Contract with America proposal exposed fissures within the Republican Party that emerged with regard to immigrants' benefits. In the Senate, Senator Simpson and Republican Senator Nancy Landon Kassebaum, two powerful GOP senators, opposed the House Republican leadership's proposal to remove authorized immigrants' access to welfare. Kassebaum, a moderate Republican from Kansas known for liberal positions on social issues like abortion, the Equal Rights Amendment, and health care, was the chair of the Senate Labor and Human Resources Committee. Her support for the bill and the endorsement of her committee would be necessary for the legislation to make its way through Congress. Simpson was the chair of the Senate Judiciary Committee. His support and the cooperation of his committee were also requirements for passage. Simpson opposed the provision, saying, "it's almost like they don't understand what a permanent resident alien is," observed Simpson. "The only thing they can't do that you and I can is vote. Period."[129] In a sense, Simpson's position and his statements echoed a traditional view of immigrants' relationship with the welfare state that was presently undergoing a large shift.

The national press attacked other elements of the proposal as well, including the proposal's support for orphanages and other forms of state-supervised residences to care for the illegitimate children of young women who would be cut from welfare rolls and thus deemed unable to support their children. After being attacked on orphanages and several other issues that made Republicans look "cruel and hard hearted," Gingrich announced in early January that he would reconsider the proposal to deny welfare benefits to authorized immigrants.[130] Nevertheless, Gingrich said the move did not represent a "change of heart" on the broader issues, and the new Speaker argued that the Republicans' position on immigration would continue to evolve, noting that the Contract With America was written before the Republicans knew they would be in power and able to find "more creative solutions."[131] Gingrich noted that the Republican Party was engaged in a complex dialogue with the American people and that "it changes over time . . . We are not going to get trapped into doing something dumb just so you all can say we're consistent."[132]

Gingrich's shift in position upset two key lieutenants on welfare reform, Congressman Clay Shaw, who headed the House Ways and Means subcommittee that was the lead on welfare reform, and Ways and Means Chairman Bill Archer of Texas who was more hardline.[133] Shaw publicly argued against Gingrich's shift, calling it problematic because the cuts in immigrant benefits paid for not only welfare reform but also many of the tax breaks for the middle class. Shaw felt it was unclear how to finance those initiatives without the savings from the proposed cuts.[134] After meetings with Gingrich, Archer and Shaw assured the press that the proposal to cut off immigrant's benefits was still a viable option. "The Speaker and I have no problems in regard to that," Shaw said.[135] The debate over immigrants' welfare access, however, was about more than how to finance the welfare bill as the savings were quite small, perhaps only $5 billion a year. At its heart, the debate was over the role immigrants played in the nation, and their relationship with the welfare state.

While generally supportive of the devolution of power to the states, many Republican governors opposed how the bill asked states to bear more responsibility without requisite additional funding and how it created onerous new regulations in their opinion. As a unified group under the auspices of the Republican Governors Association, they expressed their opposition to the bill.[136] After negotiations with the House leadership, the Republican governors backed a revised version of the Contract with America's welfare bill. They agreed to support the bill and its five-year freeze on federal welfare funding in exchange for more state control of the welfare system, which would generate the needed savings.[137] Consequently, Congressman Archer introduced the revised bill that spring, which barred authorized immigrants from approximately thirty-five means-tested programs; and made the immigrants' sponsor's pledge of financial support to those they sponsored entering the country legally binding, with an SSI exception for individuals in the country more than ten years and over age seventy-five.[138] When the bill was examined in committee, efforts to restore benefits for immigrants were unsuccessful.[139] While there was some support for retaining immigrants' benefits among liberals and those with significant immigrant constituencies, the groundswell of restrictionist support was too strong to restrain.

After passing the Ways and Means Committee, the bill was taken up by the House as a whole. In order to secure passage, the leadership made some concessions to moderates that altered some of the committee's provisions, making authorized immigrants eligible for more programs than the committee bill would have allowed, but it made qualifying for them contingent on the income of the immigrant's US sponsor.

In the Senate, controlled by Republicans after their successful midterm elections campaign, three bills made their way through their respective committees of jurisdiction over the spring and summer of 1995 and were revised into a single bill that was passed on September 19 by a vote of 87 to 12, the wide margin of the vote reflecting the bill's more moderate approach to immigration than the House version. The House bill made most authorized immigrants who were not citizens ineligible for five federal programs: SSI, cash welfare, social services block grant funds, Medicaid, and Food Stamps, while the Senate bill proposed making immigrants who arrived after enactment of the legislation ineligible for most low-income social services for a five-year period.

The bill that came out of the House-Senate conference did not go as far as the House-passed bill, but still imposed significant restrictions. The conference report specified that authorized immigrants who arrived in the United States after the bill was enacted would be denied most low-income federal social services for five years after their arrival, but immigrants who had worked in the United States for at least ten years would be exempted from these restrictions. Furthermore, those authorized immigrants already residing in the United States at the time of passage would be ineligible for SSI and Food Stamps, and states could make them ineligible for more programs.[140] Passed by the newly minted Republican Congress, the bill was vetoed by President Clinton, who attacked other provisions of the bill that he argued unfairly targeted children.[141]

With no comprehensive legislation passed in 1995, the issue of welfare reform and immigrants' benefits remained unresolved and contentious during the first half of 1996. The administration and congressional Republicans continued to spar over solutions. Framing their legislation in terms of "American" values of hard work and self-sufficiency, the House Republican Conference noted that while 90 percent of noncitizens were value-adding members of society, the remaining 10 percent "collect welfare, flouting both our traditions and the residency agreement they must sign pledging they will not become wards of the state."[142] Republicans attacked the Clinton plan for allowing noncitizens to remain eligible for benefits since benefits were an "immigration magnet."[143] Senator Bob Dole and the Republican Party also used the issue in the 1996 campaign, with the RNC releasing an ad titled "fool me once" that targeted Clinton on welfare, suggesting that Clinton supported giving welfare benefits to unauthorized immigrants.[144] Clinton countered with a tough ad "signed" that touted his border security record, "President Clinton doubled border agents . . . Signed a tough anti-illegal immigration law protecting US workers. 160,000 illegal immigrants and criminals deported, a record."[145] Both parties embraced a restrictionist tone to woo voters in 1996, a far cry from their 1992 campaign stances.

By the middle of 1996, revised versions of the Republican bills offered the previous year made their way through the House and Senate, passing both chambers by late July. The legislation offered by Congress constituted a serious blow to immigrants. If made law, beginning August 1, 1997, most currently authorized immigrants would be denied Supplemental Security Income and Food Stamps, with states given the option to deny them access to Medicaid and cash welfare (TANF) as well. Those currently receiving SSI and other supports would be cut off one year after passage. New immigrants would be excluded from SSI and Food Stamps and barred from Medicaid and TANF for the first five years they were in the United States, with the state given the option to extend benefits to them at their own expense.[146]

The White House considered their options and whether to veto the bill as they had in previous years. Bruce Reed, Deputy Assistant to the President for Domestic Policy and Clinton's lead staffer on welfare reform, urged him to sign the current proposal as he felt the White House had won strong concessions on "virtually every issue that is central." Reed admitted that three areas remained of concern: vouchers, Food Stamps, and the immigrant provisions, but he did not think it was possible to negotiate further changes in those three areas. In particular, changes on the immigrants' access to welfare provisions were unlikely, Reed felt, "because Republicans want to jam us and Democrats don't want to go out on a limb."[147] Clinton was left in a difficult position. Under pressure to pass welfare reform since he had vetoed the Republicans' earlier efforts as being too harsh, and on the record as suggesting both the House and the Senate bills were improvements over the 1995 legislation, he still felt uneasy about the welfare reform bill, saying, "You can put wings on a pig but you don't make it an eagle."[148]

On July 31, 1996, President Clinton announced that while the measure had "serious flaws," he would sign it anyway because it represented the "best chance we will have in a long, long time" to fulfill his 1992 campaign promise of "ending welfare as we know it." In his announcement, he attacked congressional Republicans over two specific areas—cuts to Food Stamps and the immigration provisions. In a statement, Clinton noted that he was "disappointed" in the immigrant provisions and he attacked the provisions as wrong based on immigrants' status as contributing to society economically and through military service. "It is just wrong to say to people, . . . You'll pay taxes. You serve in our military. You may get killed defending America. But if somebody mugs you on a street corner, or you get cancer, or you get hit by a car, or the same thing happens to your children, we're not going to give you assistance anymore."[149]

Likely to Become Public Charge

While the provisions of PRWORA restricting authorized immigrants' access to social welfare were the more prominent policy change regarding the nexus of immigration and welfare, they were not the only ones passed that fall. About a month after the passage of PRWORA, Congress passed and the president signed the Illegal Immigration Reform and Immigrant Responsibility Act of 1996 (IIRIRA), a sweeping immigration restriction bill.[150] IIRIRA not only reiterated many of the welfare restrictions passed as part of PRWORA, but it also clarified the definition of "public charge." While noncitizens who were deemed "likely to become a public charge" had long been considered ineligible for admission or adjustment of status and deportable, prior to 1996, there had been no statutory guidance on what that meant. IIRIRA changed that by requiring that the following factors be taken into account when determining whether aliens are inadmissible on public charge grounds: age; health; family status; assets, resources, and financial status; and education and skills.[151] IIRIRA also redefined the requirements for immigration sponsorship. Legal immigrants' sponsors were now required to have incomes higher than 125 percent of the federal poverty level and their affidavits of support were made legally enforceable by government agencies.

Reversing the Tide

After these bills were signed, President Clinton resorted to executive power to overturn some of the more restrictive measures imposed by the PRWORA legislation. President Clinton issued two executive actions to delay and reduce the effects of the passed immigrant benefit cuts, requesting that Secretary of Agriculture Dan Glickman give states the maximum time allowed to continue to provide Food Stamps to immigrants, and ordering Attorney General Janet Reno to reduce the bureaucratic delay for those applying for citizenship in order to help immigrants become citizens before their benefits would be cut off in August 1997.[152]

The president was not the only politician calling for a restitution of benefits. On the Republican side, several prominent leaders, including Governors Jim Edgar of Illinois, Lincoln Almond of Rhode Island, Christine Todd Whitman of New Jersey, and George Voinovich of Ohio, all called for a restitution of some benefits for authorized immigrants. New York Governor George Pataki attacked the denial of benefits retroactively, thus cutting off support for those already receiving benefits, saying the federal government was "trying to balance its budget on the back of the states," and Governor George W. Bush of Texas expressed a desire to improve the legislation "to take care of the elderly and disabled, without going backward."[153] Reflecting this growing concern, the National Governors Association began to draft a recommendation that authorized immigrants to remain eligible for aid. Senate Majority Leader Trent Lott worked to squash the statement in advance of the NGA's annual meeting, by persuading the thirty-two Republican governors to support a more muted general statement. The NGA released a statement that merely urged Congress and the Clinton administration to "meet the needs of aged and disabled legal immigrants who cannot naturalize and whose benefits may be affected."[154]

Soon after the welfare changes took effect on August 1, 1997, several lawsuits were filed challenging the constitutionality of the provisions that denied SSI benefits to authorized immigrants, one in California by advocacy organizations and two in New York by Republican New York City Mayor Rudolph Giuliani and several advocacy organizations, respectively.[155] One of the lead plaintiffs in the latter suit included Jan Tomas Abreu, a forty-one-year-old authorized immigrant who suffered a severe stroke and had been comatose for five years and was thus unable to take the exams required for citizenship. Other plaintiffs included Ekaternia Drubich, an eighty-seven-year-old Holocaust survivor who fled Ukraine in 1980 to avoid political prosecution. Partially paralyzed and unable to speak English, she was unlikely to be able to naturalize before her benefits ran out. Giuliani, in announcing the suit on behalf of New York City, said that Congress's argument that the legislation would encourage self-sufficiency and discourage illegal immigration "makes no sense," as disabled people are "by definition unable to attain self-sufficiency."[156]

While challenges to the law were pending in the courts, others pursued legislative avenues to amending the law. Across the country, individuals, interest groups, and state and local officials petitioned the White House to restore SSI and Food Stamp benefits.[157] Groups like the National Association of Counties and the United States Conference of Mayors held news conferences to highlight the harmful nature of the welfare bill's immigrant provisions.[158] Immigrants' rights and Latino advocacy organizations worked to bring awareness to the denial of benefits for immigrants by publicizing sympathetic profiles of immigrants who were going to lose support in newspapers throughout the country. This tactic was immensely successful, as Cecilia Muñoz, Deputy Vice President of NCLR, later said it "created outrage and made what happened real in a way that months of advocacy before the bill passed failed to do."[159]

The administration responded to the public outcry over the cuts in immigrants' benefits by seeking to increase pressure on House Republicans to amend the legislation. The White House rolled out a series of public events around the issue that were featured in the press, including a meeting with a bipartisan group of mayors from major cities.[160] President Clinton also highlighted overturning the ban on benefits in his February 4, 1997 State of the Union address, arguing, "to do otherwise is simply unworthy of a great nation of immigrants." In his budget request for 1997, the president asked Congress to allow authorized immigrants who became disabled after entering the country to receive SSI and Medicaid benefits and to provide Medicaid to authorized immigrant children of poor families.

Soon, leading Republicans both at the state level and on Capitol Hill began to break ranks on supporting the blockage of immigrants' access to benefits. Whereas earlier Senator Lott had convinced the NGA to mute its opposition, by April several Republican governors including Pataki, Bush, Edgar, and William Weld of Massachusetts were more publicly vocal in urging the restoration of benefits, arguing again that the legislation just shifted the burden to the states, as states would have to provide assistance to many people losing federal benefits. The looming fiscal burden on states for costs previously borne by the federal government weighed heavily on the governors' minds. Governors and other state officials also opposed the additional administrative burden of verifying the citizenship status of immigrants applying for benefits. While Democratic governors were happy to have a bipartisan coalition to attack the cuts, they were also exasperated with their Republican colleagues' late support. One Democratic member said: "Republican governors who were clamoring for this bill six months ago are now urging the repeal or softening of some of its biggest money-saving provisions. Where were they last summer?"[161]

On the Hill, under pressure from immigrants' groups, a group of moderate Republican senators introduced legislation to restore benefits to those immigrants already receiving them at the time of the bill's passage.[162] Joined by several Democratic colleagues, they argued it was a matter of fairness to those immigrants who had come to the United States under one set of rules only to find a new set imposed right under their feet. But the House and Senate Republican leadership remained largely unmoved. Ways and Means Committee Chair Archer observed that calls for change were not from members but from parties coming from "out of town," and labeled these demands for changes based on "false hope." Senate Majority Leader Lott noted that while he was "looking at concerns in these areas, I'm not inclined to go for a blanket change."[163]

In the late spring of 1997, all of the pressure to restore benefits began to pay off when a preliminary budget deal hashed out between the White House and GOP leadership promised additional funding to maintain disability benefits for authorized immigrants for the next five years. But House Republicans balked at the proposed agreement, with subcommittee chairman Shaw saying the deal went "too far" in restoring benefits.[164] Walking away from the deal with the White House, in early June House Republicans released their own budget plan that only restored benefits to those who were already disabled at the time of the welfare bill's signing.[165] The House Republican proposal drew heavy criticism from Democrats, with Senate Minority Leader Tom Daschle calling it an "extraordinary revocation" of the budget blueprint agreed to earlier that spring, and the Clinton White House charging that by 2002, 75,000 fewer authorized immigrants would qualify for SSI under this revision.[166] A reflection of the contentious and shifting nature of immigration debates, an amendment offered by Democratic Congressman Xavier Becerra of California to extend SSI benefits to authorized immigrants who were in the country in August 1996 and later became disabled was almost passed, failing by just one vote, but with three Republicans now voting with their Democratic counterparts.[167]

Eager to find a middle ground between House Republicans and the White House, Senate Republican leaders proposed a bill that would provide some benefits to immigrants who became disabled after the ratification of the welfare reform bill. Following several months of legislative wrangling, the White

House and Congress reached a budget agreement in August. Many in the White House viewed the deal as a success, as some of the benefits to those immigrants already in the United States before the passage of welfare reform were restored. Authorized immigrants who were receiving SSI and related Medicaid benefits when the welfare overhaul was signed would remain eligible. In addition, authorized immigrants who were in the country on that date and later became disabled would be eligible for SSI and Medicaid benefits. In addition, through the 1998 Agricultural Research Act, the administration successfully pushed for the restoration of approximately 225,000 authorized immigrants to Food Stamps, primarily to children and the elderly disabled.[168] However, as activists noted, this change affected only about 30 percent of those who lost Food Stamps as a result of the 1996 bill, leaving out adult authorized immigrants, even those with children.[169] Studies in the years since the passage of PRWORA have found that welfare reform had the greatest impact on legal permanent residents' use of TANF and Food Stamps, but did not show parallel declines in Medicaid or State Children's Health Insurance Program (SCHIP).[170]

Beyond those immigrants and their families directly impacted by the PRWORA policy changes, there was a much broader impact due to what has been dubbed "chilling effects." Women like Olga Manzanero, an authorized immigrant, withdrew her children, who were both US citizens, from Medicaid as she feared their enrollment in the program would, under the new IIRIA LPC policy, jeopardize her and her husband's chances to become permanent legal US residents. Withdrawing her children from the health care they qualified for, she hoped her children would not get sick and feared what would happen if they did.[171] Like Olga, many immigrants still entitled to public benefits and services did not apply for them due to confusion about their eligibility and fear that it would impact their ability to sponsor family members in the future.[172] Fear of benefit use impacting future immigration status as well as confusion about what benefits immigrants were still eligible for drove precipitous declines in immigrants' access to the welfare state. For example, studies by the US Department of Agriculture found that food stamp use fell by 53 percent among US-citizen children in families with a noncitizen parent between 1994 and 1998. In 1999, Los Angeles County reported that applications for public aid by legal immigrants fell by 71 percent while applications from citizens remained the same, whereas eligibility requirements did not change for either group.[173] The Kaiser Commission on Medicaid and Uninsured found that many immigrants did not seek public insurance after welfare reform even if they were still eligible because they feared it would affect their immigration status or ability to apply for citizenship.[174] Not only did PRWORA and IIRIRA directly remove millions of lawful permanent residents from accessing the welfare state, the legislation indirectly drove many citizens away from the welfare state because of their alienage status.[175]

By the end of the Clinton presidency, immigrants in the United States, regardless of the legality of their immigration status, were largely restricted from social welfare support and were often reticent to access those programs they were still eligible for, fearing the impact on their immigration status. Citizenship was now the basic litmus test for rights. The welfare benefit restriction marked one of the most significant successes of the anti-immigrant movement since the 1970s and signaled the emergence of a new period of immigration policy in the 1990s. Anti-immigrant sentiment was gaining traction nationwide as grassroots groups mobilized. Larger political shifts, the importance of winning California in 1996, and the centrist ideas of welfare reform drove immigration policymaking rightward in the Clinton administration. At the same time, the conservative elements of the Republican Party swept into power by the 1994 midterms and the Contract with America dominated the GOP, pushing aside more moderate and pro-immigration voices. In the 1970s, the turn against welfare helped to undermine immigrants' social rights.[176] By the 1990s, the dynamics had changed and popular nativism, partisanship, and electoral politics along with the turn toward federal welfare retrenchment led to a reduction in immigrants' rights. For various actors, the drive to reduce immigrants' rights preceded the turn against welfare, whereas for others, efforts to reduce welfare preceded an interest in immigrants' benefits. Together, these forces had a devastating impact.

Beyond the immediate restrictions, the changes made in the 1990s established a new policy framework that would ultimately reshape immigration policy over the next two decades. The slight mitigation seen through the legislative fixes and INS guidance would prove fleeting as the immigration politics of the next decade seized on the policy changes of the 1990s to fulfill their agenda. States were also driving policymaking in new ways during the 1990s. In the case of immigrants' benefits, even though the courts eventually invalidated the new restrictive California policies, federal immigration policy shifted to accommodate state pressures, with similar consequences for immigrants. As a result, the rights of immigrants in the United States were restricted, building on a foundation constructed during the two previous decades, and setting a precedent that continued to grow throughout the 1990s.

6

From the Border to the Heartland

LOCAL IMMIGRATION ENFORCEMENT
AND IMMIGRANTS' RIGHTS

ON A COLD JANUARY NIGHT IN 1995, with temperatures hovering around 30 degrees, nineteen-year-old Justin Younie fled a house party in Hawarden, Iowa, stumbling toward the street. He had been stabbed multiple times in the back and abdomen in a melee that erupted at the party. He collapsed in the street and died shortly thereafter while his friends fled from their assailants in Younie's truck.

In the eighteen months that followed, the reverberations from that killing in a rural Iowa town would reach across the country to Washington, DC and lead to a fundamental shift in the relationship between the federal government and states. The year after Younie's death, Congress passed the Illegal Immigration Reform and Immigrant Responsibility Act (IIRIRA), which authorized state and local officers to carry out immigration enforcement. The legislation reversed more than a hundred years of doctrine that supported federal supremacy in immigration enforcement. The story of how a killing in small-town Iowa caused this shift highlights several important themes.

First, although immigration policy was ostensibly and continuously a sphere of exclusively federal law, actual policymaking during this period reveals much more complex dynamics among assorted national, local, governmental, and nongovernmental actors. Federal inability to address some of the complicated issues of immigration control opened the window for state efforts at policymaking. Second, throughout this period, large structural questions about federalism and localism were answered in practice through the interrelation among formal legal rules and episodes of politically charged violence. Third, this story highlights how, by the 1990s, the battles that shaped immigration policy, once restricted to border areas, now were debated in the nation's center. But the story of the shift in local immigration enforcement policy is one that begins long before Younie's death in Hawarden. What happened in those eighteen months was the culmination of nearly two decades of political infighting that began in the 1970s over the role of state and local law enforcement in immigration and immigrants' civil liberties.

Legal Beginnings

Federal control of immigration was paramount throughout the twentieth century. However, during the colonial era and for most of the nineteenth century, state law enforcement was generally involved in efforts to control the flow of immigrants.[1] Immigration historians have long emphasized the emergence of federal immigration control during the late 1870s and early 1880s, growing out of concern with Chinese immigration on the West Coast.[2] Disturbed by the immigration of Chinese women, Congress first passed the Page Act in 1875, followed shortly thereafter by the Chinese Exclusion Act in 1882.[3] Concurrently, the Supreme Court, in a series of decisions, began to establish federal plenary power over immigration regulation that limited the role of states in immigration regulation.[4] The case *Chy Lung v. Freeman* involved nearly two dozen women who were aboard a ship that sailed from China to San Francisco bringing more than six hundred people to the United States for work.[5] At the time, California law required any ship's master transporting "lewd and debauched women" to pay $500 bonds per person to the California Commissioner of Immigration. Because the women were traveling alone, they were deemed to be prostitutes and therefore "lewd." When the ship's master refused to pay the bond, California's Commissioner of Immigration ordered the women detained onboard and then to be sent back to Hong Kong. Assisted by the local Chinese community, the women challenged the state law, arguing that it violated the federal constitution.[6]

In the first Supreme Court case ever to involve a Chinese litigant, the Court sided with the women and held that Congress has exclusive authority to regulate immigration. Justice Samuel Miller, who wrote the decision, warned that the state law would lead to extortion, invidious judgments, and discrimination at the hands of state officials. He then turned to address how the California law would allow any single state to weaken the United States' global standing by making a policy that contradicted national interests. If state governments had the power to deny immigrants entry, the Court posited, "a single State [could] at her pleasure embroil us in disastrous quarrels with other nations." Miller therefore enunciated a principle of federal preemption: "The passage of laws which concern the admission of citizens and subjects of foreign nations to our shores belongs to Congress, and not to the states."[7] The findings made in 1876 by Miller about discrimination and foreign policy implications were cited frequently by opponents of state and local immigration enforcement in the decades to follow. *Chy Lung* was followed soon after by the Supreme Court's ruling in *Henderson v. Mayor of the City of New York*, which struck down a state law that required shipmasters to post bond or pay a fee for each passenger. For the rest of the nineteenth century, and much of the twentieth century, the Supreme Court's commitment to federal preemption in immigration enforcement seen in *Chy Lung* and *Henderson* was firmly settled legal doctrine.[8]

Yet, while the Supreme Court repeatedly affirmed its support of federal preemption in the formulation of immigration policy, state and local law enforcement continued to play a role in immigration enforcement throughout the first half of the twentieth century. The Immigration Act of 1929 classified unauthorized entry as a misdemeanor, but Border Patrol often treated it as a civil offense.[9] Locally, police worked with federal authorities to deport foreign-born individuals who they deemed criminal, and federal authorities relied on the support of local police for federally initiated immigration enforcement efforts. One prime example of this was Operation Wetback, an immigration enforcement effort undertaken by the Eisenhower administration that began in June 1954 and continued through 1955. Under its auspices, immigration agents were assisted by local police in rounding up unauthorized immigrants and deporting them using inhumane methods.[10] It was not only during Operation Wetback that this cooperation occurred. In reflecting on his early days in the force, Daryl Gates, the Los Angeles Police Department chief from 1978 to 1992, recalled that local police accompanied by INS agents "used to go down to the railroad stations and pick 'em up by the dozens."[11]

The role of state and local law enforcement in immigration enforcement was explicitly defined in 1952 when Congress passed the Immigration and Nationality Act (INA). The INA created a bifurcated system of civil and criminal violations under federal immigration law. Illegal presence in the United States was defined as a civil violation of the INA, while actions like border crossing (improper entry) and trafficking unauthorized immigrants were deemed criminal. The law authorized Immigration and Naturalization Service officers and "all other officers whose duty it is to enforce criminal laws," including state and local law enforcement officers, to make arrests for criminal violations. For civil violations, only Immigration and Naturalization Service and other federal officers could make arrests. The distinction between arrests for civil and criminal violations was not discussed when the bill was passed, and the implications of that difference in enforcement clauses would not become apparent until two decades later.

Rising Jurisdictional Variation

In the two decades that immediately followed the passage of the INA, the structure established by the INA for immigration enforcement went unchallenged. With the rise of unauthorized immigration in the 1970s, local officials in many communities took matters into their own hands. Some localities responded to their growing immigrant populations by more directly engaging in immigration enforcement, while others removed themselves from immigration enforcement altogether.

In communities with greater local immigration enforcement, legal activists pushed to protect the rights of immigrants through lobbying efforts in Washington and through legal activism across the country. In response, the Carter administration outwardly pushed back against restrictionist pressure supporting a continued exclusive federal role, but privately expressed doubts about the exclusive federal role's constitutional basis in the wake of the INA enforcement provisions. Still, by the end of the decade, a court case opened the door to further incursions in immigration enforcement by state and local law agencies.

Los Angeles was one of the jurisdictions that technically removed its officers from involvement in immigration enforcement.[12] While the LAPD had played a role in enforcing immigration law before the 1970s, in the late 1970s, two Latino legal resident immigrants who had been falsely arrested on immigration-related charges sued the LAPD.[13] Under pressure from the community for cooperating too closely with INS, the Board of Police Commissioners announced "Special Order 40," which prohibited LAPD officers from questioning anyone about their immigration status, verifying status with the INS, or transferring suspects accused of minor violations of California law to immigration authorities. In announcing Special Order 40, the police commissioner emphasized that immigration enforcement was not well tied to the LAPD's primary goal of crime control in city neighborhoods.[14] As Police Chief Gates noted of their policy in the 1970s, "This[immigration enforcement] was not our responsibility, and all it did was get us into trouble."[15] Clearly it was not because of concerns with the potential for racism and discrimination that Gates announced Special Order 40, since while Gates and the LAPD were distancing themselves from enforcing immigration law, they were taking a more aggressive stance in the African American community, leading to charges of racial profiling and police brutality.[16]

Although Los Angeles and some other communities formally declined to participate in immigration enforcement, state and local immigration enforcement grew in other contexts during the 1970s. For example, in 1972, Sherriff John Duffy in San Diego County ordered taxi drivers to report suspected unauthorized immigrants to the police.[17] The Committee on Chicano Rights, a civil rights organization led by activist Herman Baca, pressured Chief Duffy to retract this policy, but similar efforts to enforce immigration law at the local level emerged across the state and nation. Tensions between Mexican American and other immigrant communities and the authorities grew following several high-profile cases of police brutality. In particular, the killing of twelve-year-old Santos Rodriguez by a Dallas police officer, and the murder of a Vietnam veteran, José Campos Torres, by Houston police officers were widely referenced as examples of the growing problem with police brutality. These specific cases portended and symbolized some of the issues and tensions that were emerging nationwide on a broader scale.

Reacting to numerous efforts at local immigration enforcement, racial profiling, and police brutality, MALDEF began a local and national campaign of resistance, joining efforts with the Ad Hoc Committee on the Police Enforcement of Immigration Laws. Recently founded in California, the committee had grown out of the work of Bob Ryan, a California state senate staffer who had reached out to MALDEF with documentation that local police were enforcing immigration laws in California. Ryan organized a series of meetings that included MALDEF and several attorneys from California Rural Legal Assistance and Peter Schey, one of the counsels in a case that had been consolidated in *Plyler*. As a result of those meetings, MALDEF became involved in two pending California court cases, *Galvan v. Duke* in Wasco, California and *Galvez v. McDonald* in San Mateo County.[18] MALDEF continued to receive complaints from communities including Reno, Huntington Park, and San Bruno, and in these new cases typically pursued damages for the injured parties, injunctive relief, and negotiations with police chiefs.[19]

MALDEF also sought to engage the federal government. In Washington, it began working with the Immigration and Naturalization Service, the Civil

Rights Division, and the Office of Legal Counsel (OLC) at the Department of Justice. MALDEF wanted the department to make some sort of public declaration that would clarify the limited role of state and local police officers in enforcing federal immigration laws. Throughout the second half of 1977 and early 1978, MALDEF leaders met with members of the DOJ including Assistant Attorney General for Civil Rights Drew Days and Deputy Attorney General Benjamin Civiletti to discuss state and local police enforcement of immigration laws as well as police brutality toward Latinos.[20] MALDEF offered three arguments against local immigration enforcement, and in doing so embraced several of Justice Miller's holdings from a century earlier.

First, MALDEF contended that local officials lacked the legal authority to enforce civil violations of federal immigration laws, and it submitted a legal analysis memorandum.[21] Second, MALDEF claimed that local enforcement would lead to discrimination and racial profiling. Finally, MALDEF maintained that local enforcement would lead to inconsistent enforcement practices across jurisdictions.[22] MALDEF provided Attorney General Bell with examples of local police enforcing civil immigration violations.[23] After their meetings, MALDEF's leaders were hopeful that justice officials would agree about the negative impacts of local immigration enforcement, and they expected the Carter administration "to concur with this view" as well.[24]

In the spring of 1978, the Attorney General met with members of the Congressional Hispanic Caucus, Vilma Martinez, MALDEF's executive director, as well as with the chief counsel of the Puerto Rican Legal Defense and Education Fund. These organizations expressed their concerns to Bell that since local police lacked knowledge of immigration law and procedures, they often harassed Latino citizens and legal residents in their zeal to track down unauthorized immigrants. The organizations warned Bell that this enforcement was creating an "extremely explosive situation" in some communities between police and Mexican Americans, Puerto Ricans, and other Latino residents.[25] While the department had a long-standing policy that state and local law enforcement should leave immigration enforcement to federal officials, members of the Hispanic Caucus asked the attorney general to publicly emphasize that it was official national policy, and Bell agreed.

Following the meeting with MALDEF and other Latino groups, the Justice Department released a directive reaffirming that the enforcement of immigration laws "rests with [federal immigration authorities], and not with state and local police." The statement further urged state and local police not to "stop and question, detain, arrest, or place an 'immigration hold' on any persons not suspected of crime, solely on the ground that they may be deportable aliens."[26] Vilma Martinez praised the directive, saying that it would help local police understand "they should not run about trying to enforce immigration laws which they know nothing about."[27]

But while Bell acquiesced to the request for a public statement, the department's internal position on the role of state and local police in immigration was far more complex. Responding to the legal memo MALDEF had submitted about local immigration enforcement, the INS general counsel wrote a letter to MALDEF in August, stating, "Our study of the question leads us to conclude that state and local peace officers are not precluded . . . from making arrests for violations of the immigration laws."[28]

With the statement from Bell and the INS letter, MALDEF attorneys felt that the campaign was in "limbo" and that the administration would go no further on the issue. MALDEF determined that unless there was a "major crisis" or significant positive change in the Department of Justice, future policy shifts would have to come from litigation.[29] With that, MALDEF resigned itself to waiting to see if some outside influence would press the matter again. It turns out the group would not wait long before litigation provided just such an opportunity.

Gonzales v. Peoria

MALDEF's next litigation challenge would come from Arizona. Peoria, Arizona was a small town outside of Phoenix, about 200 miles from the US-Mexico border and at the edge of numerous citrus groves. Between 1977 and 1983, the Peoria police engaged in immigration enforcement on many occasions, several of which would be challenged as violations of the preemption doctrine. In the first, Peoria officers received a request from the US Border Patrol to detain people who would arrive at a local market, Saliba's. Officers did not charge them with any state or local criminal offense but held the individuals for release to the Border Patrol. In another incident at Saliba's, several individuals were loading groceries into a truck when a local police officer approached them. The officer claimed that he was drawn by the truck's interference with the traffic flow, and because the men "fit the profile of" unauthorized immigrants. He questioned the men, asked them for immigration papers, took them into custody, and then called Border Patrol. In another incident, city officers responding to a call about a fight questioned bystanders about their immigration status and detained one man until he persuaded the officers he was a US citizen. The officers arrested the other men for improper entry, a criminal violation of the INA. Staff of the local farmworkers' union had heard about many of these incidents from their membership and connected the potential plaintiffs with Community Legal Service in Phoenix.[30]

Kenneth Schorr, a young legal aid lawyer who had recently been hired as the litigation director at Community Legal Services (CLS) in Phoenix, was assigned the case. For the first few years out of law school he had worked in Little Rock for the newly formed Association of Community Organizations for Reform Now, and in other labor law jobs. Schorr, on behalf of the plaintiffs, argued that city police officers detained people of Mexican descent based on their appearance under the auspices of immigration violations, in violation of the Fourth and Fourteenth Amendments, as well as the doctrine of preemption that precluded state and local police from enforcing immigration laws. The plaintiffs turned to a familiar group of allies from MALDEF and other groups in order to make their case.

During the trial, Schorr produced evidence that official city policies allowed broad discretion to make arrests for immigration violations. A department policy from 1978 stated that the city's "law enforcement officers have the authority to make arrests for federal violations." The following year, the department issued a contrary memorandum providing that "at no time will any illegal alien be arrested because he is an illegal alien." Three years later in 1982, the city changed its policy again, allowing officers to detain persons suspected of unauthorized entry for up to twenty-four hours.[31] The plaintiffs argued that some of these city ordinances contradicted the preemption doctrine dating from Justice Miller's opinion in 1876.

The case was argued before federal District Judge Walter Craig. Judge Craig was a fourth-generation lawyer who was appointed to the bench by President Kennedy in 1963, and who later served as special counsel to the Warren Commission that investigated Kennedy's assassination. Prior to his appointment, he practiced law in Phoenix and was president of the American Bar Association.[32] A current of racism permeated the case, in significant part because of Judge Craig himself. At trial, when Schorr asked a police officer to clarify what he meant in stating that the plaintiff matched "the profile of illegal aliens," Judge Craig leaned toward the officer and said, "They looked like wetbacks, right? I understand what he means." When Schorr asked the police officer to explain his use of the term "usual garb of illegal aliens," the judge interrupted the testimony and said, "They wear hats that were 'heco in Mexico.'

You can spot them a mile away."[33] Consistent with his gratuitous comments during the trial, Judge Craig ruled against the plaintiffs.

Stretched thin for resources following the departure of his co-litigation director, Schorr sought outside assistance in order to appeal the district court's decision.[34] From the beginning of the trial, there had been widespread interest in the case, and the National Council of La Raza filed an amicus brief in support of the plaintiffs. Armando De Leon, a Phoenix attorney who produced the NCLR amicus brief, reached out to MALDEF and convinced them to help with its appeal.[35] Morris Baller, with the assistance of Linda Wong in MALDEF's Los Angeles office, drafted the plaintiffs' brief for the US Court of Appeals.[36]

The MALDEF and legal aid lawyers were not successful in their appeal. In the Ninth Circuit's decision upholding Judge Craig's opinion, the court ruled that state and local enforcement of the criminal provisions of the INA did not inherently conflict with federal interests. The court reasoned that neither the structure nor the legislative history of the INS demonstrated an intent by Congress to preclude state or local enforcement of the INA's criminal provisions. In *Gonzales*, the Ninth Circuit drew a line between the criminal and civil provisions of the INA, clarifying a distinction made in the INA thirty years earlier and suggesting that civil provisions were a "pervasive regulatory scheme . . . as would be consistent with the exclusive federal power over immigration."[37]

Pursuant to this adverse ruling, Morris Baller wrote to Schorr, urging him not to file a petition to have the case heard by the Supreme Court. Already stretched by other litigation, Schorr and his Community Legal Services colleagues Mario Moreno and Jerome Blake agreed.[38] Despite not having produced a Supreme Court precedent, the *Gonzales* opinion shifted the immigration law landscape by cementing state and local authority to enforce criminal violations of the INA. The long-held federal supremacy of immigration enforcement was eroding at the edges, a trend that would continue for the next two decades.

Expansion Enthusiasm

Interest to expand the role of state and local law enforcement in the early 1980s came from some members of Congress. One of the first signals that Congress was moving toward expanding the role of state and local immigration enforcement came from Republican Senator Charles Grassley of Iowa. A farmer by trade, Grassley had served in the Iowa statehouse and then as a congressman before his election to the Senate in 1980. Grassley argued that the Griffin Bell directive had "chilled the cooperative effort previously enjoyed by the INS and local police." To remedy the chill and address what he felt was an underfunded INS, Grassley introduced an amendment to the proposed Simpson-Mazzoli immigration bill to facilitate cooperation between federal immigration authorities and local law enforcement agencies.[39]

While the Reagan administration eventually welcomed an expansion of the role of state and local police, the Department of Justice and INS did not support the specifics of the Grassley amendment.[40] Civil rights groups also opposed the measure. A *Los Angeles Times* editorial also opposed the Grassley measure, urging that immigration enforcement should be left to federal officials who were trained in "the nuances of often complex regulations."[41] Lacking widespread support, Grassley's legislation quietly died.

Soon after these legislative efforts failed, the Reagan Justice Department signaled eagerness to increase state and local immigration enforcement and moved to institute its own changes. Grassley and members of the administration met to discuss the issue, and the Griffin Bell directive was put under bureaucratic review. In September 1982, when INS Commissioner Alan Nelson was questioned about DOJ policy by Senator Grassley during a Judiciary Subcommittee on Immigration and Refugee Policy hearing, Nelson noted that the INS and the Justice Department believed that "the Griffin Bell directive was not really appropriate and it should be changed," calling it a "bar to effective coordination between federal and state authorities."[42]

In the months after the hearing, the Justice Department revised its policy on state and local immigration enforcement through a public memorandum from the Office of Legal Counsel. The new memo argued for greater involvement by state and local police in the enforcement of criminal immigration laws, but emphasized that federal authorities "remain responsible for all arrests for [civil] immigration violations," replicating the position enunciated in *Gonzales*.[43] When critics objected to this policy shift, an INS spokesman noted that the administration's interpretation "does not encourage police to pick up people for immigration violations." Instead, it merely represented a change of "spirit and perception" as the Bell directive had been misinterpreted to prohibit all intergovernmental cooperation.[44] In late 1984, the INS further clarified its position, declaring that state and local law enforcement officers acting alone could not arrest unauthorized immigrants unless there was suspicion of criminal activity. However, state and local officers could request authorization from the INS to hold a suspected unauthorized immigrant for up to twenty-four hours if that person would be likely to flee.[45]

As the federal government delegated greater authority to local officials and facilitated greater cooperation, some local communities manifested growing resistance to local police enforcement of immigration laws. During the 1980s, the concept of community-oriented policing, which required a close partnership between the police and local residents to help reduce crime and disorder, gained popularity. The adoption of community policing methodologies led some state and local police forces to conclude that cooperating with federal immigration officials might undermine their bonds with communities.

In Santa Ana, California, Police Chief Ray Davis sent a critical letter to immigration officials, which included photographs of immigration officials questioning people on bus benches and cruising residential neighborhoods to find unauthorized immigrants. Davis suggested that, while his officers would aid immigration services in cases involving federal crimes such as smuggling unauthorized individuals, local police would have no role in general immigration enforcement. "In order for the illegal aliens to trust us and report crimes, we can't be seen as an extension of the INS," he wrote, to explain his department's lack of cooperation in immigration enforcement. Reagan INS official Howard Edzell denounced Davis's actions.[46]

In San Jose, a series of federal raids on city residents and continuing harassment by the INS prompted elements of the community to oppose any cooperation by local police. Latino reform advocates, church workers, local union heads, city council members, and business leaders in San Jose denounced the INS's activities. As a result, the San Jose City Council directed the local police chief to avoid cooperating with the INS, and the mayor asked the national INS commissioner to remove the local INS chief.[47] INS quickly retreated by sending the national commissioner to meet with local officials, examining the management of the local office, and reducing the number of INS raids in the region. Local news reports commented on the cause of the retreat, saying, in an election year "when Hispanics are courted by Democrats and Republicans alike, the administration has discovered that heavy-handed enforcement tactics won't help its vote-getting effort."[48]

For the next decade, some local communities carved out their own policies with regard to local immigration enforcement, but the *Gonzales* opinion and the Reagan OLC memorandum cemented the formal legal ability of state and local law enforcement to enforce criminal violations of the INA, slowly eroding the federal supremacy of immigration enforcement but maintaining for federal immigration officers a substantial amount of authority with respect to the exclusive enforcement of civil violations.[49]

Changes in the Rural Midwest

It was the killing of Justin Younie in Iowa that would provide the spark to drastically expand the role of state and local law enforcement more than a decade later. Younie was at the party because one of his friends was invited by one of the residents of the house, Rafel Mellado, who worked with Younie's friend at a small manufacturing facility in Hawarden.[50] Mellado lived with twenty-year-old Guillermo Escobedo and eighteen-year-old Cesar Herrarte. Escobedo and Herrarte were unauthorized migrant workers from Mexico and Guatemala respectively who worked at local meatpacking facilities in Hawarden.

Younie and his friends arrived at the party after several hours of drinking at a party in Akron and driving around in Younie's Chevrolet Blazer.[51] Later in the evening, a fight broke out between some of the men who lived in the house and one of Younie's friends. As the fight escalated, Herrarte testified that Younie briefly grabbed Herrarte by the throat. Herrarte and Escobedo pulled two knives from a kitchen drawer and stabbed Younie and slashed one of his friends. Escobedo testified that Younie was coming toward him when the stabbing occurred. He said that he and Herrarte followed Younie outside and smashed the passenger window of Younie's Blazer, occupied by three of his friends who then fled. Younie collapsed in the street, was picked up by a local ambulance, and died in the hospital.[52] Later that evening, Herrarte and Escobedo were arrested for Younie's murder.

The mere presence of unauthorized immigrant workers like Herrarte and Escobedo in rural Iowa was a relatively recent development in 1995. During the previous decade, Iowa underwent demographic changes as a result of large shifts in agribusiness. A farm crisis in the 1980s caused jobs to disappear as family-owned farms gave way to larger corporate enterprises. At the same time, immigrants emerged as an important labor source in the meatpacking industry.

Across the country, meatpacking jobs were largely unionized, well paid, and urban at the turn of the twentieth century. Workers were generally male and of European descent. Beginning in the 1960s, and exploding in the 1980s, meatpacking underwent a dramatic shift as companies eliminated skilled labor, moved operations to rural areas or states with right-to-work laws, slashed wages, and sped up production, despite higher risks for workers. Deunionization and declining wages tracked other industries that experienced similar economic shifts at the time. A 1986 ruling by the US Supreme Court accelerated these changes by permitting meatpacking companies to consolidate in a merger wave that left four companies controlling 80 percent of the industry.[53] Wages in meatpacking fell 50 percent in the 1980s, while the speed of kill lines increased by 50 percent.[54] Meatpackers responded by recruiting immigrant labor.[55] Between 1980 and 2000, the share of Hispanics in the meatpacking workforce rose from 9 percent to 29 percent, and the foreign-born percentage of those workers rose from 50 percent to 82 percent.[56]

Several meatpacking plants opened in Iowa, and the state's population between 1990 and 2000 grew by 5.4 percent, to nearly 2.9 million, with approximately two-thirds of this growth owing to immigration. In the 1990s, the state's Latino population swelled by 153 percent.[57] The Census Bureau estimated that 75 percent of immigrants to Iowa came from Mexico. But these totals may have been conservative, not including many workers who arrived in the state illegally. Verne Lyon, the director of the Des Moines Hispanic Ministry, said of the Census Bureau's figures that one could "double them and you'd still be under" the true population total.[58]

In 1995, the *Des Moines Register* ran a five-day front-page investigative series: "Hispanics in Iowa." Those articles highlighted the dangers of crossing the Mexican border illegally, the challenges faced by immigrants within the United States, the rise of Latino evangelicalism in Iowa, and the ways that state institutions adapted to this new population's needs.[59] Examples were drawn from small towns like Lennox, Storm Lake, Perry, Marshall Town, and Columbus Junction alongside larger cities like Davenport, Sioux City, and Des Moines. Many of these municipalities tried to provide language services in schools and translators at the police department.[60]

But while the *Des Moines Register* highlighted many communities' acceptance of recent immigrants, not all Iowans were happy with the new arrivals. In January 1995, Mayor Mose Hendricks characterized Hawarden as "a small town in the middle of Iowa, where the people aren't used to outsiders."[61] In 1992, five Hawarden residents admitted to beating three Latino men in a racially motivated attack.[62] The next year, Julie Junker, a local teenager, was riding her bicycle with a friend and was killed in a hit and run accident.[63] The car that hit her was linked to Ramiro Rodriquez, an unauthorized immigrant who worked at a local meatpacker, creating more tension between long-time White residents and newer Latino residents.[64] In November 1994, reportedly under pressure from the Junker family as well as political and public pressure, the INS raided Rodriquez's workplace, arresting half of the company's eighty-eight-person labor force. Three detainees were released after providing valid immigration documents, while the rest of the group, thirty-six men and five women, were found to be unauthorized and deportable.[65] Among those de-ported were Guillermo Escobedo and Rafel Mellado.[66]

Soon after the arrest of Herrarte, Escobedo, and Mellado in connection with Younie's death, many Hawarden residents were upset to learn that the local police department knew that the men had returned to Hawarden after their deportation, but the police department had not arrested them. The police noted that they had not taken any action because they did not have authority to enforce civil immigration laws.[67] As one resident wrote in the local paper, "[i]f they don't have the authority, they better change the laws and get some authority." Another Hawarden resident called for laws that "guaranteed good immigrants and guaranteed that as an immigrant you became a self- support-ing, responsible, taxpaying, law-abiding member of society."[68] Following Younie's death, racial tensions ran high. "Anyone looking Hispanic was yelled at," the police chief said. "Even an Indian kid got yelled at from a group passing by in a car, 'get out of town spic.'"[69]

In September 1995, the case against Herrarte and Escobedo went to trial, and a jury found the men guilty of murder in the first degree, willful injury, and ag-gravated assault. Some critics accused the prosecutor, Sioux County Attorney Mark Schouten, of implanting race into the proceedings by describing Escobedo as "Hispanic" and Younie and his friends as "the White guys."[70] Schouten denied that he had raised race impermissibly, but he conceded in a press conference after sentencing that, "[i]n a broader sense, this is a case about race. It is a case about what happens when people from different races and cultures who do not understand one another meet, and the tragic consequences that can follow."[71]

Even before the Younie verdict, many Iowa residents worried that unau-thorized immigrants were the root cause for escalating crime trends, and state politicians from both parties fed those unfounded beliefs and fears for elec-toral gain.[72] The Republican Party's hold on state politics was unstable, with the GOP losing the state in both the 1988 and 1992 presidential elections. Thus, state politics in the 1990s was a mix of elected Democrats, Republicans, and Independents that spanned the ideological spectrum.[73] Iowa's population had declined by 140,000 due to the 1980s farm crisis, and the state faced a sagging economy and an increase in crime. Iowa politicians of all persuasions re-sponded by blaming the flood of immigration into the state. Echoing the views of most political leaders, Republican Governor Terry Brandstad said that Iowa "was a peaceful rural community not accustomed to having violence and crime," and he ordered a review of state immigration policy after the Younie murder trial.[74]

The panel conducting this review was led by Jay Irwin, an assistant to the Iowa public safety commissioner, who justified the panel's work based on "concern from Iowans about criminal activities of illegal immigrants."[75] Ultimately, the review recommended a law that would make it a felony for a foreign national to use a fraudulent document to gain employment or to extend a stay in the United States.[76] Similar legislation had failed during the previous session, but after the special panel's report, the Iowa legislature criminalized possession of forged INS and federal documents, such as green cards and Social Security cards.[77] The Iowa Senate approved this measure by a vote of forty-nine to zero.[78]

As the governor and state legislature enhanced immigration enforcement within the state, Iowans and politicians remained eager for the federal government to address unauthorized immigration. One Hawarden resident urged her fellow citizens to "[tell] our Congressmen we are tired of being abused as taxpayers, help us stop the use of forged documents they hide behind."[79] Advocating greater state and local roles in immigration enforcement, the Hawarden police chief said, "[i]f a town has a problem and wants to address it, then it should be able to. If [it] has a problem, it needs to act."[80]

Responding to the groundswell in their state, Republican Senator Grassley and Democratic Senator Tom Harkin both called for an increased INS presence in Iowa and pressured the Clinton administration to respond quickly. At the time, the INS office nearest to Iowa was the one in Omaha, which oversaw more than two hundred meatpacking plants across the two states.[81] Invoking Justin Younie's murder, Grassley asked Attorney General Janet Reno to increase INS presence in the state.[82] Senator Harkin also urged Reno to boost INS resources, noting that the INS in the previous two years had experienced staff cuts even as its criminal immigrant workload had increased by 25 percent. Harkin said the combination of the cuts and rising crime created "severe and negative effects on Iowa and the ability of Iowa law enforcement to handle problems from our fast-paced growth of illegal aliens."[83]

In early March, the INS responded by announcing two new offices in Iowa, one in Des Moines and one in Cedar Rapids. The political importance of unauthorized immigration became even more apparent when Harkin and Grassley openly bickered over who deserved credit for the INS's announcement.[84] The Justice Department's actions did not satisfy Grassley, and his press secretary noted that the Des Moines INS office "is great ... but it's not the only thing that's needed."[85]

Pressure on Washington

Pressure mounted on Congress and congressional leaders to take further action against illegal immigration. Those pushing for change began to target the congressional leadership, and Mayor Max Bacon of Smyrna, Georgia lobbied Speaker of the House Newt Gingrich and other congressmen from the state to address illegal immigration, repeating many of the fiscal arguments used by the supporters of Proposition 187. Mayor Bacon asserted that immigration made it "increasingly difficult for our community to operate without an increase in cost to our taxpayers" due to the cost of social welfare and education programs for unauthorized immigrants, and he argued that immigrants were taking jobs from local residents.[86]

After meeting with Bacon, Gingrich asked his staff to learn whether local law enforcement officials could demand proof of legal immigration status if they suspected an individual was in the United States without authorization, and he was surprised when a subcommittee staffer said that only an INS agent could ask for proof of legal status.[87] The Justice Department's Office of Legal Counsel issued a similar opinion, echoing *Gonzales*, finding that while state and local police were not preempted from making arrests for criminal immigration violations, they "lacked recognized legal authority" to enforce the civil provisions of the INA.[88]

With the issue now on the radar of federal governmental leadership, Congressman Tom Latham of Iowa introduced an amendment to the pending IIRIRA bill on March 20, 1996 to give state and local law enforcement officers authority to seek and apprehend unauthorized immigrants for violating deportation orders, and to detain such unauthorized immigrants for transfer to federal custody. Latham's legislation also allowed the Justice Department to deputize state and local officials for purposes of immigration enforcement.[89]

In the upper chamber, Senator Grassley introduced his own amendment to the pending IIRIRA bill.[90] Grassley had initially planned on sponsoring a measure to allow federal pilot training of local police officers in seven states. After the Younie murder, however, he expanded his proposal to allow Justice Department agreements with any states or localities that wished to enforce federal immigration laws.[91] These amendments fit well with the GOP's broader agenda of shifting power away from the federal government toward states and localities.

Civil rights and Latino interest groups voiced opposition to the Latham and Grassley proposals. Gregory Nojeim, of the legislative council for the

American Civil Liberties Union, said that "Congress is callously seeking to hand over US Border Patrol responsibilities to the local police, while we are seeing firsthand the problems with using untrained local law-enforcement to do the job of the federal government."[92] Georgina Verdugo, regional counsel with MALDEF, argued that police had to be adequately trained "to differentiate someone crossing the border from someone fleeing an armed robbery."[93]

The Latham amendment was fiercely debated when it reached the floor of the House. Supporters of the measure argued that the legislation was critical because such a wide cross-section of communities across the country were directly impacted by unchecked immigration. Hawarden's representative in the House, Greg Ganske, pointedly reminded his fellow legislators, "When we discuss the immigration problem plaguing our country, we immediately think of California, Florida and Texas. What many may not realize is that this crisis also affects America's heartland . . . it is also Des Moines, Perry and Hawarden."[94] Supporters of the legislation also cited the federal government's fiscal responsibility and the amendment's potential impact on the efficacy of policing at the state and local levels, suggesting that the lack of immigration authority was seriously impeding local police. Congressman Latham argued that his proposal would end impediments to local policing. Describing local law enforcement officials as "the frontline," Latham said allowing them to assist INS officials in apprehending lawbreakers was vital for states to "protect their communities."[95]

Commenting on some opponents' federalism concerns, Congressman Brian Bilbray of California said, "This is not an issue of the Federal Government encroaching out into the community . . . We are talking about the fact of doing what we talk about here, allowing the local community to contribute to the federal effort."[96] This rhetoric resonated with the devolution of power to the states and the reinvigoration of the Tenth Amendment were key planks of the Republican revolution platform. However, President Clinton had also supported a restrained notion of shifting power back to the states, noting "I believe we should ship decision-making responsibility and resources from bureaucracies in Washington to communities, to states and, where we can, directly to individuals."[97]

The arguments of Latham's legislative opponents echoed those made in the Supreme Court's century-old decision in *Chy Lung v. Freeman*, as well as those made by advocates for MALDEF and other groups since the 1970s. They claimed that devolving immigration enforcement power away from the federal government would increase racial profiling and discrimination. Representative

Xavier Becerra of California warned that increasing state enforcement authority would make local police forces "entrappers of individuals who may look different or speak a different language." Opponents also cautioned it would harm the community policing efforts and effectiveness of state and local police, because as Representative Sheila Jackson-Lee of Texas commented, the devolution of immigration enforcement authority would force local police "to do a job that is not theirs" and in turn would prevent them from doing their "real job, which is to protect those communities and protect the larger communities and to engender trust in the community so that they can get the job done."[98] Congressman Becerra and others opposed to the measure argued it would devolve federal jurisdictional supremacy. Becerra noted "[t]his amendment . . . actually breaks the ground of what we have had in this entire country of jurisdictional responsibility for law enforcement."[99]

Proposals to increase local immigration enforcement put some members of Congress in very difficult positions. For example, Senator Harkin attempted to acknowledge the positions of both sides, as his Democratic colleagues mostly opposed the Grassley and Latham amendments, but he felt intense pressure from Iowan constituents to support it. Harkin agreed with many Democrats about the potential to increase discrimination and decrease local policing, saying that the amendment "takes away from their [police] main function, which is to keep our streets safe. That's . . . what they ought to be doing—not trying to check to see what kind of card you're carrying."

Harkin ultimately supported the Latham and Grassley amendments, however, as he feared that unauthorized immigration was being "dumped on localities," but noted that in his view ideally the issue would be addressed with a beefed-up INS presence.[100] After debate in both chambers, the Latham and Grassley amendments were successfully passed and added to the larger pending Illegal Immigration Reform and Immigrant Responsibility Act of 1996.

While Congress considered this larger piece of legislation, local communities' debates over immigration remained contentious. The City Council in Smyrna, Georgia resolved that the federal government should give local jurisdictions "more direct power to deal with the problem" of a perceived illegal immigration "epidemic."[101] Meanwhile, the INS in Iowa addressed concerns over unauthorized immigration by conducting two large workplace raids in May 1996, one at the Iowa Beef Processors packing plant in Storm Lake and one at a chicken processing plant in Charles City.[102]

For the most part, there was continued support across Iowa for a stronger INS response and for greater delegation of authority to state and local police.

As the *Des Moines Register* reported on its front page in June, Iowa's INS office was so swamped that it regularly failed to answer phone calls from employers, or even from state troopers who had stopped suspected unauthorized immigrants.[103] When questioned about this lack of responsiveness, the INS district director admitted that such calls were a low priority for INS agents who were primarily focused on removing criminal immigrants.[104] Against this backdrop, residents and politicians in Iowa continued to call for the passage of IIRIRA as the only effective solution to an increasingly urgent problem.

Some Iowans cheered the raids and praised the crackdown, but others were less enthusiastic. Mayor Madsen of Storm Lake thought the raids would not deter illegal immigration, which he believed was driven by broad and unchanged economic conditions in Mexico and the United States. "If we insist on ignoring the economics and simply keep rounding up and using force and threat, those who work here ... will live behind closed doors in anger and fear. I'm more concerned that we have a stable community with families and openness," he said.[105]

The IIRIRA was passed in September, and the Latham amendment in its final form amended Section 287 of the INA to permit the delegation of immigration enforcement functions to state and local officers. The Clinton White House did not oppose the Latham amendment, as the INS General Counsel David Martin later recalled, because it seemed more acceptable than some earlier proposals, and the administration had successfully negotiated other issues in IIRIRA that they had opposed more vehemently.[106]

After IIRIRA, Section 287(g) of the Immigration and Nationality Act authorized the attorney general to:

> enter into a written agreement with a State, or any political subdivision of a State, pursuant to which an officer or employee of the State or subdivision, who is determined by the [Secretary of Homeland Security] to be qualified to perform a function of an immigration officer in relation to the investigation, apprehension, or detention of aliens in the United States (including the transportation of such aliens across State lines to detention centers), may carry out such function at the expense of the State or political subdivision and to the extent consistent with state and local law.[107]

For the first time in more than a century, the federal government had relinquished its jurisdictional supremacy over civil immigration enforcement to state and local forces.

Community Consternation and Resistance

The passage of the legislation was a watershed moment in immigration law, but its implementation was far more complex. Even after all of the various political demands to delegate immigration authority, for the first few years after its ratification, not a single state or municipality signed a 287(g) agreement with the Department of Justice. Only one even came close—Salt Lake City, Utah. The story of that episode exposes vital limits concerning the implementation of immigration policy, as it highlights the difference between federal policy and realities on the ground.

Salt Lake City, like Utah as a whole, was a first-hand witness to demographic shifts that affected the entire country during the 1970s. Between 1980 and 2000, Utah's Latino population increased dramatically, including a significant influx of immigrants.[108] Utah's Hispanic population grew by 40.3 percent from 1980 to 1990, and it grew even more rapidly in the next decade, more than doubling to 201,599 by 2000. Overall, Utah's Hispanic population grew 234.2 percent between 1980 and 2000.[109] Latinos' integration in Utah was uneasy, and the relationship between a White Mormon majority and immigrant populations that were 60 percent Catholic and 10 percent Pentecostal was sometimes difficult.[110]

Despite virtually no scientific studies tying immigrants to rising crime rates, some residents and government officials, like Salt Lake City Police Chief Ruben Ortega, sought to blame the city's rising drug crime rates on unauthorized immigrants.[111] Senator Orrin Hatch called for more federal support, saying, "Utah is experiencing a growing problem with criminal illegal aliens, a problem some in Washington have failed to realize is not limited to border states." As chairman of the Senate Judiciary Committee, Hatch pressed the Justice Department to allow Salt Lake City to enter into a memorandum of understanding as part of the 287(g) program in order to better coordinate federal and state efforts to combat unauthorized immigration.[112]

Attorney General Janet Reno responded that the Justice Department would authorize a 287(g) memorandum with Salt Lake City as a pilot.[113] At a press conference discussing the need for such a program, Reno said, "What we're talking about is the frustration sometimes of a sheriff who picks up someone who he knows to be an illegal alien. There is no one that can respond, or someone says 'Well, we can't really do anything.'"[114]

Despite Senator Hatch and the federal government's enthusiasm, however, the plan was highly contentious in Salt Lake City. Latino activists noted that even without a 287(g) deputization, immigrants were already being targeted and subject to racial profiling by city police.[115] A 287(g) agreement would further exacerbate the situation, they suggested. As local Latino leader Robert Archuleta argued, "if officers are already doing things like this [targeting immigrants] on their own, imagine what will happen if they have more authority."[116] Michael Comfort, the acting head of Denver's INS office, unsuccessfully tried to assuage fears among the Latino community and others concerned by calling it "a delegation of authority, not deputization," and assured opponents that the authority to make immigration arrests would only be used by a handful of well-trained officers.[117]

While many Latinos in Utah opposed the measure, some saw it as inevitable; therefore, they sought to ameliorate the program's implementation. The board of the Utah coalition of La Raza voted to offer training for the deputized local law enforcement officers, with one member commenting, "[I]f Janet Reno and Orrin Hatch are going to make it happen—if this gets forced down our throats—then why don't we help in training and bringing awareness to these officers?"[118] One group, La Allianza Latina, promised not to mobilize critics against the program in exchange for representation on an oversight board that would have addressed discrimination complaints, though this offer was ridiculed by many Latinos as "sleeping with the enemy."[119]

New avenues for both support and protest against the program became available after it became apparent that the 287(g) pilot project needed City Council approval.[120] In late July 1998, one of Salt Lake City's Republican congressmen, Chris Cannon, tried to build support for a 287(g) agreement by convincing House Judiciary Immigration Subcommittee chairman Lamar Smith to hold a field hearing on Utah's rising illegal immigration and its ties to rising crime rates. At the hearing, Cannon pressured city authorities and the Justice Department to formally sign a 287(g) agreement. Police Chief Ortega fully embraced the measure, and he testified that Mexican unauthorized immigrants were responsible for most of the city's drug trade. Other law enforcement officials, like Salt Lake County Sheriff Aaron Kennard, were more ambivalent about a 287(g) agreement but ultimately signaled support.[121] Kennard said, "Let me reaffirm that I have no intention of cross-deputizing my deputies so they can enforce INS laws. I have enough to do in Salt Lake County with the local laws." Instead, Kennard pushed for a more limited use of state and local authorities to address detention issues.[122]

By the fall, the potential 287(g) agreement went before the City Council. During a four-hour meeting, more than seventy residents testified, and

90 percent of them were opposed to the measure. One council member, Joanne Milner, disputed Chief Ortega's efforts to blame unauthorized immigrants for the city's drug issues and instead charged him with racial profiling.[123] At the end of the hearing, City Council rejected the 287(g) proposal by a 4 to 3 vote. The deciding vote, Rodger Thompson, later said that the overwhelming response of the Latino community had changed his mind against the measure.[124]

After Salt Lake City rejected the 287(g) agreement, no other state or municipality seriously tried to produce such a collaboration for the rest of the decade. Even in Iowa, Sioux City rejected a proposed collaboration following local opposition.[125] Local political pressure had spurred Congress to weaken federal supremacy by passing section 287(g), yet local dissenters ensured that federal control of immigration enforcement remained almost completely exclusive.

Immigration Federalism and the War on Terror

The relationship between the federal and state governments in immigration enforcement that was negotiated in the 1990s was profoundly recalibrated in the wake of the 9/11 terrorist attacks.[126] Immigration authority morphed from a matter of detaining unauthorized immigrants to a tool in the global "war on terror." One of the hijackers on 9/11 had been pulled over on a traffic violation only days earlier, but the officer was unaware of his visa overstay. This episode of terrorism and violence resurrected calls for greater state and local involvement in immigration enforcement. The first 287(g) agreement was signed between the Department of Justice and the Florida Department of Law Enforcement in 2002.

In June 2002, other measures aimed at increasing immigration cooperation between federal, state, and local authorities were announced, including creation of the National Security Entry-Exit Registration System, which would require registration for noncitizens from certain nations both at their ports of entry and throughout their residence in the United States. The Justice Department announced this new policy as fully "within the inherent authority of the states."[127]

Shortly thereafter, several immigrants' rights organizations requested clarification of the Department's comments and sought the OLC memorandum approving the system's creation. The department refused to disclose the OLC opinion, and litigation ensued. In 2005, the US Court of Appeals for the

Second Circuit ordered the Justice Department to release the document under the Freedom of Information Act. The memo reversed and called "mistaken" the 1996 OLC opinion stating that state and local police could make arrests for criminal immigration violations but "lacked recognized legal authority" to enforce the civil provisions of the INA.[128] The 2002 OLC opinion stated that, in fact, state and local law enforcement did have authority to enforce civil provisions of the INA. Many immigrants' rights groups opposed the new policy. National Immigration Forum, the Leadership Council on Civil Rights, the American Immigration Lawyers Association, the Arab American Institute, MALDEF, and other groups wrote to President Bush that "expanding the purview of state and local law enforcement officers to include civil immigration law could have serious detrimental effects on community safety."[129]

Within the law enforcement community, reactions to the new OLC opinion were mixed. Groups such as the National Association of Police Officers and the Fraternal Order of Police supported the measure, arguing that civil immigration enforcement would help local police to fight the war on terror. Lieutenant Margo Hill of the Boston Police Department told reporters that local police needed such authority as "it's incredibly difficult to detain people who have been targeted with al Qaeda connections . . . This would be a huge contribution to the anti-terrorism effort by local law enforcement."[130]

Other municipalities and law enforcement organizations condemned the policy switch as counterproductive, as one Chicago Police Department official called it, "political dynamite . . . We have an executive order from the mayor's office where we don't do anything with immigration. When we stop someone, we don't ask them what their alien status is."[131] Many police organizations, including the International Association of Chiefs of Police, the Police Executive Research Forum, and Major City Chiefs (MCC), also opposed the shift toward greater state and local enforcement power. The MCC argued that immigration enforcement by local police would cause immigrants to avoid any police contact out of fear that they or their family members might be deported. Police groups also opposed the new policy as fiscally unjustifiable and suggested that it might prompt an increase in racial profiling. Nevertheless, by March 2010, more than 1,075 local officers were trained and certified through the program under sixty-seven active 287(g) agreements signed in twenty-four states.[132]

The relationship between immigration and federalism is complicated. While the overarching legal framework for federal control over immigration enforcement was established in the Constitution and spelled out in *Chy Lung v. Freeman*, local realities ensured that state and local law enforcement continued to play a role in immigration enforcement in the first half of the twentieth century. In the 1990s, state and local law enforcement gained a formal authorized role in immigration enforcement as the result of state and local reactions to an act of violence and to transformative demographic trends throughout the United States. This newfound devolution of power was contested in local communities as all initially shunned the recent authority granted to local law enforcement. However, the violence of 9/11 caused a recalibration of federalism in practice. Whereas a decade earlier, communities and activists had successfully pushed back against the implementation of this newfound authority, the politics of fear and anti-terrorism allowed the federal government and the states to act together to enforce immigration law locally in communities across the country.

Epilogue

AT THE END OF THE TWENTIETH CENTURY, immigrants lived and worked in the United States, making essential contributions to both the American economy and society, but were facing greater harassment and more limited protections on a daily basis. By the turn of the twenty-first century, immigrants—both legal residents and unauthorized—had lost many of their claims on the state, creating sharpened distinctions between people who had full citizenship status and rights and those who did not. This loss of rights did not mean that immigrants had disappeared, as they continued to be a critical component of the economy and society whether as farm workers or physicians.[1]

While the narrative of the constitutive role that immigrant labor plays for the economy is well publicized, less well known is the role immigrants play in sustaining the welfare state. Today, both authorized and unauthorized immigrants are essential to financing the entitlement programs of the welfare state. The Social Security Administration estimates that more than three quarters of unauthorized workers in the United States contribute payroll taxes. Beginning in the late 1980s, the Social Security Administration began a file called the "earning suspense file" for the large number of W-2 earnings reports with incorrect Social Security numbers. It is no surprise that this file emerged soon after the passage of employer sanctions in 1986, which spurred many unauthorized workers to buy fake identification documents to get jobs and enabled many companies to assert that they believed all their workers were legal by paying them on the books with payroll tax deductions. During the 1990s, $189 billion worth of wages were recorded in the suspense file. In the first part of the 2000s, the suspense file was generating $6–$7 billion in Social Security tax revenue and about $1.5 billion in Medicare taxes per year.[2] By 2013, Stephen Goss, chief actuary for the Social Security Administration, estimated that unauthorized workers contribute about $15 billion a year to Social Security through payroll taxes, and have contributed nearly 10 percent of the Social Security Trust Fund.[3] In other words, unauthorized immigration is essential to the solvency of the fundamental programs of the welfare state.

But while immigrants were making fundamental contributions to the United States, their own relationship with it has been under attack for the last forty years. Debates over immigration, citizenship, and rights were reinvented in the wake of the shift to a post-industrial economy and the large demographic changes that resulted from the passage of the Hart-Celler Act of 1965. The Act not only transformed the nation's demographic profile, but it also changed the politics of immigration policy. While progressive in its removal of the national origins quotas and its diversification of immigration, the Hart-Celler Act drove an evolution in the anti-immigrant movement that would eventually restrict immigrants' rights within the United States. It was a unique moment when shifts in the economy and their consequences for workers combined with changes in notions and patterns of immigration and the emergence of a strengthened anti-immigrant movement. This confluence of forces led to massive fractures, fissures, and realignments regarding immigration policy at local, state, and federal levels.

As the demographic profile of immigrants changed and it became clear that stemming the flow of immigration at the border was impossible, restrictionist sentiment, particularly within the Republican Party, caused such individuals to turn their efforts toward limiting immigrants' rights. Initially, immigrants' rights activists and the Supreme Court expanded immigrants' rights in *Plyler* and liberalism persisted, even within the Reagan administration as the administration argued for extending equal protection rights to unauthorized individuals in the *Plyler* case. The expansive notions of the Equal Protection and Due Process clauses of the Fourteenth Amendment created during the civil rights movement had changed the contours of American politics, giving immigrants access to resources and networks that they were able to successfully harness to expand their claims on the state. While thwarted in *Plyler*, the roots of restrictionist sentiment within both the Democratic and Republican parties seen in the *Plyler* case would grow over the following decades.

Identifying immigrants as costly burdens to the state, restrictionists drew upon arguments that appealed to those who saw the massive growth of Latino and other unauthorized immigrant populations as an indication of the new economy—an economy that had shifted the ground beneath their own feet. Employer sanctions were seen by restrictionists as a way to preserve jobs for themselves and their constituents, but the reality was that those jobs no longer existed, as a result of the destruction of the union movement and changes in the political economy, including the rise of the service industry. Individuals for and against employer sanctions battled over whether movement and population shifts would actually drive American economic development. In that way, not only was their disagreement about immigration policy itself, but immigration was in some ways a vehicle for a larger conversation about the structure and order of a transitioning American economy. Those supporting employer sanctions struggled to gain power and shape policy within both parties. Employer sanctions, and immigration issues more broadly, divided the parties internally and interest groups struggled to forge the unusual alliances needed to enact policy change. Restrictionist efforts were further stunted by the fractured federal legislative process and institutional structures at the state and local levels. The obstacles to restrictionist reform and the ensuing failures to change policy made anti-immigrant activists more resolute and fueled restrictionist sentiment over the decades.

As shown in this book, the politics of immigration changed significantly in the 1990s—a pivotal decade. Citizenship status became the litmus test for basic rights. A new, restrictive era had begun, in which citizenship—rather than resident status—was the new boundary for access to certain rights and the welfare state. The intra-party fracturing exposed during the 1986 passage of the Immigration Reform and Control Act continued throughout the political debate over the removal of immigrants' access to welfare benefits. This internal dissension over immigration policy within the Democratic and Republican parties complicates the story of increased polarization and party homogeneity that scholars often ascribe to the 1980s and 1990s. The passage of welfare reform also highlights clearly how efforts to restrict immigrants from rights furthered the deterioration of rights for citizens. Removing noncitizen immigrants from welfare enabled the removal of millions of citizens from welfare under welfare reform. At the same time, the concern with entitlement spending overall drove the removal of authorized immigrants from welfare. These debates were fundamentally intertwined.

During this period, despite the preemption doctrine and its conception of exclusive federal control over immigration policy, states and localities played significant roles in forming immigration policy. Federal inaction in addressing complex immigration issues created opportunities for state and local participation in making policy. At times, states pressured the federal government to delegate authority. One example is the path from Younie's death to IIRIRA Section 287(g) discussed in chapter 6. At other times, states and localities have themselves confronted federal inaction by passing and implementing their own immigration policies. Courts have sometimes invalidated state-level immigration policies, as with California's employer sanctions and Proposition 187, but the extralegal force of these state policies nevertheless pressured the federal government to enact its own employer sanctions and welfare reform policies. In the years to come, pro-immigration activists would turn to the restrictionist playbook, and increasingly embrace state- and local-level efforts to defend alienage rights and push for immigrant integration in the two decades after 2000 with varying success.[4]

By June 2019, Americans were anything but apathetic toward the issue of immigration, listing immigration as the top problem facing the United States, with 23 percent of poll respondents choosing immigration over issues such as health care and dissatisfaction with government.[5] Both those supporting increased immigration and those pushing for restriction felt something needed to be done.[6] The battle over immigrants' rights and citizenship benefits remains fierce. While at the forefront of voter minds today, current immigration political and policy battles reflect the historical developments of the last fifty years. In the wake of the 2016 election, news outlets decried what they viewed as a recent rise of anti-immigrant sentiment in the United States. But the anti-immigrant movement that spurred Donald Trump into the presidency was not a recent phenomenon; instead, its shape and strategy were the result of the decades-long shifts traced in this book.

The anti-immigrant movement that emerged in the 1970s was successful at framing immigrants as a threat not just to citizens' jobs, but as a burden on the state, taking government benefits away in a moment when the new economic order was leaving many citizens without economic security and turning toward the welfare state's safety net. This narrative continued with Donald Trump's first general election television ad in 2016 ominously warning that, in Hillary Clinton's America, "The system stays rigged against Americans . . . Illegal immigrants convicted of committing crimes get to stay. Collecting Social Security benefits, skipping the line. Our border open. It's more of the same, but worse."[7] While famous for his calls to build a wall, Trump's anti-immigrant policies extend far beyond border and admissions policies to targeting the rights of immigrants already residing within the United States.

The period studied in this book influences not only today's anti-immigrant movement and rhetoric but the legal frameworks and enforcement tools upon which many of today's contested policies and programs are built. In recent years, policymakers on both sides of the aisle have turned to these rulings, precedents, and policies, especially those passed in the 1990s, to accomplish their various immigration policy agendas. The George W. Bush, Obama, and Trump administrations undertook large-scale deportation efforts using tools created by the 1990s legislation. IIRIRA and the Anti-Terrorism and Effective Death Penalty Act, also passed in 1996, radically expanded the crimes that made an immigrant eligible for deportation and created expedited deportation procedures for removal of certain noncitizens without a hearing before an immigration judge.[8] Before the passage of these laws in 1996, internal enforcement had not played a very significant role in immigration enforcement. For the several decades before the mid-1990s, annual deportations had not exceeded 50,000. After the passage of these laws, as sociologists Douglas Massey and Karen Pren have shown, internal enforcement rose "to levels not seen since the deportation campaigns of the Great Depression," with annual deportations just under 200,000 by 2000. With the further strengthening of enforcement measures under the Patriot Act in 2001, deportations increased again under the George W. Bush administration, reaching approximately 350,000 per year by 2008.[9] Current estimates suggest that the Obama administration removed more than 3 million people through immigration orders, a figure that does not include the number of people who "self-deported" or were "returned" or turned away to their home country at the border by US Customs and Border Protection.[10]

While the Trump administration gained notoriety for its calls for building a wall, and increased border enforcement, the other side of its policy agenda highlights the ways in which the previous fifty years had fostered an inextricable link between immigrants' rights and the politics of immigration control. Like its predecessors, the Trump administration looked to the tools of the 1990s to forward its restrictionist agenda. As discussed in chapter 5, under the passage of IIRIRA in 1996, there were new guidelines for the definition of "Likely to Become Public Charge" (LPC) that could be used for admission and adjustment of status. While the 1990s put these and other new anti-immigrant regulations on the books, the politics at the time meant that many of the immediate changes were somewhat mitigated in implementation.[11] In February 2020, the Trump administration adopted new guidance to define LPC. The new guidance directed immigration officials weigh a wide swath of assistance previously excluded from consideration, including SNAP and housing benefits, CHIP, Medicaid, and Medicare Part D, and refundable tax credits like the EITC. This guidance and similar efforts sought to stymie access to these legally entitled benefits for fear of restrictive immigration enforcement, challenging the family-, employment-, and diversity-based immigration system installed in the Hart-Celler Act.

Immigrants in the United States today have dramatically different access to rights and the welfare state than they did fifty years earlier. These changes have enormous consequences, not just for immigrants and their families, but for native-born Americans as well. Immigrants' relationship to the administrative state is what has explicitly changed, but there are implicit consequences for all Americans who face a vastly reduced welfare state. Although many of today's immigration debates pit immigrants versus native-born American workers, these debates ultimately undermine the notion of citizenship, creating a new reality for all living in the United States.

ACKNOWLEDGMENTS

I AM FOREVER indebted to Julian Zelizer for his steadfast mentorship and the guidance he has given this project and me from beginning to end. His deep knowledge and thorough edits at every stage improved this project in immeasurable ways. His work ethic and dedication to the field always motivate me to do better. Kevin Kruse has provided wisdom, advice, and kind reassurance for the past decade. His commentary has enriched this project, and his enthusiasm for excellent scholarship is infectious. His pep talks have picked me up when I doubted myself. It was a conversation with Dan Rodgers that started this project, and the wisdom of Margot Canaday, Rosina Lozano, and Dirk Hartog has improved it. Meg Jacobs has provided both warm encouragement and blunt directives in just the right combination when needed. I am grateful for the wonderful support and community that I found at Princeton.

Gary Gerstle did not hesitate when I asked him to sign on to this project; he pushed me to make bold arguments and his commentary strengthened every chapter. His belief in this project has sustained it throughout this long process. David Gutiérrez's incisive feedback on a very early draft of the entire manuscript helped me reframe it. Debbie Kang read many chapters and provided wise advice both on this book and academia for which I am most grateful. This work has benefited tremendously from the comments of Cybelle Fox, Madeline Hsu, Dan Tichenor, Carl Bon Tempo, and Ruth Gomberg-Muñoz, who reviewed and commented on portions of the book. Brian Balogh, Jefferson Decker, Katie Benton-Cohen, Gerry Cadava, Maggie Elmore, Eugene Hillsman, Lori Flores, Adam Goodman, Lily Geismer, Niki Hemmer, Hidetaka Hirota, Max Felker-Kantor, Julian Lim, Beth Lew-Williams, Kelly Richter, Will Schultz, Tom Sugrue, Andrew Sandoval-Strausz, and Jeremi Suri have been generous interlocutors about this project in its various stages. Thank you for generously sharing your wisdom and time.

I would never have become a historian without the unfailing encouragement and care of Glenda Gilmore and Jonathan Holloway. They introduced me to archival research and the craft, guided me to graduate school, and still offer wise counsel.

A post-doctoral fellowship at the Center for Presidential History at Southern Methodist University provided the time to write that made this book a reality. Thank you to Jeff Engel for giving me those two years. My time at SMU was made all the more fruitful by the engaging community, and many thanks are due to Neil Foley, Brian Franklin, Andy Graybill, Tom Knock, Evan McCormick, and Paul Renfro.

I have found a welcome home at Texas State University. Jeff Helgeson and Angela Murphy have been supportive chairs and protected my time to research and write. Jeff also somehow found time to comment on many chapters of this manuscript. I have learned so much from my colleagues and I am thankful for the insights of Sara Damiano, Paul Hart, John McKiernan-González, Josh Paddison, Jessica Pliley, Carrie Ritter, and Louie Valencia that have strengthened this project. Ana Romo not only edited chapters, but also gave crucial advice at a late stage.

Several other institutions have supported my research: The Society of Woodrow Wilson Fellows, the Graduate School and the History Department at Princeton University, the Eisenhower Institute, the Immigration and Ethnic History Society's Outstanding Dissertation award, the Hagley Library and Museum, and the Miller Center at the University of Virginia. These programs and institutions have been most generous and I am grateful.

No academic project is complete without rigorous debate and peer review. This work has benefited from opportunities to present at various conferences and from the insightful comments from workshops at the University of Pennsylvania Program on Democracy, Citizenship and Constitutionalism; the Miller Center at the University of Virginia; the annual meetings of the OAH, WHA, and the AHA; the fellowship of Woodrow Wilson Scholars and Modern America Workshop at Princeton; the Newberry Library Borderlands and Latino/a Studies Seminar; Purdue University; and the Swinney faculty writing group at Texas State University.

Archivists can make or break a project, and I am indebted to the following archivists who filled requests, dug out long untouched materials, and guided me through thousands of folders and boxes to help tell this story: Kary Charlebois at the Reagan Library, Joseph Geller at Stanford University Special Collections, Jeremy Brett at A&M Clements Collection, Dan Linke at the

Mudd Library at Princeton, Sam Kidd at the Smith County Historical Society, the staff of the Tyler Independent School District Records Office, the NARA staff at the Carter and Clinton Libraries, Blynne Olivieri at the University of West Georgia. Thanks to Sarah Sadlier, who provided some key research assistance at Stanford. I would also like to thank Kenneth Schorr, Michael Wise, Ron Haskins, David Martin, and Tom Epstein for graciously agreeing to my interview requests.

At Princeton University Press, Eric Crahan has supported this project from its early days. Bridget Flannery-McCoy, Karen Carter, Thalia Leaf, Alena Chekanov, and Layla Mac Rory got it across the finish line and made it beautiful. Thank you to Karen Verde for her copyediting and to Tobiah Waldron for his indexing. Thank you to the editors of the Politics and Society in Modern America Series for including it in the series. Thank you as well to the anonymous reviewers for Princeton University Press for their incisive readings. I am grateful to everyone who helped make this a better book. All errors are my own.

Thank you to my former Senate, campaign, and White House colleagues for a political education that has provided great insights for my project as well as revealed the necessity and potential applications of this work. In particular I would like to thank Ron Klain, Alan Hoffman, Tino Cuellar, Phil Weiser, Brian Levine, Stefanie Feldman, Tobin Marcus, Herbie Ziskend, and Terrell McSweeny. Ron Klain has always provided kind guidance. From day one, Terrell McSweeny has been a mentor and a great friend.

Graduate school introduced me to four incredible historians and a scientist, Dov Groshgal, Aaron Goldman, Craig Green, Molly Lester, and Kathryn McGarr, who have become dear friends for whom I am most grateful. Kathryn McGarr has inspired, encouraged, assisted, and refined this project in more ways than can be noted, and I owe her more than she will ever know.

For their decades of friendship, thank you to Jenny Baine, Anne Dudley, Carolina Galvao, Danielle Hertz, Eileen Jones, Benet Kearney, Christine Lee, Elizabeth Laws, Erin Suhr, Charlotte Taft, Thomas Dolan, Carl Dietz, Joe Ghory, and Alex Ramsay. Friends are the family you choose, and I am so lucky. Thank you to Julie Edwards, Juliet Eurich, Karen Lavine, and Donald Kilpatrick for your encouragement and support. Thank you to Marcia and John Goldman and Janie and Cappy McGarr for opening your homes to me repeatedly throughout this project. When I found myself in Texas for the last four years, the atx crew made it a soft landing. Thank you for the tennis games, margaritas, and laughter that provide a welcome respite from academia. Thank you to Shannon Wardlaw for translating Texan and laughing with me on this parenting adventure. I am indebted to Nola Rudolph, Sellers Webb, Claudia Vasquez, and my mother, who took care of my children with such love so that I could have time to write.

Thank you to my family. The Barnards have welcomed me into their family and adapted as deadlines crept their way into holidays. My sister Rebekah Coleman is a gifted writer and provided a sounding board and supportive ear as I embarked on my own writing project. Bek, Ian, Hannah, Kate, and Erin have also provided key moments of comic relief throughout. My parents, Marj and Bill Coleman, have always been my biggest supporters and my most beloved readers. They show me every day the definition of unconditional love.

Finally, my deepest gratitude goes to Nick Barnard. He has celebrated every milestone along this long journey, and no one is more excited for it to be done. Cole and Etta Barnard, to whom this book is dedicated, you each noisily entered the world and interrupted this project, and while the book might not be, my world is infinitely better because of it. No words are enough to express my love for you two.

NOTES

Introduction

1. The history of the phrase and notion "a nation of immigrants" has been the subject of significant critical scholarship. For an analysis of its use as a keyword, see Gabaccia, "Nations of Immigrants: Do Words Matter?" For an overview of the historiography surrounding the notion, see Gabaccia, "Is Everywhere Nowhere?" Daniel Kanstoom traces the myth of the nation of immigrants in the 1790 law limiting naturalization to White aliens. Donna Gabaccia dates the invention of this notion to the decades of the Civil War. When the invention of the United States as a nation of immigrants began in the decades of the Civil War, there was a shift from calling recent arrivals emigrants to calling them immigrants. Aristide Zolberg points to its origins in the anti-Chinese debates of the 1860s and 1870s. See Kanstroom, *Deportation Nation*. See also Gabaccia, "Nations of Immigrants: Do Words Matter?" 7; Zolberg, *A Nation by Design*. Mae Ngai's forthcoming work, *Nation of Immigrants: A Short History of an Idea* (under contract with Princeton University Press) will provide great insight into these developments. In light of these interventions, scholars have suggested alternative descriptive frameworks for the United States. Aristide Zolberg has described it as "a nation by design"; whereas Erika Lee offers that the United States should be seen as a "gatekeeping nation" in the years between 1870 and 1930; and Daniel Kanstroom has called it a "deportation nation." Several scholars have argued that the United States has been defined by notions of competing ideals. Gary Gerstle has traced how "civic nationalism" and "racial nationalism" have played key roles in shaping the twentieth-century United States. Erica Lee has suggested that the United States is simultaneously "a nation of immigrants" and "a nation of xenophobia." See Gerstle, *American Crucible*, and Lee, *America for Americans*.

2. For scholarship on border and admissions restrictions during this period, see Tichenor, *Dividing Lines*; Zolberg, *Nation by Design*. For scholarship on deportation during this period, see Goodman, *The Deportation Machine*. For a broader history of undocumented migration during this period, see Minian, *Undocumented Lives*. For a discussion of alienage rights, see Bosniak, *The Citizen and the Alien*. For the influence of rights on border and admissions policy during this period, see Carolyn Wong, *Lobbying for Inclusion*. For analysis of post-2005 immigration policy, see Tom K. Wong, *Politics of Immigration*. Wong's excellent work argues that from 2005, immigration policy has been characterized by a sharpening of the partisan divide, changing demographics that are shifting electoral incentives and increasing debates over what it means to be an American. During the earlier period that this work examines, one does not yet see the entrenched partisan divides that Wong highlights in the post-2005 moment, but one can

see the ways in which debates over immigration policy are intimately tied to notions of social citizenship and what it means to be American. In addition, in this earlier period, one can start to see some early roots of immigrant political agency shaping immigration policymaking, which Wong traces to its more full development in his analysis of post-2005 voting records. Many scholars have looked at the importance of citizenship to rights. Some, like Yasemin Soysal, have argued that in recent years, national citizenship was becoming less important for access to basic rights in many Western countries. See Soysal, *Limits of Citizenship*. While Soysal and others have negated the importance of national citizenship to rights, other scholars have suggested that we need to look at how various forms of citizenship beyond national citizenship impact rights. Andrew Gordon and Trevor Stack have studied the rise of a modern tradition of "urban citizenship" in Mexico. See Gordon and Stack, "Citizenship Beyond the State." In the wake of the changes in immigration federalism that are documented in this book, Ramakrishnan and Coburn have argued that what has emerged is a notion of "state citizenship." This state citizenship, they argue, "runs parallel to national citizenship and is enduring, immune from constitutional challenge." See Colbern and Ramakrishnan, "Citizens of California," and *State Citizenship*. Other scholars have considered the ways in which race and ethnicity have and continue to play a larger role than citizenship in impacting rights. For example, Leo Chavez, using innovative media analysis, has shown how in recent debates race has played a larger role than citizenship, as the "Latino Threat" narrative gained currency and caused a crisis over the meaning of citizenship, leading US-born Latinos to be cast as "'alien-citizens,' perpetual foreigners despite their birthright." See Chavez, *The Latino Threat*. Finally, scholars like Cybelle Fox have pointed to the ways in which legal status has played a key role in the development of rights for those without citizenship status. For a more extended discussion of Fox's work and the relationship between legal status, citizenship, and rights, see chapter 5 of this work. In addition, there is excellent scholarship exploring how, historically, the rights accorded to and denied immigrants has put pressure on different notions of citizenship, at times extending it beyond a narrow legal definition to include economic and cultural rights and at times contracting it. Most famously, T. H. Marshall has argued for the sequential development of civil, political, and social citizenship and a corresponding range of rights. For an extended and thoughtful review of the scholarship on distinct understandings of citizenship, see Chavez, *The Latino Threat*, Introduction, and Bosniak, "Universal Citizenship and the Problem of Alienage."

3. Ngai, *Impossible Subjects*.

4. On the historical patterns and development of nativism and xenophobia, see Higham, *Strangers in the Land*; Lee, *America for Americans*; Perea, *Immigrants Out!*; Gerstle, "The Immigrant as Threat"; Reimers, *Unwelcome Strangers*; Schrag, *Not Fit for Our Society*.

5. A note on terminology. Throughout the book, the terms "restrictionist" and "anti-immigrant" are used to describe a range of policies or people who support policy positions that support greater immigration enforcement and the decreased ability of immigrants to access public goods, services, and benefits, and who oppose the more full inclusion of immigrants into American society.

6. The concern about immigrants, poverty, dependency, and their potential burden on communities has a long history in the United States, dating from colonial times. This nativist rhetoric has arisen at various points over the last three centuries. For more on the colonial era and the use of poverty and the "likely to become public charge" rule to restrict Irish immigration,

see Hirota, *Expelling the Poor*. "Likely to become pubic charge" was used in the early twentieth century to deny entry to Jewish immigrants at Ellis Island and South Asians on Angel Island, see Lee, *America for Americans*, 10. Throughout the twentieth century, the "likely to become public charge" clause was increasingly targeted toward Mexican immigrants.

7. As a contested category subject to frequent refashioning, I use the term Latino to reflect current terms of identity within scholarship, while Hispanic is used in this work only when the original sources such as the census or polling data would have used that terminology in assigning identification.

8. For a thoughtful discussion of the relationship between immigration law and policy and alienage law and policy, see Bosniak, *The Citizen and the Alien*, 37–76. Immigration law scholars often distinguish between "immigration law" and "alienage law" in that the term immigration law applies to those laws regulating entry and exit and the terms of remaining in the United States, vesus alienage law, which would apply to other laws that affect immigrants, a distinction that Pratheepan Gulasekaram and S. Karthick Ramakrishnan note remains "important in modern judicial appraisals of state and local laws that affect immigrants." However, this distinction is often complicated because, as seen in this work and others, alienage laws are often created by governments to influence immigration decisions. For more see, Gulasekaram and Ramakrishnan, *The New Immigration Federalism*.

9. Bosniak, *The Citizen and the Alien*, 68–69.

10. The federal government played a limited role in regulating immigration from its founding through the 1860s, with its two most notable actions being the passage in the 1790s of several naturalization laws and the passage of the Alienage and Sedition Acts of 1798, which provided the president with limited removal authority for those deemed to be "dangerous to the peace and safety of the United States." During this period, immigration regulation was primarily the purview of state and local authorities. In *Expelling the Poor*, Hidetaka Hirota shows how state-level regulation in New York and Massachusetts emerged during the middle half of the nineteenth century, targeting Europeans, and in particular the Irish, as a matter of economic and cultural nativism that focused on concerns about their poverty. Beth Lew-Williams in *The Chinese Must Go* outlines how anti-Chinese violence in California and the Pacific Northwest drove exclusionary policymaking.

11. For more on these cases, see chapter 6.

12. Pratheep Gulasekaram and S. Karthick Ramakrishnan have written an excellent narrative of the historical antecedents, legal development, and doctrinal shifts in immigration federalism. For more detail on immigration federalism during what they call "the second era of immigration federalism," see Gulasekaram and Ramakrishnan, *The New Immigration Federalism*, 24–41.

13. Other scholars, notably Gulasekaram and Ramakrishnan, have also argued for the emergence of a new period of immigration federalism post–Hart-Celler. However, Gulasekaram and Ramakrishnan trace its slow development between 1965 and 2004 and focus on the "flurry" of state-level restrictive legislation between 2004 and 2012. This work suggests that states were already playing a larger role by the 1990s. In their analysis, Proposition 187 failed to have an immediate impact, pointing to its failure to be implemented in California as well as its failure to successfully push other copycat legislation. The authors view Prop. 187 as important for its longer term impact for two reasons; as the moment "national groups began to recognize the potential for states to serve as battlegrounds over immigration policy"; and as a model that

taught restrictionists lessons in the 2000s when they began a proliferation of state-level initiatives. Their analysis, while correct in addressing the long-term impact of Prop. 187, underplays the transformative effect Prop. 187 had *immediately*. By looking to national politics, and in particular looking at how Proposition 187 had a dramatic effect in the politics of the Clinton White House as is explored in chapter 5, one can see the important role that California held in the 1990s, directly influencing national policy and the adoption of PRWORA. Similarly, Gulasekaram and Ramakrishnan read the 287(g) program in a way that suggests it is noteworthy only once states began signing MOUs in the wake of 9/11. But if one looks at the development and legislative history of 287(g) as discussed in chapter 6, one can see the way in which Iowa is driving national policy and getting the program on the books. Its mere passage is a product of increasing state power and shows how states are driving immigration policy. All taken together, while there is more widespread adoption of state-level immigration legislation post-2004, I believe that Gulasekaram and Ramakrishnan under-read the importance of these developments in the 1990s and the role that states were already playing in defining immigration policy well before 2004.

14. In the 2000s, state-level efforts to defend alienage rights would emerge. With states having emerged as playing a central role in shaping immigration policy and facing increased surveillance and a reeducation in immigrants' access to the social welfare states, immigrants' rights activists in the 2000s began an immigrant integration campaign that was successful in several states. See Ramakrishnan and Colbern, "The 'California Package.'" Other scholars including Kelly Richter, Jonathan Bell, and Mark Brilliant have shown the ways in which California has been at the forefront of many political debates about inclusion and the formative role that California has played in forging federal policymaking in the postwar period. In response to those works on California, this project presses that idea further by showing that many other states, including those in the nation's interior and Midwest, played important roles in forging immigration policy. Brilliant, *Color America Changed*; Bell, *California Crucible*; Richter, "Uneasy Border State."

15. Wilentz, *The Age of Reagan*.

16. Lassiter, "Political History Beyond the Red-Blue Divide."

17. Ngai, *Impossible Subjects*, 24.

18. Ngai, *Impossible Subjects*, 50–54. For an overview of the history of the racial classification of persons of Mexican dissent and citizenship, see Neil Foley, *Mexicans in the Making of America*, 50–63.

19. For more on exclusion, expulsion, and repatriation during this period, see Adam Goodman, *The Deportation Machine*, 37–72 and Ngai, *Impossible Subjects*, 64–75. For more on the rise of the Border Patrol and expulsion during this period, see Kelly Lytle Hernández, *Migra!*.

20. Tichenor, *Dividing Lines*, 215 and Jewish Telegraphic Agency, Daily News Bulletin, June 2, 1965. Accessed June 30, 2017. http://pdfs.jta.org/1965/1965-06-02_106.pdf.

21. Ngai, *Impossible Subjects*, 261.

22. Radford and Noe-Bustamante, "Facts on U.S. Immigrants, 2017."

23. Pew Research Center, "Modern Immigration Wave."

24. US Constitution, preamble.

25. Chetty et al., "The Fading American Dream."

26. Judith Stein, *Pivotal Decade*; McCartin, *Collision Course*; Cowie, *Capitol Moves*. While the declension narrative is most prominent, there has been excellent work on late-twentieth and early-twenty-first-century working-class activism and militancy. See Bloemraad, Voss, and Lee, "The Protests of 2006"; Boris and Klein, *Caring for America*; Cobble, *The Sex of Class*; Fine, *Worker Centers*; Fink, *The Maya of Morganton*; Fink, "Labor joins *la marcha*"; Hing and Johnson, "The Immigrant Rights Marches of 2006," 99.

27. A number of both legal and administrative decisions during the period show the growth of immigrants' rights during the period. *Graham v. Richardson* 403 U.S. 365 (1971) recognized the right of aliens to receive state welfare benefits. For more on *Graham*, see chapter 5 and Fox, "Unauthorized Welfare." *Almeida-Sanchez v. U.S.*, 413 U.S. 266 extended Fourth Amendment protection. Immigrants' due process rights in deportation and detention were also expanded during the period through cases such as *Landon v. Plasencia*, 459 US. 21 (1982), which cemented the right to procedural due process for a returning alien in an exclusion hearing, as well as *Bolanos v. Kiley*, 509 F.2d 1023 (2d Cir. 1975), which extended the right of aliens, including unauthorized aliens, to sue, and *Matter of Marin*, 16 I&N. Dec 581 (1978), which established a balance of equities in determining relief in deportation cases. There were also notable defeats for immigrants' rights activism during the period, including *Mathews v. Diaz*, 426 U.S. 67 (1976), which allowed Congress to deny federal benefits based on alienage status as part of its authority to regulate immigration, which is discussed in greater detail in chapter 5 of this work. See also Motomura, *Curious Evolution of Immigration Law*.

28. Katz, *In the Shadow of the Poorhouse*; Orleck, *Storming Caesars Palace*; Kornbluh, *The Battle for Welfare Rights*.

29. Kornbluh and Mink, *Ensuring Poverty, Welfare Reform*.

Chapter 1: The Rose's Sharp Thorn

1. Winter, "A Supreme Court Case 35 Years Ago."

2. In *Yick Wo v. Hopkins*, 118 U.S. 356 (1886) decision, the Supreme Court held that resident aliens enjoyed the protection of the Fourteenth Amendment, noting that the terms of the Fourteenth Amendment are "not confined to the protection of citizens . . . These provisions are universal in their application, to all persons within the territorial jurisdiction, without regard to differences of race, of color or of nationality. . . . The questions we have to consider and decide in these cases, therefore, are to be treated as involving the rights of every citizen of the United States equally with those of the strangers and aliens who now invoke the jurisdiction of the court."

3. Bosniak, *The Citizen and the Alien*, 54.

4. *Yick Wo v. Hopkins*, 118 U.S. 356 (1886).

5. For more on these cases, see Parker, *Making Foreigners*, 160–163; and Gulasekaram and Ramakrishnan, *The New Immigration Federalism*, 34–41. Some examples include *Patsone v. Pennsylvania* (1914), which upheld a Pennsylvania law banning noncitizen hunting; *Truax v. Raich* (1915), which struck down an Arizona law requiring businesses to hire mostly citizens; *Ohio v. Deckenback* (1927), which upheld a Cincinnati law barring noncitizens from operating billiard halls; *Hines v. Davidowitz* (1941), which struck down a Pennsylvania alien registration law; and *Takahashi v. Fish and Game Commission* (1948), which struck down a California law denying commercial fishing licenses to noncitizens.

6. Cybelle Fox and Tom Guglielmo have traced these efforts between the 1920s and 1940s, and David Gutiérrez and Shana Bernstein explored the provision of old-age pensions in California for long-term resident aliens during the 1960s. See Fox and Guglielmo, "Defining America's Racial Boundaries"; Gutiérrez, *Walls and Mirrors*, 172; Bernstein, "Interracial Activism."

7. Massey, Durand, and Malone, *Beyond Smoke and Mirrors*, 43–44.

8. Minian, *Undocumented Lives*, 56.

9. Ibid., 45.

10. Gallup Immigration Polling, https://news.gallup.com/poll/1660/immigration.aspx. Accessed December 10, 2018. It should be noted that the Gallup polling referred to throughout this book looks not at immigrants' rights, but at admissions levels. I rely on these figures to access the general public sentiment at the moment as there is no consistent polling data on immigrants' rights and Gallup has not historically conducted polls on immigrants' rights. While sentiment toward immigrants' rights and admissions levels is often related, the two are not the same and should not be taken as synonymous.

11. This anti-Mexican nativism and language of invasion was not new in US history, as it had reared its head in earlier periods such as during the US-Mexican War, the repatriation campaigns of the 1930s, and during Operation Wetback.

12. Minian, *Undocumented Lives*, 220.

13. "The Newest Americans: A Second Spanish Invasion," *U.S News and World Report*, July 9, 1974, 34–36, quoted in Gutiérrez, *Fertile Matters*, 78.

14. Calavita, "Employer Sanctions Legislation," 77.

15. For more on the politics of immigrant and Mexican American reproduction in the 1970s and 1980s, see chapter 5 in this text; also Chavez, *The Latino Threat*, and Gutiérrez, *Fertile Matters*.

16. Kovach, "Eased Immigration Laws," 1.

17. Gutiérrez, *Fertile Matters*, 25.

18. Ibid.

19. Ibid., 78.

20. Johnson, "The New Nativism," 172.

21. Ibid.

22. On grassroots mobilization, see Payne, *I've Got the Light of Freedom*; John Dittmer, *Local People*; Countryman, *Up South*. For legal activism see Klarman, *From Jim Crow to Civil Rights*.

23. For more on this transition see chapter 3 of this work as well as Gutiérrez, *Walls and Mirrors*. For more on earlier positions, see Vargas, *Labor Rights Are Civil Rights*.

24. Minian, *Undocumented Lives*, 159–160. As Minian notes, other organizations that fought at a grassroots level for undocumented workers with mixed success were the Texas Farm Workers and Centro de Acción Social Autónomo (CASA).

25. As noted earlier, I use the term Latino to reflect current terms of identity within scholarship, while Hispanic is used in this work as seen here, only when the original sources such as the census or polling data would have used that terminology in assigning identification. http://www.census.gov/population/www/documentation/twps0056/tab58.pdf

26. University of Texas at Austin. Bureau of Business Research, "Texas Fact Book 1980" (Austin, TX: Bureau of Business Research), 13.

27. US Supreme Court, "*Plyler v. Doe* Oral Arguments" (1981).

28. Attorney General Opinion H-586 (1975). This was not the first time the issue of unauthorized tuition policies had arisen in Texas, as two previous Attorneys General Opinions in the early twentieth century held that unauthorized children had the same right to attend public schools for free as do the children of citizens. These were Attorney General Opinion No. 2318, Book 55 at 338 (1921) and Attorney General Opinion O-2318 (1914). *In Re Alien Children Ed. Litig.,* 501 F. Supp. 544, 554 (S.D. Tex. 1980).

29. *In Re Alien Children Ed. Litig.,* 501 F. Supp. 544, 554 (S.D. Tex. 1980).

30. Belejack, "A Lesson in Equal Protection." Larry Daves Case file for *Plyler v. Doe,* Miscellaneous Manuscript No. 212, Benson Latin American Collection, General Libraries, the University of Texas at Austin.

31. Larry Daves Case file for *Plyler v. Doe,* Miscellaneous Manuscript No. 212, Benson Latin American Collection, General Libraries, the University of Texas at Austin.

32. Larry Daves Interview, Texas After Violence Project Collection of Oral History Interviews, Human Rights Documentation Initiative, University of Texas Libraries, the University of Texas at Austin, [http://av.lib.utexas.edu/index.php?title=TAVP:Larry_Daves_3].

33. Winter, "A Supreme Court Case 35 Years Ago."

34. The Robles family would later submit their 1040 forms dating back to 1969 to the court as supporting evidence of their claims. Robles 1040 forms in Daves Case file for *Plyler v. Doe,* Miscellaneous Manuscript No. 212, Benson Latin American Collection, General Libraries, the University of Texas at Austin.

35. Winter, "A Supreme Court Case 35 Years Ago."

36. Larry Daves Case file for *Plyler v. Doe,* Miscellaneous Manuscript No. 212, Benson Latin American Collection, General Libraries, the University of Texas at Austin.

37. Davis, *Brutal Need,* 11.

38. Houseman and Perle, "Securing Equal Justice."

39. Kelly, "Legal Aid Still Open."

40. Cochran, "'Outsider' Lawyers," 2.

41. Reaves, "Legal Aid Fights Its Bitter Success."

42. For more on these cases, see Richards, *Once Upon a Time in Texas,* 160–169.

43. East Texas Legal Services would eventually establish an office in Nacogdoches in 1977.

44. Larry Daves Interview, Texas After Violence Project Collection of Oral History Interviews, Human Rights Documentation Initiative, University of Texas Libraries, the University of Texas at Austin, [http://av.lib.utexas.edu/index.php?title=TAVP:Larry_Daves_1]

45. Richards, *Once Upon a Time in Texas,* 165.

46. Kemerer, *William Wayne Justice,* 4–71.

47. Ibid., 76.

48. Alice Murphy, "Pete Tijerina Firing Requested by Ford"; Karen O'Connor and Lee Epstein, "A Legal Voice for the Chicano Community."

49. Gonzales, *Hispanic American Voluntary Organizations,* 129–130.

50. For more detail on this transition, see chapter 3 of this work and Gutiérrez, *Walls and Mirrors.*

51. Daves Oral History and Peter Roos Deposition, Record Group 5, Box 1170, Folder 3, Mexican American Legal Defense and Educational Fund (MALDEF) Records, M673, Special

Collections and University Archives, Stanford University Libraries. See also Guadalupe San Miguel, *Chicana/o Struggles for*, 62.

52. Peter Roos Deposition, Record Group 5, Box 1170, Folder 3, MALDEF Records.

53. Kemerer, *William Wayne Justice*, 238.

54. Michael Wise Interview, December 12, 2014.

55. Roos to Castillo Letter, Record Group 5, Box 115, Folder 5, MALDEF Records.

56. Carlton Stowers, "Alien Issue Triggers Uneasiness in Tyler," *Dallas Morning News*, September 14, 1977, 2A.

57. Dan Watson, "Aliens Get No Protection from Court in School Suit," *Dallas Morning News*, September 16, 1977, 8.

58. Roos to Castillo Letter, Record Group 5, Box 115, Folder 5, MALDEF Records.

59. Baller to Resnick Letter, Record Group 5, Box 1162, Folder 4, MALDEF Records.

60. Baller to Serrano Letter, Record Group 5, Box 1162, Folder 4, MALDEF Records.

61. Roos to Garcia Letter and Garcia to MALDEF Letters, Record Group 5, Box 115, Folder 4, MALDEF Records.

62. Riles Memo, Record Group 5, Box 203, Folder 9, MALDEF Records.

63. Woliver Memo dated 9/28/78, Record Group 5, Box 203, Folder 9, MALDEF Records.

64. *Doe v. Plyler*, 458 F. Supp. 569, 585 (E.D. Tex. 1978) aff'd, 628 F.2d 448 (5th Cir. 1980) aff'd, 457 U.S. 202, 102 S. Ct. 2382, 72 L. Ed. 2d 786 (1982).

65. School funding was already a contested issue in many of these school districts following the Supreme Court's 1972 ruling in *San Antonio Independent School District v. Rodríguez* which held that the San Antonio Independent School District's financing system, based on local property taxes, was not an unconstitutional violation of the Fourteenth Amendment's Equal Protection Clause even if it caused inter-district expenditure disparities.

66. The Litigator, Winter 1981 #1, Mountain States Legal Foundation Box 1, Hoover Institution Archives, Stanford, CA.

67. For more on the conservative public interest legal movement, see Decker, *The Other Rights Revolution*; Teles, *The Rise of the Conservative Legal Movement*; Southworth, *Lawyers of the Right*.

68. Zumbrun, "Life, Liberty and Property Rights," 45.

69. Mountain States Legal Foundation Annual Report 1977–1978, Mountain States Legal Foundation Box 1, Hoover Institution Archives.

70. Mountain States Legal Foundation: Summary of Legal Activity 1977–1980, Mountain States Legal Foundation Box 1, Hoover Institution Archives.

71. Ibid.

72. The Litigator, Winter 1981 #1, Mountain States Legal Foundation Box 1, Hoover Institution Archives.

73. Ibid.

74. Ibid.

75. Roos to Torres Letter dated May 1979, Record Group 5, Box 61, Folder 10, MALDEF Records.

76. Solis Memo, Record Group 5, Carton 1479, Folder "Brownsville Correspondence," MALDEF Records.

77. Those filing in support of the students before the Fifth Circuit included Mexican American Bar Association of Houston, League of United Latin American Citizens, American Friends Service Committee, American Immigration Lawyers Association, United Church of Christ Board of Homeland Ministries, The General Board of Church and Society of the United Methodist Church, American Jewish Committee, the Bishop of the Episcopal Diocese of Dallas, Texas, Legal Aid Society of San Francisco, Washington Lawyers' Committee for Civil Rights Under Law, the National Education Association.

78. Roos to Feinberg Letter, Record Group 5, Box 61, Folder 8, MALDEF Records.

79. Roos to Days Letter dated March 28, 1979, Record Group 5, Box 61, Folder 8, MALDEF Records.

Chapter 2: "A Subclass of Illiterates"

1. Bell with Ostrow, *Taking Care of the Law*, 24.

2. For greater detail see ibid., 24–36.

3. For more on these developments, see chapter 3.

4. Stein, *Pivotal Decade*, 151.

5. Kalman, *Right Star Rising*, 178. Zelizer, *Jimmy Carter*, 49.

6. HEW Staff Memorandum undated, DPS White, Box 5, Files "Doe v. Plyler" (3) Jimmy Carter Library.

7. When constitutional questions of equal protection are implicated, legislation and executive action are subject to different levels of judicial review by the federal courts. From most rigorous to least rigorous, these include strict scrutiny, intermediate scrutiny, and rational basis review. The applicable standard depends on the nature of the policy at issue. The more rigorous levels of scrutiny are used for laws or policies that allegedly infringe on a fundamental constitutional right or discriminate based on a suspect or quasi-suspect classification. Fundamental rights typically have included those included in the Bill of Rights or the Fourteenth Amendment's Due Process Clause. Suspect and quasi-suspect classifications have come to include race, national origin, religion, sex, "legitimate" parentage, and gender. To satisfy the most rigorous level of review, strict scrutiny, a law or policy must be justified by a "compelling governmental interest," and be narrowly tailored to achieve that interest. To satisfy intermediate scrutiny, the law or policy must further an "important government interest" and be closely or substantially related to that interest. Where the law or policy affects no fundamental right and no suspect or quasi-suspect classification, courts apply rational basis review. In this default level of review, the challenged law or policy must merely be rationally related to a legitimate government interest. It does not matter whether that interest is real and supported by evidence or is merely hypothetical.

8. HEW Staff Memorandum undated, DPS White, Box 5, Files "Doe v. Plyler" (3) Jimmy Carter Library.

9. Lake noted the Universal Declaration was not a treaty and thus not a legal obligation, and the United States was not a party to the International Covenant as it had not been ratified by the Senate. As Lake wrote, "However, while education, in our judgment, is a fundamental right in U.S. law." Lake to Days Letter, Folder SG/ *Doe v. Plyler*, Box 100, Subject Files of the Attorney General Griffin B. Bell 1977–1979.

10. Zelizer, *Jimmy Carter*, 57. Griffin Bell's appointment as Attorney General had concerned civil rights activists. Bell had previously been a law partner of Carter confidant Charles Kirbo, and his appointment was interpreted as a form of patronage for a campaign veteran. As even Carter noted, Bell was a "southern gentleman," who as a federal judge did not push for the integration of public schools. He also belonged to several exclusionary White clubs. Bell's appointment was applauded by conservatives including Senator Strom Thurmond, and African American leaders were concerned that as the head of the Justice Department he would not push civil rights litigation. See also Kalman, *Right Star Rising*, 181, 94.

11. Landsberg, *Enforcing Civil Rights*, 157.

12. Days Memo, Folder 880 Civil Rights Division Illegal Aliens *Doe v. Plyler*, Box 202, Subject Files of the Assistant Attorney General William Bradford Reynolds, 1981–1988, Office of the Assistant Attorney General, Civil Rights Division, General Records of the Department of Justice, Record Group 60.

13. Ibid. The Helsinki Accords signed in 1975 included several provisions relating to protecting human rights. For more on *Chy Lung v. Freeman* 92 U.S. 275 (1875), see chapter 5 and Gulasekaram and Ramakrishnan, *The New Immigration Federalism*, 19–24.

14. Days Memo, Folder 880 Civil Rights Division Illegal Aliens *Doe v. Plyler*, Box 202, Subject Files of the Assistant Attorney General William Bradford Reynolds.

15. Ibid.

16. Claiborne to SG memo dated June 25, 1979, Folder 880 Civil Rights Division Illegal Aliens *Doe v. Plyler*, Box 202, Subject Files of the Assistant Attorney General William Bradford Reynolds.

17. The decisions in *Mathews v. Diaz* 426 U.S. 67 (1976) and *De Canas v. Bica* 424 U.S. 351 (1976) bothered Claiborne for several reasons. The *Mathews* decision troubled Claiborne because, although it expressly distinguished state from federal action, in his own mind, "If the federal government can withhold its 'bounty' simply because the alien is not yet sufficiently committed to the country, why cannot the State do likewise?" Claiborne was "less than comfortable with [the] explanation" of the Court that the "strength of the tie between the claimant and the State was irrelevant as the State could not equally exclude those from other states." Nevertheless, Claiborne supposed that "The Court's distinction will survive and puts out of danger our own discriminatory programs." Turning to *De Canas v. Bica*, Claiborne felt that the difference between education and employment was enough to distinguish the cases, as "in the employment context, lawfully admitted aliens and 'illegals' are significantly different, and hiring the latter prejudices the former, both directly and indirectly. Nothing comparable can be said in defense of a law excluding illegal alien children from free schooling." Nevertheless, Claiborne felt "it does not tell us whether the Court would uphold the Texas law on the ground that admitting the 'illegals' to the schools would 'depress' educational values."

18. He felt proving the "hostile intent" or "invidious nature" of the state statute would not be easy. He was also concerned about several recent Supreme Court decisions, including one that had allowed for the regulation of employment for immigrants. Claiborne to SG memo dated June 25, 1979, Folder 880 Civil Rights Division Illegal Aliens *Doe v. Plyler*, Box 202, Subject Files of the Assistant Attorney General William Bradford Reynolds.

19. Beale Memo, Folder 880 Civil Rights Division Illegal Aliens *Doe v. Plyler*, Box 202, Subject Files of the Assistant Attorney General William Bradford Reynolds.

20. Ibid.

21. Ibid.

22. For more detail on this policy, see chapter 5.

23. Claiborne directed Brian Landsberg, head of the Appellate Section of the Civil Rights Division, to research and write on the topic for him. Landsberg argued that supporting the students in the case would have no impact on the federal government's ability to regulate and restrict welfare benefits to those without citizenship status. Landsberg felt the restriction on unauthorized immigrants' access to federal welfare programs could be defended because there was a difference between the "invidious" nature of the Texas statute which was aimed at a child as opposed to the federal programs which "do not work directly against the children, but against the family; they are directed at the parent who has violated federal law." Landsberg argued that welfare, and not education, was an important factor in the flow of immigration and since there was legitimate federal supremacy over immigration, "the federal programs have a substantial basis for support which would not be affected by our attack on Texas' action." Landsberg to Claiborne Memo, Folder 881 Civil Rights Division, Illegal Aliens *Doe v. Plyler*, Box 202, Subject Files of the Assistant Attorney General William Bradford Reynolds.

24. Dong believed that supporting the students would be embraced by the Mexican government, the State Department, and the Latino community, but he echoed concerns expressed by Claiborne and others that if the department were to support the students, "almost certainly we would have to make some inconsistent arguments" as well as be viewed with "hostility by the communities where the strain of illegal immigrants on public services is beginning to reach critical proportions." Dong to Bell Memo, Folder SG/ *Doe v. Plyler*, Box 100, Subject Files of the Attorney General Griffin B. Bell.

25. Following a clash between the president's legal and political advisors over the content of the amicus brief in the *Bakke* case concerning the constitutionality of affirmative action, the Attorney General had requested an opinion from the Office of Legal Counsel that outlined the relationship between the Attorney General and the Solicitor General in formulating the government's position before the Supreme Court. While reserving "rare instances" where the Attorney General should decide the government's position, the memo asserted the Solicitor General's relative independence from the Attorney General and general political interference. Bell's reluctance to express his "personal" view of the case to his Solicitor General likely reflects the residual effects of the *Bakke* skirmish. For more on the memo, see Caplan, *The Tenth Justice*, 48–50.

26. Given the tension over the politicization of the department, Bell's staff worked to make sure that McCree "understood this was not an order but merely [Bell's] opinion on the matter as it stood." Dong to Bell Note dated July 10, 1979, Folder SG/ *Doe v. Plyler*, Box 100, Subject Files of the Attorney General Griffin B. Bell.

27. Ibid.

28. HEW Staff Memorandum Undated, DPS White, Box 5, Folder "Doe v. Plyler" (3), Jimmy Carter Library.

29. Christopher to McCree Letter, Folder SG/ *Doe v. Plyler*, Box 100, Subject Files of the Attorney General Griffin B. Bell.

30. Dong to Bell Note dated July 10, 1979, Folder SG/ *Doe v. Plyler*, Box 100, Subject Files of the Attorney General Griffin B. Bell.

31. Jordan to White Memo, Folder SG/ *Doe v. Plyler*, Box 100, Subject Files of the Attorney General Griffin B. Bell.

32. Jordan to White Note dated July 17, 1979, DPS White, Box 5, Files "Doe v. Plyler" (3) Jimmy Carter Library.

33. At his confirmation hearings, Civiletti was opposed by Latino leaders who charged that he had not aggressively pursued cases of police brutality and other civil rights violations against Latinos, including the Lozano case. Crewdson, "Hispanics Angered," A12.

34. White to Eizenstat Memo Dated 7/25/79, DPS Eizenstat, Box 299, File Undocument[ed] Aliens, Jimmy Carter Library.

35. Ibid.

36. Ibid.

37. Eizenstat to White note dated 8/03/79, DPS Eizenstat, Box 299, File Undocument[ed] Aliens, Jimmy Carter Library.

38. "Justice Reportedly to Back Illegal Alien's Free Education," *Houston Post*, October 12, 1979, in Governor William P. Clements Jr. Records, Mexico and Latin American Relations [MALAR] Records, Box 19, Folder 3, Cushing Library, Texas A&M University.

39. MALDEF press release dated November 5, 1979, Record Group 4, Box 127, Folder 8, MALDEF Records.

40. Roos memo to MALDEF Executive Committee dated October 11, 1979, Record Group 5, Box 62, Folder 1, MALDEF Records.

41. Days to Attorney General letter, Folder SG/ *Doe v. Plyler*, Box 100, Subject Files of the Attorney General Griffin B. Bell 1977–1979, Civil Rights Division, Office of the Assistant Attorney General, General Records of the Department of Justice, Record Group 60, National Archives at College Park, MD.

42. "U.S. Asks to Join in Court Challenge of Texas Tuition Law for Illegal Aliens," *Washington Post*, January 17, 1980, A6.

43. Stevens, "Education of Aliens at Issue in Texas."

44. *In re Alien Children Ed. Litig.*, 501 F. Supp. 544, 564 (S.D. Tex. 1980).

45. Price, "Texas to Appeal Aliens Decision," in Box 13, Folder 7 of Judge Woodrow B. Seals Papers, Houston Metropolitan Research Center, Houston Public Library.

46. Garcia to Clements Memo dated July 23, 1980, Governor William P. Clements Jr. Records, Mexico and Latin American Relations [MALAR] Records, Box 19, Folder 1, Cushing Library, Texas A&M University.

47. The Litigator, Spring, 1981 #2, page 2, Mountain States Legal Foundation Box 1, Hoover Institution Archives, Stanford, CA.

48. Justice to Seals Letter dated July 25, 1980, Box 13, Folder 3, Judge Woodrow B. Seals Papers, Houston Metropolitan Research Center, Houston Public Library.

49. Yarborough to Seals letter dated July 24, 1980, Box 14, Folder 11, Judge Woodrow B. Seals Papers, Houston Metropolitan Research Center, Houston Public Library.

50. While these events were occurring, the Catholic Church in Houston and other dioceses established temporary schools to educate students who were excluded from the public schools during the litigation.

51. Hyatt to Eizenstat Memo dated August 7, 1980, DPS Hyatt, Box 21, Folder undocumented aliens/refugees [1], Jimmy Carter Library.

52. Smith, "Texas Looming as a Close Battle between President and Reagan," A1.

53. William K. Stevens, "Reagan Forces Have Eye on Texas," *New York Times*, September 22, 1980 B4.

54. Ibid.; Smith, "Texas Looming as a Close Battle between President and Reagan."

55. LaFranchi, "Courting the Hispanic Vote."

56. Background and Talking Points for POTUS Corpus Christi trip, DPS Hyatt, Box 21, Folder undocumented aliens/refugees [1], Jimmy Carter Library.

57. Dyke Briefing Memo, DPS Hyatt, Box 21, undocumented aliens/refugees [2], Jimmy Carter Library.

58. Transcript, https://www.reaganlibrary.archives.gov/archives/speeches/1980/04231980 .html.

59. https://www.wpafilmlibrary.com/videos/121506.

60. Dan Balz, "Texas Asks Who's to Pay for Education of Aliens," *Washington Post*, July 19, 1982, p. A1.

61. Dyke Briefing Memo, DPS Hyatt, Box 21, undocumented aliens/refugees [2], Jimmy Carter Library.

62. "Questions That May Ensue From Our . . ." Memo, DPS Hyatt, Box 21, undocumented aliens/refugees [2], Jimmy Carter Library.

63. Draft Q and A, DPS Hyatt, Box 21, undocumented aliens/refugees [2], Jimmy Carter Library.

64. Ibid.

65. Hyatt to Eizenstat and Carp Memo dated Oct 9, 1980, DPS Hyatt, Box 21, undocumented aliens/refugees [2], Jimmy Carter Library. The Department of Education was taken out of the Department of Health, Education and Welfare in 1979 and began operating as its own department in 1980.

66. Hyatt found that many DOE leaders "believe that accepting Federal responsibility for education of unauthorized alien children could be taken as approval of their parents' presence in the U.S." Department of Education staff also worried that since Texas was the only state currently not enrolling unauthorized children, crafting a program that would fund for the education of these students would essentially reward Texas for its "neglect of these children." DOE staff questioned whether the federal government should let "Texas off the hook at the very time that courts are forcing the state to accept responsibility." Hyatt found that DOE also worried that a program funding the education of unauthorized children "might be a two-edged sword politically, even within the Hispanic community in Texas," as she noted that some middle-class Mexican Americans resented the presence of unauthorized immigrants. For more on the shifting views of Mexican American organizations on unauthorized immigration during this period, see chapter 3. Hyatt to Eizenstat and Carp Memo Attachment B, DPS Hyatt, Box 21, undocumented aliens/refugees [2], Jimmy Carter Library.

67. Ibid.

68. Ibid.

69. It was technically difficult in Fisher's mind due to the inability to accurately predict program impact or cost. Fisher also feared that federal aid would be portrayed as sanctioning the presence of those not legally admitted to the country. Furthermore, he believed that the deeper involvement of the federal government would be opposed by those in Texas who viewed

the growth of the Mexican American population as a threat, including Mexican Americans who viewed the "influx of Mexican migrants as a threat to their own well-being." Fisher Memo to Carp, DPS Hyatt, Box 21, Folder undocumented aliens/refugees [1], Jimmy Carter Library.

70. Ibid.

71. Hyatt to Eizenstat and Carp Undated Memo, DPS Hyatt, Box 21, Folder undocumented aliens/refugees [2], Jimmy Carter Library.

72. Mondale Laredo prepared remarks, DPS Hyatt, Box 21, Folder undocumented aliens/refugees [2], Jimmy Carter Library.

73. *Doe v. Plyler*, 628 F.2d 448 (5th Cir. 1980) *aff'd*, 457 U.S. 202, 102 S. Ct. 2382, 72 L. Ed. 2d 786 (1982).

74. Letter to Mark Rosenbaum, Record Group 5, Box 63, Folder 6, MALDEF Records. Letter to Nathan Dershowitz of the American Jewish Congress, Record Group 5, Box 63, Folder 7, MALDEF Records.

75. Solis to Vasquez Letter, Record Group 5, Carton 1497, Folder "*Doe v. Plyler* Correspondence," MALDEF Records. Roos to Solis Letter 9/10/81, Record Group 5, Box 11, Folder "*Doe v. Plyler* Miscellaneous 2," MALDEF Records.

76. Letter to Ms. Beni Hall, Record Group 5, Box 63, Folder 6, MALDEF Records.

77. Roos to Martinez Memo, Record Group 5, Box 63, Folder 6, MALDEF Records.

78. Roos Letter to Undersecretary Clohan dated May 20, 1981, Record Group 5, Box 63, Folder 6, MALDEF Records.

79. Remarks of the Attorney General Before the Federal Legal Council, Reston, Virginia, October 29, 1981, http://www.justice.gov/ag/aghistory/smith/1981/10-29-1981.pdf. Accessed January 17, 2014.

80. Caplan, *The Tenth Justice*, 81.

81. Babcock, "Justice Officials Move to Control Sensitive Civil Rights Division," A2.

82. Barnett to Reynolds Memo, Folder 881 Civil Rights Division Illegal Aliens *Doe v. Plyler*, Box 202, Subject Files of the Assistant Attorney General William Bradford Reynolds.

83. Caplan, *The Tenth Justice*, 43.

84. For more detail on scrutiny, see chapter 2, note 7.

85. Wallace to Solicitor General memo, Folder 883 Civil Rights Division *Doe v. Plyler*—Corres. Box 202, Subject Files of the Assistant Attorney General William Bradford Reynolds.

86. Brief for the United States as Amicus Curiae in No. 80–1538 and Brief for the United States in No. 80–1934, James PLYLER, et al., Appellants, v. J. and R. DOE, as Guardians Ad Litem for I. Doe, et al. In re: Alien Children Education Litigation State of Texas and Texas Education Agency, Appellants, v. Certain Named and Unnamed Undocumented Alien Children., 1981 WL 390001 (U.S.); and McDaniel, "Justice Dept. Pulling Out of Alien Case," 1, 22.

87. Taylor Jr., "Conflict over Rights of Aliens," A1; McDaniel, "Justice Dept. Pulling Out of Alien Case," 1, 22; Hines, "Issue of Illegals' Schooling."

88. McDaniel, "Justice Dept. Pulling out of Alien Case," 1, 22.

89. Craig, "Lulac Head Thinks Officials Made Deal," in Governor William P. Clements Jr. Records, Mexico and Latin American Relations [MALAR] Records, Box 19, Folder 4, Cushing Library, Texas A&M University.

90. Ibid.

91. Verboon, "U.S. Will Leave Alien Tuition to Court," in MALAR Records, Box 19, Folder 4, Clements Papers.

92. Balz and Thornton, "U.S. Won't Intervene in Alien School Case," in MALAR Records, Box 19, Folder 4, Clements Papers.

93. "US, in Shift, Says Alien Case a Texas Issue," 30.

94. "Ideas & Trends: Government Pulls Back on Two School Cases," E22.

95. Babcock, "Shifts in Rights Policy and Turmoil at Justice," 3.

96. Groups filing in support of the students included the Mexican Bar Association of Houston, American Friends Service Committee, United Church of Christ Board of Homeland Ministries, General Board of Church and Society of the United Methodist Church, National Board of Jesuit Social Ministries, the Lutheran Council in the USA, American Immigration Lawyers Association, American Jewish Committee, Legal Aid Society of San Francisco, Edgewood Independent School District, Washington Lawyers Committee for Civil Rights Under Law, the Bishop of the Episcopal Diocese of Dallas, Texas Impact, the California State Board of Education, the NEA, LULAC. Those filing in support of the state included the Federation for American Immigration Reform, the Texas Association of School Boards, the Legal Foundation of America, Harlingen Consolidated Independent School District, Mission Independent School District, Brownsville Independent School District, National School Boards Association, Pacific Legal Foundation, and the Mountain States Legal Foundation.

97. To hear oral arguments and view transcript, visit http://www.oyez.org/cases/1980-1989 /1981/1981_80_1538.

98. *Gideon v. Wainwright* (1963), *Shapiro v. Thompson* (1969), *Baker v. Carr* (1962).

99. Paul Sracic, *San Antonio v. Rodriguez and the Pursuit of Equal Education*, 34. In *Harper*, Virginia residents challenged a $1.50 poll tax on Virginia residents, which was a precondition to voting in state elections.

100. "High Court Hears Views on Free Schooling," A28.

101. Babcock, "Treatment of Alien Children in Texas," A11.

102. Newton, "The Brennan Memos."

103. *Plyler v. Doe*, 457 U.S. 202, 210, 102 S. Ct. 2382, 2391, 72 L. Ed. 2d 786 (1982).

104. Ibid.

105. *San Antonio Independent School District, et al. v. Demetrio P. Rodriguez*, et al. 411 U.S. 1, 93 S. Ct. 1278; 36 L. Ed 2d 16; (1973).

106. *Plyler*, 457 U.S. at 238–39.

107. *Plyler*, 457 U.S. at 244.

108. Kuhl and Roberts *Plyler v. Doe* Memo to Attorney General, Folder 13, Box 8, Correspondence Files of Carolyn B. Kuhl 1981–1982, Department of Justice, Record Group 60.

109. WHORM Subject File JL004–092338PD, Ronald Reagan Library.

110. "Bell Questions Court Decision," 32.

111. Ibid.

112. "Texas Isn't Shocked by Schooling Order for Alien's Children: But . . .", *Wall Street Journal*, June 16, 1982, 24.

113. FAIR Immigration Report July 1982, Folder 5, Box 2, Federation for American Immigration Reform (FAIR) records, Special Collections Research Center, George Washington University.

114. "The Rights of Illegal Aliens," A30.

115. Babcock, "Aid for Illegal Aliens' Children," A25.

116. Solis to Garza Memorandum, Record Group 5, Carton 1497, Folder "*Doe v. Plyler* Correspondence," MALDEF Records, M673, Special Collections and University Archives, Stanford University Libraries.

117. Michel Olivas's work focuses on the legal regime *Plyler* established and its implementation, and traces *Plyler's* legacy to the DREAM act. Others have focused on *Plyler's* impact on Equal Protection. See for example Olivas, *No Undocumented Child Left Behind* and Hutchinson, 167–194.

118. Tichenor, *Dividing Lines*, 241.

Chapter 3: "Heading into Uncharted Waters"

1. Calavita, *California's "Employer Sanctions,"* 26.

2. For more on the role these groups played in the passage of the Hart-Celler Act, see Tichenor, *Dividing Lines*, 201–205.

3. Tichenor, "Strange Bedfellows."

4. BLS Unemployment Rate Data.

5. Cowie, *Stayin' Alive*, 12.

6. Ibid., 222.

7. Katz, *In the Shadow of the Poorhouse*, 285.

8. Minian, *Undocumented Lives*, 60. See also Pitti, *The Devil in Silicon Valley*.

9. Tilly, "Short Hours, Short Shrift."

10. Massey, *Beyond Smoke and Mirrors*, 61.

11. Minian, *Undocumented Lives*, 61.

12. Reimers, *Still the Golden Door*, 208.

13. Minian, *Undocumented Lives*, 56.

14. Gallup poll cited in Minian, *Undocumented Lives*, 58.

15. "Curbing Illegal Immigration," A4.

16. Minian, *Undocumented Lives*, 69.

17. Reimers, *Still the Golden Door*, 209.

18. Tichenor, *Dividing Lines*, 226–227.

19. Ibid., 225.

20. Fine and Tichenor, "A Movement Wrestling."

21. Ibid., 104.

22. Calavita, *California's "Employer Sanctions."*

23. Sutton, "Illegal Immigrants Swamp State," 15.

24. Ibid. Also see "Illegal Aliens: Bill to Bar Them Is Under Pressure," 16.

25. West, "State Measure to Ban Hiring of Illegal Aliens."

26. [KTLA news (Los Angeles, Calif.). 1971-11-24—excerpt and/or outtakes. Demonstration protesting Dixon-Arnett Law and its impact on undocumented workers. MM4540], ULCA Television and Film Archive.

27. *Dolores Canning Co. v. Howard*, 115 Cal. Rptr. 435, 442 (Ct. App. 1974).

28. *De Canas v. Bica*, 424 U.S. 351 (1976).

29. Calavita, "Employer Sanctions Legislation in the United States," 77.

30. Calavita, *California's "Employer Sanctions": The Case of the Disappearing Law*. This shift is explored in greater depth later in the chapter.

31. Legislators in Texas again introduced employer sanctions legislation, but it fell to heavy opposition from agricultural interests and the Latino community. In addition, bills were introduced in Delaware, Florida, Illinois, Indiana, Kansas, Maine, Massachusetts, Montana, Nebraska, New Hampshire, New Jersey, Nevada, Ohio, Oregon, Rhode Island, Vermont, and Virginia. Florida: State Bill 68 (1977) Indiana: House Bill 1306, Nebraska: Labor Bill 507, Illinois: 1977; For more, see Record Group 4, Box 91, Folder 8, MALDEF Records.

32. Schwarz, "Employer Sanctions Law," 98–99.

33. Kansas convicted one employer, Montana won two default judgments, and Virginia had two convictions. See ibid., 84.

34. Kaufman, "Former Rep. Peter W. Rodino Jr, Is Dead at 95."

35. Perrotti, "Resolving Policy Conflict," 89.

36. *Espinoza v. Farah Mfg. Co.*, 414 U.S. 86 (1973).

37. Tichenor, *Dividing Lines*, 227.

38. Roybal was born in New Mexico and had grown up on the east side of Los Angeles in the barrios near Boyle Heights. After serving in the army and as a public health worker, Roybal co-founded the Community Service Organization (CSO), which sought to develop a grassroots movement against discrimination in housing, employment, and education as well as improve voter registration within the Mexican American community in Los Angeles. The group would become well known for their role fostering Cesar Chavez and Dolores Huerta. Roybal served as the group's first president and its primary spokesperson and used his work with the group to make a successful run for city council, where he served for thirteen years.

39. Tendayi Kumbala, "Bill on Illegal Aliens Called 'Discriminatory,'" 16.

40. Perrotti, "Resolving Policy Conflict," 86.

41. Gottron, "Illegal Alien Curbs," 637–641.

42. US Department of Justice, "A Program for the Effective and Humane Action on Illegal Mexican Immigrants: Final Report of the Special Study Group on Illegal Immigrants from Mexico," cited in Cárdenas, "United States Immigration Policy toward Mexico," 66–91.

43. Le May, *Anatomy of a Public Policy*, 31. Chiswick Testimony June 1985 Before Senate Sub-Committee on Immigration in Immigration Reform Legislation; 1982–1983; American Civil Liberties Union Records: Subgroup 3, Regional Offices Files Series, Box 4268; Public Policy Papers, Department of Rare Books and Special Collections, Princeton University Library.

44. Katz, *In the Shadow of the Poorhouse*, 285.

45. George Gallup, "Illegal Aliens' Job Prohibition Favored 6 to 1."

46. Westoff, "The Commission on Population Growth."

47. Rockefeller had founded the Population Council in 1952 which focused on population growth in developing nations, and he was a co-chair with Wilbur Cohen of President Johnson's Committee on Population and Family Planning. The President's Committee had made several recommendations, including the creation of a Commission to assess the consequences of population trends in the United States.

48. "One Billion Americans?" E10. Commission on Population Growth and the American Future, 8–9.

49. Keely, "Immigration Recommendations."

50. Reimers, *Unwelcome Strangers*, 48.

51. Zolberg, *Nation by Design*, 360, and Kulish and McIntire, "Why an Heiress Spent Her Fortune Trying to Keep Immigrants Out."

52. Even after her death, May would continue to provide vital support for the anti-immigrant movement. May's Colcom foundation would provide $179.9 million between 2005 and 2017 to conservative immigration and population control groups. For more, see Kulish and McIntire, "Why an Heiress Spent Her Fortune Trying to Keep Immigrants Out."

53. Gutiérrez, *Walls and Mirrors*.

54. Del Olmo, "Chavez Union Does a Turnabout," 3. For more detail on the history of UFW and the shift, see Gutiérrez, *Walls and Mirrors*, 198–199.

55. Del Omo, "Illegal Alien Union Targets," 8A.

56. For more on this crumbling, see chapter 5.

57. For more detail on this shift, see Gutiérrez, *Walls and Mirrors*, 193–194.

58. Wong, *Lobbying for Inclusion*, 7.

59. Sierra, "The Political Transformation of a Minority Group," 211–212.

60. La Raza Organizational History, http://www.nclr.org/index.php/about_us/history/initiation_of_research_policy_efforts/#sthash.YOAhBFiU.dpuf. Accessed March 1, 2014.

61. Cortés, "Policy Analysts and Interest Groups," 357.

62. Baller to Exec Cmte Memo 8/7/1977, Record Group 4, Box 89, Folder 6, MALDEF Records.

63. Sutton, "Illegal Immigrants Swamp State."

64. Previous USCC Position Document in Unlabeled folder; 1982–1984; American Civil Liberties Union Records: Subgroup 3, Regional Offices Files Series, Box 4475; Public Policy Papers, Department of Rare Books and Special Collections, Princeton University Library.

65. Del Olmo, "Dole Hits Plan to Penalize Employers of Illegal Aliens."

66. Marro, "Carter Aides to Map New Policy on Aliens," 1.

67. Hower and McCartin, "Marshall's Principle."

68. Leroy Aarons, "Secretary of Labor Ray Marshall Was the Cabinet's Invisible Man and Then the Miners Walked Out," *People Magazine* 9, no. 4 (April 10, 1978).

69. Miller Center, "Interview with Ray Marshall," University of Virginia, May 4, 1988. Accessed July 1, 2016, http://millercenter.org/president/carter/oralhistory/ray-marshall.

70. Bernstein, "U.S Maps Action on Aliens," 1.

71. Perrotti, "Resolving Policy Conflict," 94.

72. Knapp to Eizenstat Memo dated 5/10/1977, JDPS Eizenstat, Box 299, Folder Undocumented Aliens (General) [AO6245], Jimmy Carter Library.

73. Gutierrez to Eizenstat dated 3/25/1977, DPS Eizenstat, Box 299, Folder Undocumented Aliens (General) [AO6245] 2), Jimmy Carter Library.

74. Eizenstat to President Memo dated 5/3/1977, DPS Eizenstat, Box 299, Folder Undocumented Aliens (General) [AO6245] 1), Jimmy Carter Library.

75. President to Eizenstat note, 5/4/1977, JC-DPS, Eizenstat, Box 299 Folder Undocumented Aliens (General) [AO6245] 1), Jimmy Carter Library.

76. Eizenstat to President Memo dated 7/13/77, DPS, Eizenstat, Box 299, Folder Undocumented Aliens (General) [AO6245] 4), Jimmy Carter Library.

77. George Mayo to File Memo re June 18 1977 Meeting with House Staff, Record Group 4, Box 89, Folder 1, MALDEF Records.

78. Ibid.

79. "Presidential Statement: Carter Proposes Illegal Aliens Legislation."

80. MALDEF statement on Carter Plan, Record Group 4, Box 85, Folder 3, MALDEF Records. MAPA Resolution, Record Group 4, Box 85, Folder 5, MALDEF Records.

81. US Chamber Testimony, Box 16, Folder 3, Herman Baca Papers, MSS 649. Special Collections & Archives, UC San Diego.

82. "Carter Unveils Illegal-Alien Proposals," 5.

83. "Illegal Aliens."

84. Perrotti, "Resolving Policy Conflict," 95.

85. Schacht Memo dated February 7, 1978, Record Group 4, Box 91, Folder 1, MALDEF Records.

86. Yzaguirre Memo Re; Roybal Meeting, 8/5/77, Record Group 4, Box 85, Folder 3, MALDEF Records.

87. Yzaguirre Memo Re; Roybal Meeting, 8/5/77, Box 85, Folder 3, MALDEF Records.

88. Perez Immigration Strategy Memo 11/25/1977, Box 91, Folder 2, MALDEF Records.

89. Al Perez to V. Martinez Memo, May 2, 1977, Record Group 4, Box 89, Folder 1, MALDEF Records.

90. Perez Immigration Strategy Memo 11/25/1977, M673, Record Group 4, Box 91, Folder 2, MALDEF Records.

91. Sierra, "The Political Transformation of a Minority Group," 246.

92. Gutiérrez, *Walls and Mirrors*, 202.

93. Perrotti, "Resolving Policy Conflict," 96; Tichenor, *Dividing Lines*, 238.

94. The Select Commission was composed of four public members, four cabinet secretaries, and eight members of Congress. The chair was Father Theodore Hesburgh, the president of Notre Dame and former head of the Civil Rights Commission. They held regional hearings and visited immigration- related sites in twelve cities and heard testimony from 698 witnesses. The Commission's final 1981 report was 450 pages (with a supplemental report that totaled 900 pages), identified unauthorized immigration as "the most pressing problem," and ultimately recommended the implementation of employer sanctions with a system of employer identification.

Chapter 4: "A Riverboat Gamble"

1. Zelizer and Jacobs, *Conservatives in Power*, 20.

2. Jones, "Reagan Answer to Mexican 'Illegals.'"

3. Latham, *Ronald Reagan*, 43.

4. Meese and Baker Memo to the President date June 1, 1981, Folder "Immigration and Refugee Matters (2), Box OA6518, Edwin Meese Files, Ronald Reagan Library.

5. The White House also sought to distance the president from the report by having Vice President Bush receive it publicly. Gray and Hodsoll to Meese, Baker and Deaver, Feb 24, 1981, Folder Immigration (1 of 4), Box CFOA 86, Martin Anderson Files, Ronald Reagan Library.

6. Richard Wirthlin to Meese, Baker and Deaver Memo dated 5/28/81, Folder "Immigration and Refugee Matters (1)," Box OA 6518, Edwin Meese Files, Ronald Reagan Library.

7. Hodsoll to Baker Memo dated 4/3/81, Folder "Immigration and Refugee Matters (1)," Box OA 6518, Edwin Meese Files, Ronald Reagan Library.

8. Ibid.

9. WH Staff, Folder "Immigration and Refugee Matters (1)," Box OA 6518, Edwin Meese Files, Ronald Reagan Library.

10. Hodsoll to Baker Memo dated 4/3/81, Folder "Immigration and Refugee Matters (1)," Box OA 6518, Edwin Meese Files, Ronald Reagan Library.

11. Richard Wirthlin to Dick Richards Memo dated 6/18/81, Folder "Immigration and Refugee Matters (1)," Box OA 6518, Edwin Meese Files, Ronald Reagan Library.

12. Ibid.

13. Niskanen to Fuller dated 6/30/81, Folder "Immigration and Refugee Matters (3)," box OA 6518, Edwin Meese Files, Ronald Reagan Library.

14. Nofziger to Reagan Memo July 27, 1981, Folder "Immigration and Refugee Matters (4)," Box OA 6518, Edwin Meese Files, Ronald Reagan Library.

15. Schweiker to Fuller Memo and Bell to Fuller Memo dated 6/30/81, Folder "Immigration and Refugee Matters (3)," Box OA 6518, Edwin Meese Files, Ronald Reagan Library.

16. Anderson, *Revolution*, 316–317; Tim Miller, "Sharp Differences on Immigration Law Changes Could Doom a Bill This Year," *National Journal*, February 20, 1982, 336, in Folder "Immigration-Press Clippings," Box OA9445, Michael Uhlmann Files, Ronald Reagan Library.

17. Latham, *Ronald Reagan*, 107–108.

18. Moore Memo to Anderson, Cavaney, Dole, Gribbin, Hillier, Hodsol, Medas, Nofziger, and Ursomarso Memo dated July 13, 1981, Folder "Immigration- Consultations (1)," Box 3, Kate Moore Files, Ronald Reagan Library.

19. Meeting attendees included the Hispanic Chamber of Commerce, the Cabinet Committee on Hispanics, National Council of La Raza, and the GI Forum.

20. "American Survey: The Ins and Outs of Immigration Policy," *The Economist*, August 8, 1981, 17.

21. US Congress Senate Committee on the Judiciary. Subcommittee on Immigration and Refugee Policy. *Proposed Regulation Changes for Refugee Assistance: Hearing Before the Subcommittee on Immigration and Refugee Policy of the Committee on the Judiciary.*

22. Ibid.

23. Clements's other efforts to court the Latino vote included supporting a Democratic Latino candidate in a state senate race over the GOP candidate, and appointing a Mexican American to a key judicial vacancy. Balz, "As the Hispanic Vote Emerges," A3. Balz, "Texas Governor Breaks Ranks on Reagan Immigration," A14.

24. Balz, "Texas Governor Breaks Ranks on Reagan Immigration," A14.

25. *AFL-CIO Free Trade Union News* 26, no. 10 (October 1981), Folder "Draft NFTC Status Report & Other Publications, 1981," Box 124, National Foreign Trade Council (NFTC) records (Accession 2345), Hagley Museum and Library, Wilmington, DE 19807.

26. United States Congress Senate Committee on the Judiciary. Subcommittee on Immigration and Refugee Policy. *Proposed Regulation Changes for Refugee Assistance: Hearing Before the Subcommittee on Immigration and Refugee Policy of the Committee on the Judiciary.*

27. Polling memo, Folder Polling [1 of 2] Box F007, Elizabeth Dole Files, Ronald Reagan Library.

28. Memo, Folder "Immigration-1982 [3 of 3]," Box F0004, Elizabeth Dole Files, Ronald Reagan Library.

29. The quiet campaign included pushing for the passage of amendments by Senators Tower and Kennedy that aimed at weakening and sunsetting employer sanctions, but those amendments were defeated. See Hiller to AG memo dated August 23, 1982, Folder "Immigration: Senate Passage of 222," Box OA9445, Michael Uhlman Files, Ronald Reagan Library. In the House, the Reagan administration privately engaged House Judiciary Committee members (where the bill would first be examined) seeking to weaken the bill's employer sanctions proposals. Hiller to AG Briefing memo dated 9/12/82, Folder "Immigration: Hiller memo to AG re house markup," Box OA9445, Michel Uhlmann Files, Ronald Reagan Library. Cabinet Council on Legal Policy Memo dated April 16, 1982, Folder "Immigration-1982 [3 of 3]," Box F0004, Elizabeth Dole Files, Ronald Reagan Library.

30. Smith to CCLP Memo Dated 4/20/1983, Folder "Immigration: CCLP Papers on Immigration 4/21/1983," Box OA9445, Michel Uhlmann Files, Ronald Reagan Library.

31. Torres Testimony Before Senate Subcommittee February 25, 1983 in Immigration Reform Legislation; 1982–1983; American Civil Liberties Union Records: Subgroup 3, Regional Offices Files Series, Box 4268; CBC letter to O'Neill, December 2, 1982, in Untitled Folder, 1976–1983; American Civil Liberties Union Records: Subgroup 3, Regional Offices Files Series, Box 4475; Public Policy Papers, Department of Rare Books and Special Collections, Princeton University Library.

32. "A National Identity Card?" *Wall Street Journal*, September 2, 1982,16.

33. Balz, "As the Hispanic Vote Emerges."

34. Dole "Erosion of Hispanic Support" memo to Baker dated April 6, 1982, Folder Hispanics Jan–June 1982 (1 of 5), Box F004, Elizabeth Dole Files, Ronald Reagan Library.

35. Dole to Meese, Baker, and Deaver, "Hispanic Strategy" memo dated 5/7/1982, Folder Hispanics Jan–June 1982 (1 of 5), Box F004, Elizabeth Dole Files, Ronald Reagan Library.

36. Barnes, "GOP Governors Criticize Reagan," A9.

37. Smith to CCLP Memo Dated 4/20/1983, Folder "Immigration: CCLP Papers on Immigration 4/21/1983," Box OA9445, Michael Uhlmann Files, Ronald Reagan Library; Torres LULAC testimony before House Committee on Agriculture, June 15, 1983, Folder 3, Box 397, National Council of La Raza Records, M0744, Dept. of Special Collections, Stanford University Libraries, Stanford, CA.

38. CoC Tysee to Day Letter 3/31/1983, in Unmarked Folder in 1976–1983; American Civil Liberties Union Records: Subgroup 3, Regional Offices Files Series, Box 4475; Public Policy Papers, Department of Rare Books and Special Collections, Princeton University Library. The change in strategy paid off in the House when the Judiciary Committee adopted by 18 to 10 an amendment offered by Ohio Republican Rep. Thomas N. Kindness that targeted and diluted the use of the sanctions. See "O'Neill Blocks Immigration Bill in House.".

39. Draft ABA position paper May 1983, in Immigration Reform Legislation; 1982–1983; American Civil Liberties Union Records: Subgroup 3, Regional Offices Files Series, Box 4268; Public Policy Papers, Department of Rare Books and Special Collections, Princeton University Library.

40. Stockman to Meese Memo dated 4/19/1983, Folder "Immigration: CCLP Papers on Immigration 4/21/1983," Box OA9445, Michael Uhlmann Files, Ronald Reagan Library.

41. Ibid.

42. Ibid.

43. Verstanding to Baker and Deaver Memo dated 9/20/1983, Folder "Immigration + Refugees (1)," Box OA12425, Andrew Card Files, Ronald Reagan Library.

44. AG to Rodino letter dated July 27, 1983, Folder Immigration-AG's letter to Rodino 7/83, Box OA9445, Michael Uhlmann Files, Ronald Reagan Library.

45. Talking Points, Folder "Immigration: Talking Points done with C. Collins 10/1/83," Box OA9445, Michael Uhlmann, Files, Ronald Reagan Library.

46. Reid, "O'Neill Exercised Power, Bars Immigration Bill."

47. Ibid.

48. Tolchin, "O'Neill, in a Reversal, Supports Immigration Bill," A19.

49. Pear, "Bill on Aliens a Divisive Issue for Democrats."

50. "Sending a Message on Immigration," A18.

51. Henderson Memo, "Battle Still Not Over" dated July 9, 1984, M0744, Box 347, Folder 9, La Raza Files.

52. House members repeatedly raised discrimination concerns with the bill, discussing their familial histories of immigration to the United States, and making reference to Jews wearing yellow stars in Germany and Japanese internment camps during World War II. "Bill to Curb Illegal Immigration: House Debate Reflects Diversity of Nation," New York Times, June 17, 1984, A20.

53. Ibid.

54. Jasinowski, "Immigration: Save Reform," and "Assessing the passage of HR 1510," Record Group 2, Carton 70, Folder 32, MALDEF Records, August 1, 1984.

55 Ibid.

56. Ibid.

57. Margaret Shapiro, "Angry Hispanic Activists Declare Immigration Bill a Lost Cause," Washington Post, June 16, 1984, A6.

58. John Dillin, "Democrats in California," 1.

59. Smothers, "Texas Caucuses Spotlight Role of Hispanic Voters."

60. Rangel, "Rise in Status Gives a Hispanic Group Growing Pains," B14.

61. Germani, "Hispanic Demand," 4.

62. Taylor and Coleman, "Minority Blocs Step Up Pressure for Platform Modifications," A9.

63. Frank Del Olmo, "Labor Leaders Seeking to Avert Latino Boycott," 7.

64. Germani, "Hispanic Demand."

65. Gorney, "Hispanic Delegates Split," A10.

66. Pear, "White House Calls House Immigration Measure Unacceptable."

67. Cannon, "Hispanic Voter's Reaction to Signing Aliens Bill," A2.

68. Rollins to VP Memo "Hispanics" dated September 22, 1983, Folder Hispanics (5), Box 3, Mike McManus Files, Ronald Reagan Library; Grier, "US Politicians Court Hispanics," 1.

69. Wiker, "A Success Story," E23.

70. Cannon, "Hispanic Voter's Reaction to Signing Aliens Bill."

71. Wirthlin to Baker, Deaver, Fahrenkopf, Laxalt, Rollins, and Spencer Memo dated July 26, 1984, Folder [Reagan-Bush 1984] attitudes on immigration prepared by Reagan Bush 1984 (1), Box 65, Michael Deaver Series VI, Ronald Reagan Library.

72. Pear, "Reagan Raises New Obstacles to House Bill on Immigration."

73. Ibid.

74. McWilliams, "Hispanics Tell Democrats to Halt Immigration Bill," in Immigration Reform Legislation; 1982–1983; American Civil Liberties Union Records: Subgroup 3, Regional Offices Files Series, Box 4268; Public Policy Papers, Department of Rare Books and Special Collections, Princeton University Library.

75. Kruse and Zelizer, *Fault Lines*.

76. National Immigration, Refugee & Citizenship Forum Information Bulletin, No. 5. August 31, 1984, in Immigration Reform Legislation; 1982–1983; American Civil Liberties Union Records: Subgroup 3, Regional Offices Files Series, Box 4268; Public Policy Papers, Department of Rare Books and Special Collections, Princeton University Library.

77. Laffer, "Curbing Illegals Would Hurt Them and U.S. Economy."

78. McWilliams, "Hispanics Tell Democrats to Halt Immigration Bill," in Immigration Reform Legislation; 1982–1983; American Civil Liberties Union Records: Subgroup 3, Regional Offices Files Series, Box 4268; Public Policy Papers, Department of Rare Books and Special Collections, Princeton University Library.

79. Wong, "Strategy Memo on Simpson-Mazzoli," dated August 31, 1984, Record Group 2, Carton 70, Folder 32, MALDEF Records.

80. "Amid Charges, Immigration Bill Dies," A16.

81. Chavez, *Latino Threat*, 32.

82. Cody, "US Beckons Mexicans as Economy Falters," A21.

83. Acuna, "Capture of Illegal Aliens in Western U.S. Jumps 39%," A1.

84. Pear, "New Restrictions on Immigration Gain Public Support," A1.

85. Roybal later contended that he introduced the legislation as "bait" in order to get Sen. Simpson to introduce an even more extreme bill that would increase the chances that it would be blocked. Still, others believed that Roybal's bill was an attempt by elements of the Congressional Hispanic Caucus to move a compromise bill into law. Sierra, "In Search of National Power," 145.

86. Ibid., 146.

87. Perrotti, "Resolving Policy Conflict," 305.

88. Ibid., 306.

89. For unification as a triumphant moment see Gutiérrez, *Walls and Mirrors*, 202–203.

90. Tichenor, *Dividing Lines*, 260

91. Sierra, "Latino Organizational Strategies on Immigration Reform," 83; Perrotti, "Resolving Policy Conflict," 307.

92. Perrotti, "Resolving Policy Conflict," 311.

93. "Simpson/Mazzoli: Appraisal of the legislation's prospects and the role the White House might play," Folder Immigration-WH Legislative Position on Simpson Mazzoli, Box OA9445, Michael Uhlmann Files, Ronald Reagan Library.

94. Nadine Cohodas, "Combination of Penalties, Amnesty."

95. Perrotti, "Resolving Policy Conflict," 311.

96. Michael J. Wishnie, "Prohibiting the Employment of Unauthorized Immigrants: The Experiment Fails," *University of Chicago Legal Forum*, 2007, 193–217.

97. Ibid.

98. Pear, "President Signs Landmark Bill on Immigration," A12.

99. Handwritten note, Folder [Immigration Bill] (2 of 4), Box OA19146, Alan Charles Rauel Files, Ronald Reagan Library.

100. Wallison to Chew Signing Statement Memo, Folder [Immigration Bill] (1 of 4), Box OA19146, Alan Charles Rauel Files, Ronald Reagan Library.

101. "Description and Brief Analysis of the Frank Amendment," Folder [Immigration Bill] (2 of 4), Box OA19146, Alan Charles Rauel Files, Ronald Reagan Library.

102. Robert Pear, "Law Sets Off Dispute on Legal Alien's Jobs Rights," 1986, 1.

103. Glickman, "Dispute over Antibias Hiring Clause in New Immigration Law." See also "Congress Clears Overhaul of Immigration Law."

Chapter 5: "To Reward the Wrong Way Is Not the American Way"

1. Lesher and Lichtblau, "O.C. Group Helps Fuel Anti-Immigrant Furor," 1.

2. Literature examining the link between immigration and PRWORA has focused largely on the connection post–PRWORA passage. A notable exception is Ron Haskins (who was interviewed for this chapter), who has given an account of the history of these events from a participant's perspective in Ron Haskins, "Limiting Welfare Benefits for Noncitizens: Emergence of Compromises," in Michael Fix, ed., *Immigrants and Welfare: The Impact of Welfare Reform on America's Newcomers* (New York: Russell Sage, 2009). R. Kent Weaver notes in his account of welfare reform the role immigration played in financing the legislation. Weaver, *Ending Welfare As We Know It*. For work exploring the impact of PRWORA on immigrants and their families, see for example Marianne P. Bitler and Hilary W. Hoynes, "Immigrants, Welfare Reform, and the U.S. Safety Net," in D. Card and S. Raphael, eds., *Immigration, Poverty, and Socioeconomic Inequality* (New York: Russell Sage, 2013). See also Michael E. Fix (ed.), *Immigrants and Welfare*. Other works have looked at the organizing that immigrant communities undertook to restore benefits at the state and federal levels in the wake of PRWORA. See Ellen Reese, *They Say Cut, We Say Fight Back!*; Lynn Fujiwara, *Mothers Without Citizenship*. Hana Brown has examined the link between immigration and state level welfare reforms in California and Arizona; see Hana E. Brown, "Race, Legality, and the Social Policy Consequences of Anti-Immigration Mobilization."

3. This work focuses on the impact upon lawful permanent residents as PRWORA primarily focused on them but other "qualified immigrants" impacted by the PRWORA changes included some refugees and some other small categories of legal noncitizens. PRWORA contained a carve-out exempting three discrete noncitizen populations from its larger restrictions: refugees during their first 5 to 7 years in the United States; immigrants with 40 quarters of work history; and noncitizens who had served in the US military.

4. Other scholars have pointed to the 1990s as a key moment as well in various other aspects of immigration activism. For example, Kitty Calavita looks at how changes in the political economy and the ensuing rise of balanced-budget conservatism led to the rise of Prop. 187, and the ways in which Prop. 187 signaled a new kind of symbolic politics, where voters used the ballot knowing it was a "purely symbolic function." see Calavita, "The New Politics of Immigration"; Robin Dale Jacobson sees it as a turning point in the redefinition of racial categories and the meanings of citizenship in California. See Jacobson, *The New Nativism*.

5. This split in the Republican Party is categorized by Dan Tichenor as "Classic Exclusionists" versus "Free Market Expansionists." My interpretation of this moment in the 1990s and more specifically IIRIRA (discussed in chapter 6) and welfare reform differs from Tichenor in that I view Tichenor's "Classic Exclusionists" as more dominant than he does, especially when one shifts away from focusing on admissions levels and looks at the long-term implications of these bills with regard to immigrants' rights, interior enforcement, detention, and deportation. Tichenor, writing in 2002, sees this moment as "a triumph for free-market expansionists, who allied with pro-immigration liberals to sustain unprecedented legal admissions and with anti-immigrant conservatives to trim alien substantive and procedural rights." Tichenor also highlights the increase in naturalization immediately following the passage of the 1996 welfare restrictions. I view this moment as much more restrictive, in particular when one looks at the ways in which the changes in the 1990s created the legal framework for some of the more draconian deportation policies of the contemporary period, as well as other policies that restrict immigration and immigrants' rights, including President Trump's "likely to become public charge rule" change. For more on Tichenor's argument, see Tichenor, *Dividing Lines*, 276–288.

6. Gulasekaram and Ramakrishnan in *The New Immigration Federalism* have argued that post-1965 is a new period in immigration federalism, an argument I agree with. However, they point to post-2004 as a transformative moment in states forging policy and interpret Prop. 187 as having no immediate restrictionist policy impact, pointing to its blockage by the Court in California and the failure of copycat legislation to pass. In their argument, Prop. 187 is important because it served as a wake-up call to national groups on the ability of states to serve as immigration policy battlegrounds. However, as evidence in this chapter makes clear, Prop. 187 did have an immediate impact on national politics and policy, showing one example of how states were playing a critical role in forging immigration policy in the 1990s. See introduction, note 13 for a longer discussion of *The New Immigration Federalism* and the ways in which this book complicates their arguments.

7. See epilogue for discussion of post-2000 policy implications and further suggested readings.

8. While there were not de jure alienage restrictions, unauthorized immigrants faced many other barriers to accessing public assistance, including durational residency restrictions and racial discrimination. See Fox, *Three Worlds of Relief*; Molina, *Fit to Be Citizens?*

9. Robert A. Moffitt, "The Deserving Poor, the Family, and the U.S. Welfare System," *Demography* 52, no. 3 (2015): 729–749.

10. See also Orleck, *Storming Caesars Palace*, and Kornbluh, *The Battle for Welfare Rights*.

11. Chavez, *The Latino Threat*, 30.

12. Gallup Study of Attitudes toward Illegal Aliens, 16–17, cited in Minian, *Undocumented Lives*, 63.

13. Gutiérrez, *Fertile Matters*, 26.

14. Minian, *Undocumented Lives*, 66.

15. Chavez, *Anchor Babies*.

16. For more on these early efforts in California and New York, and particularly the role of welfare retrenchment and the federal judiciary in these developments, see Cybelle Fox, "'The Line Must Be Drawn Somewhere': The Rise of Legal Status Restrictions in State Welfare Policy in the 1970s," *Studies in American Political Development* 33, no. 2 (2019): 275–304.

17. State poor laws had a history of restricting public assistance to individuals by requiring a "settlement" for an extended period. These restrictions were based on the notion that members of the community were entitled to support during difficult times, but transients were not. Fox, "Unauthorized Welfare," 1053.

18. Motomura, *Americans in Waiting*, 40.

19. Fox, "Unauthorized Welfare," 1051–1074. While Fox has rightly elucidated this moment in the 1970s as a seminal moment in the restrictive turn in federal policy making, she also argues that it was at this moment that "national citizenship eclipsed state and local citizenship as a key boundary of social citizenship." I would instead suggest that national citizenship gained its key importance in the 1990s, as authorized immigrants without citizenship status still had access to welfare between the changes Fox describes in the 1970s until the changes in 1996.

20. Ibid.

21. Text of *Graham* footnote: "We have no occasion to decide whether Congress, in the exercise of the immigration and naturalization power, could itself enact a statute imposing on aliens a uniform nationwide residency requirement as a condition of federally funded welfare benefits."

22. *Mathews v. Diaz*, 426 U.S. 67 (1976).

23. Weaver, *Ending Welfare as We Know It*, 230–231.

24. George H.W. Bush, *Statement on the Signing of the Immigration Act of 1990*.

25. "Clinton Maps Ideas from Inner City to Persian Gulf."

26. "Bush vs. Clinton: What Would Be Best Immigration Policy?" B6.

27. Sciolino, "Clinton Says U.S. Will Continue Ban on Haitian Exodus."

28. Leah Perry, *The Cultural Politics of U.S. Immigration*.

29. Sontag, "Calls to Restrict Immigration Come from Many Quarters," E5.

30. Zolberg, *Nation by Design*, 386.

31. Census 2000 data in Elizabeth Greico, "Characteristics of the Foreign Born in the United States: Results from Census 2000," Migration Policy Institute, December 1, 2002.

32. Zolberg, *Nation by Design*, 383–385.

33. Suro, "California's SOS on Immigration," A1.

34. Durand, Massey, and Charvet, "The Changing Geography of Mexican Immigration to the United States."

35. Zolberg, *Nation by Design*, 385.

36. Wroe, *The Republican Party*, 29.

37. Mydans, "A New Tide of Immigration Brings Hostility to the Surface."

38. This is not the first time that rising concern and a turn against welfare spending helped to undermine immigrant rights and notions of social citizenship. See Fox, "'The Line Must Be Drawn Somewhere."

39. For examples of this rhetoric, see Sontag, "Calls to Restrict Immigration Come from Many Quarters"; Fitzgerald, "Welfare for Illegal Aliens?"

40. Zolberg, *Nation by Design*, 409.

41. Weaver, *Ending Welfare*, 231.

42. "Benefits for Illegal Aliens," GAO Testimony before Task Force on Illegal Immigration, September 29, 1993. http://www.gao.gov/assets/110/105221.pdf

43. Chavez, *Anchor Babies*.

44. Zolberg, *Nation by Design*, 392.

45. James Bornemeier, "Immigrant Cost Study Draws Fire," *Los Angeles Times*, June 28, 1994. Reimers, *Unwelcome Strangers*, 49.

46. Hector Tobar, "Study of Immigrants' Cost to L.A. County Fuels Debate," *Los Angeles Times*, November 12, 1992, A14.

47. Fix and Passel, "Immigration and Immigrants."

48. Schmos, "In Recession, Illegal Aliens Find a Cold Reception on L.I."

49. Wroe, *Republican Party*, 42.

50. "The Unfair Immigration Burden," *New York Times*, January 11, 1994.

51. Epstein to Emanuel Memo, National Security Council, Speechwriting Office, and Robert Boorstin, "Immigration—Key Policy Issues," Clinton Digital Library, accessed January 1, 2016, http://clinton.presidentiallibraries.us/files/original/b87b5feob313802fa9f9fee65e7c9cc7.pdf

52. Stall and McDonnell, "Wilson Urges Stiff Penalties."

53. Maria Puente, "65% Want Immigration Cut Back," *USA Today* in Domestic Policy Council, Carol Rasco, and Subject Series, "Immigration Info '92/'93 [2]," Clinton Digital Library, accessed December 13, 2015.

54. Handwritten note, Domestic Policy Council, Carol Rasco, and Subject Series, "Immigration Info '92/'93 [2]," Clinton Digital Library, accessed December 13, 2015.

55. Christopher Edley Testimony, US Commission on Civil Rights, Presentation on Civil and Human Rights Implications of U.S. Southwest Border Policy, November 14, 2002, http://www.usccr.gov/pubs/migrant/present/trans.htm.

56. Bornemeier, "Putting California Spin on Clinton Policies."

57. Interview with Committee Staff Director Ron Haskins, February 17, 2016.

58. House Republican Press Release, May 1993 in DPC, Kathryn Way Files, Box 3, Folder Republican Welfare Reform Plan [OA/ID 4045], William J. Clinton Presidential Library.

59. Rick Santorum, "Its Called SSI and It May Be Our Worst Social Program," *Washington Times*, May 12, 1993 in Domestic Policy Council, Kathryn Way Files, Box 3, Folder: Republican Welfare Reform Plan, William J. Clinton Presidential Library.

60. Weaver, *Ending Welfare*, 206.

61. DeParle, "Welfare Plan Seeks Limit on Benefits."

62. "On Not Blaming Immigrants First," *Washington Post*, May 9, 1994, A16.

63. Rasco to Reed and Way Memo January 1994, in Domestic Policy Council, Kathryn Way Files, Box 3, Folder: Rollout [1], William J. Clinton Presidential Library.

64. Shalala to POTUS memo, Domestic Policy Council, Kathryn Way Files, Box 3, Folder: Rollout [1], William J. Clinton Presidential Library.

65. Reed, Ellwood, and Bane memo to POTUS November 29, 1993, in Domestic Policy Council, Kathryn Way Files, Box 3, Folder: Rollout [1], William J. Clinton Presidential Library.

66. "Key Questions in Welfare Reform March 30, 1994," Memo.

67. "Stan Greenberg and Joe Goode, Re: Welfare Reform—Priorities and Funding Memo, 5/20/1994," Domestic Policy Council, Cathy Mays Files, Box 2, Folder "Correspondence and Memos for the President [Binder] [4]," William J. Clinton Presidential Library.

68. Weaver, *Ending Welfare*, 245.

69. Pear, "The Nation; Deciding Who Gets What in America."

70. Shogren, "Clinton Unveils Welfare Reform."

71. Domestic Policy Council, Bruce Reed, and Welfare Reform Series, "Letters—SSI/Immigration [1]," Clinton Digital Library, accessed December 21, 2015, http://clinton.presidentiallibraries.us/items/show/32094.

72. Martinez and Carvajal, "Creators of Prop. 187 Largely Escape Spotlight Ballot," 1.

73. Lesher and Lichtblau, "O.C. Group Helps Fuel Anti-Immigrant Furor."

74. Ibid. "Boxer Won't Back Riordan Plan for LAX." *Santa Cruz Sentinel*, July 11, 1993, A6.

75. Lesher and Lichtblau, "O.C. Group Helps Fuel Anti-Immigrant Furor."

76. Reinhold, "A Welcome for Immigrants Turns to Resentment."

77. Kulish and McIntire, "Why an Heiress Spent Her Fortune Trying to Keep Immigrants Out."

78. Wroe, *Republican Party*, 61–62.

79. Suzanne Espinosa Solis, "New Group to Battle Illegal Immigration," *San Francisco Chronicle*, July 28, 1994, A17; Ed Mendel, "Immigration Control Could Zoom Into Law—If Its Time Has Come," *San Diego Union-Tribune*, August 1, 1994 A3.

80. Stefanic, "Funding the Nativist Agenda,"128–129.

81. HoSang, *Racial Propositions*, 178; Wroe, *Republican Party*, 66.

82. Wroe, *Republican Party*, 66, 71.

83. Feldman, "Prop 187."

84. Wroe, *Republican Party*, 73.

85. "Prop 187: Foes on the Attack," Proposition 187 Campaign Ephemera, f 94 00632, Volume 1, University of California, Berkeley, Institute of Governmental Studies.

86. HoSang, *Racial Propositions*, 181.

87. "Taxpayers Against 187 Pamphlet," Proposition 187 Campaign Ephemera, f 94 00632, Volume 1, University of California, Berkeley, Institute of Governmental Studies.

88. Podger, "Ballot Measures Attract Big Money," B3.

89. Wroe, *Republican Party*, 72–73.

90. Ibid., 64.

91. Burdman, "Democrats Blame Wilson For Immigration Problem."

92. Krikorian and Lesher, "Huffington Declares Support for Prop. 187."

93. Ayres Jr., "Feinstein Faults Aliens Proposal," 9.

94. "Wilson Endorses Proposition 187," *Oakland Tribune*, November 16, 1994, in Proposition 187 Campaign Ephemera, f 94 00632, Volume 1, University of California, Berkeley, Institute of Governmental Studies.

95. HoSang, *Racial Propositions*, 169–170.

96. Ibid., 192.

97. Ayres Jr., "Feinstein Faults Aliens Proposal."

98. Everett Brandon, "How Prop. 187 Threatens Democracy," *San Francisco Independent*, November 4, 1994 in Proposition 187 Campaign Ephemera, f 94 00632, Volume 3, University of California, Berkeley, Institute of Governmental Studies.

99. Rahm Emanuel and Ron Klain to Leon Panetta "Immigration Strategy" Memo, September 29, 1994 in Domestic Policy Council, Bruce Reed, and Subject Files, "Immigration [1]," Clinton Digital Library, accessed December 10, 2015.

100. Marcus, "Clinton Assails California Proposal," A29.

101. Ibid.

102. A federal district court judge in California concluded in 1995 that many of Prop. 187's provisions were preempted by federal law in *League of United Latin American Citizens v. Wilson*, 908 F. Supp 755 (C.D. Cal 1995). The judge invalidated the provisions that required notifying federal authorities and the provisions' refusal to educate unauthorized immigrants, yet the judge allowed some provisions denying benefits. In 1997, following the passage of PRWORA, a California federal judge ruled that the benefit denial of Prop. 187 was preempted by congressional actions on the matter in *League of United Latin American Citizens v. Wilson*, 997 F. Supp 1244 (C.D. Cal 1997).

103. "Prop. 187 Supporters Field Calls for Advice," *Oakland Tribune*, November 5, 1994 in Proposition 187 Campaign Ephemera, f 94 00632, Volume 3, University of California, Berkeley, Institute of Governmental Studies.

104. Miller, "Creators Set Prop. 187 for National Stage, Immigration," A1.

105. Draft Roscoe to POTUS Memo, Domestic Policy Council, Bruce Reed, and Subject Files, "Immigration [2]," Clinton Digital Library, accessed December 11, 2015.

106. Melissa Healy, "House GOP Charts California Agenda Congress," *Los Angeles Times*, November 13, 1994.

107. Brownstein, "Wilson Proposes U.S. Version of Prop. 187 Immigration," 1.

108. Ibid.

109. Ibid.

110. Oleszek, *The Use of Task Forces in the House*.

111. Wroe, *Republican Party*, 121.

112. Report to the Speaker, Task Force on Immigration Reform, cited in Wroe, *Republican Party*, 121.

113. Ibid., 122.

114. Wroe, *Republican Party*, 121–122.

115. Ibid.

116. Sandalow, "Republicans Battle Over Immigration," A3.

117. Broder, "Clinton Administration Readies Centrist Strategy."

118. "Greenberg Public Polling Update: Immigration," Office of Communications and Don Baer, "Immigration," Clinton Digital Library, accessed June 24, 2016, http://clinton.presidentiallibraries.us/items/show/34550.

119. Ibid.

120. White House Immigration Issue Undated Memo, in Domestic Policy Council, Kathryn Way Files, Box 3, Folder Personal Responsibility Act Welfare Provisions in Republican Contract with America, William J. Clinton Presidential Library.

121. Draft Roscoe to POTUS Memo, Domestic Policy Council, Bruce Reed, and Subject Files, "Immigration [2]," Clinton Digital Library, accessed December 11, 2015.

122. Ibid.

123. Clinton, "1995 State of the Union."

124. Pear, "Clinton Will Seek Spending to Curb Aliens, Aides Say," A1.

125. Domestic Policy Council, Carol Rasco, and Meetings, Trips, Events Series, "POTUS Immigration Briefing and Announcement 7 Feb. 1995 10:35—11:15am," Clinton Digital Library, accessed December 11, 2015.

126. For more detail, see Weaver, *Ending Welfare*, 263.

127. Suro, "GOP Would Deny Legal Immigrants Many U.S. Benefits."

128. Rector and Lauber, "America Is Becoming a Deluxe Retirement Home."

129. Engelberg, "G.O.P.'s Voice on Aliens Roars to Challenge the Party," B20.

130. Trout and Kuntz, "GOP May Reconsider Proposal to Deny Benefits to Legal Aliens," A22.

131. Interview with Ron Haskins, February 17, 2016; "Gingrich Changes Mind, Backs Immigrant Benefits."

132. Ibid.

133. Jost, "Cracking Down on Immigration."

134. Merid and Havemann, "Gingrich Softens Stance Against Aliens' Benefits," A1.

135. *Congressional Quarterly Weekly Report*, January 14, 1995, 162.

136. Weaver, *Ending Welfare*, 266–267.

137. "Gingrich Changes Mind, Backs Immigrant Benefits."

138. Weaver, *Ending Welfare*, 282.

139. Amendments offered by liberal Congressman Pete Stark of California to retain full social services benefits for authorized immigrants who had paid US taxes for at least five years, and by Congressman Charles Rangel from New York to retain full social services benefits to legal immigrants who were veterans, were both defeated and not included in the bill. "Welfare Bill Clears Under Veto Threat."

140. Ibid.

141. Pear, "Welfare Bill Cleared by Congress," A1.

142. House Republican Conference Release "Defining Issue: Welfare Reform dated July 31, 1996," Box 11, Folder 25, Richard Armey Papers, Carl Albert Center, University of Oklahoma.

143. Ibid., and House Republican Conference Talking Points, February 1, 1996, Box 11, Folder 25, Richard Armey Papers, Carl Albert Center, University of Oklahoma.

144. RNC Press Release and Ad Transcript, Domestic Policy Council, Bruce Reed, and Welfare Reform Series, "Illegal Immigrants," Clinton Digital Library, accessed December 17, 2015, http://clinton.presidentiallibraries.us/items/show/31754.

145. "Signed," Clinton/Gore '96 General Committee, 1996, Museum of the Moving Image, The Living Room Candidate: Presidential Campaign Commercials 1952–2012, accessed June 22, 2016, www.livingroomcandidate.org/commercials/1996/signed.

146. Edelman, "The Worst Thing Bill Clinton Has Done"; Zolberg, *Nation by Design*, 416.

147. Reed to POTUS Memo "Welfare Reform Conference" dated 7/23/96, Domestic Policy Council, Bruce Reed, and Welfare Reform Series, "Signing [1]," Clinton Digital Library, accessed December 2, 2015, http://clinton.presidentiallibraries.us/items/show/31944.

148. Purdum, "Clinton in a Box."

149. "Text of President Clinton's Welfare Announcement."

150. IIRIRA's other provisions are discussed in greater depth in chapter 6.

151. Notably, it did not include guidance on what factors were to be considered in determining whether an immigrant is deportable. Congressional Research Service, "Public Charge Grounds of Inadmissibility and Deportability: Legal Overview," February 6, 2017. Batalova, Fix, and Greenberg, "Chilling Effects." For a longer history on the "public charge" restriction see Torrie Hester et al., "Historians' Comment on DHS Notice," 2018 public paper in author's possession.

152. Associated Press, "Clinton Moves to Protect Legal Aliens' Welfare Benefits," A6.

153. Domestic Policy Council, Bruce Reed, and Welfare Reform Series, "Immigration [2]," Clinton Digital Library, accessed December 17, 2015, http://clinton.presidentiallibraries.us /items/show/31758.

154. "$13 Billion in Welfare Cuts Restored."

155. Ellis and McDonnell, "Suit Targets U.S. Cuts in Aid for Immigrants," A4.

156. Havermann, "Civil Rights Groups, N.Y. Mayor Challenge Welfare Cutoff," A23.

157. Assorted petitions, Domestic Policy Council, Cynthia Rice Files, Box 25, Folder Welfare-Budget Conference Immigrants, William J. Clinton Presidential Library.

158. Dugger, "Giuliani Uses Conference to Rally Immigrant Cause," B3.

159. Dugger, "New Alliances and Attitudes on Aid," A23.

160. Immigration Memo, Elena Kagan Files, Domestic Policy Council, Box 63, Folder 001, William J. Clinton Library.

161. Pear, "G.O.P. Governors Seek to Restore Immigrant Aid."

162. This group included John Chafee of Rhode Island, Alfonse D'Amato of New York, and Mike DeWine of Ohio.

163. Havermann, "Republicans Start to Break Ranks on Welfare Cutoff," A19.

164. Georges and Rogers, "Senate Delays Cutoff in Immigrant Aid," 24.

165. Pear, "GOP Backing Off Deal to Restore Aid to Immigrants."

166. Democrats were further angered when the Ways and Means Human Resources Subcommittee adopted an amendment offered by Congressman Jim McCrery of Louisiana to deny SSI benefits in perpetuity for immigrants whose sponsors made $40,000 or more a year, but the amendment was dropped in the full committee.

167. "$13 Billion in Welfare Cuts Restored."

168. "A Record of Restoring Benefits to Legal Immigrants" Factsheet, "2011–0320-F—Illegal Immigration Reform and Immigrant Responsibility Act (IIRIRA)," Clinton Digital Library, accessed December 2, 2015, http://clinton.presidentiallibraries.us/items/show/14840.

169. National Immigration Forum Update on Various Immigration Policy Issues Email dated July 9, 1998, Folder WHO [Welfare Residence & Immigration Responsibility Act] [04/01/1997–05/22/2000], Box FOIA Request 2011–0320-F, William J. Clinton Library.

170. Randy Capps, Michael E. Fix, and Everett Henderson, "Trends in Immigrants' Use of Public Assistance after Welfare Reform," in Fix, ed., *Immigrants and Welfare.*

171. Karen Brandon, "When Benefits Hurt," *Chicago Tribune,* January 5, 1999, 1.

172. Francisco I. Pedraza and Ling Zhu, "The 'Chilling Effect' of America's New Immigration Enforcement Regime," Pathways, Spring 2015 cited in Batalova et al., "Chilling Effects," 15.

173. Brandon, "When Benefits Hurt," 10.

174. Batalova et al., "Chilling Effects," 15.

175. To try and reduce the "chilling effect" of the IIRIA changes, immigration activists pushed for clarification on what would be considered in an LPC designation. Beyond immigration activists, states were increasingly frustrated with the lack of clarity around the LPC designation, and state health officials in California repeatedly asked for guidance as they felt fear of being designated an LPC was impacting parents who were enrolling their children in the state CHIP program. (See Jean H. Lee, "Fear Keeps Aliens from Seeking Care," *Santa Maria Times,* January 24, 1999, 11.) Senator Feinstein began to force the White House to act on the

issue by threatening to introduce her own bill to address the issue (See Domestic Policy Council and Elena Kagan, "Immigration—Public Charge," Clinton Digital Library, accessed December 6, 2018, https://clinton.presidentiallibraries.us/items/show/26357). Vice President Al Gore announced new INS guidance during a stop in Texas in May 1999, saying the guidance would "improve the health of our families by addressing widespread confusion." The INS guidance narrowly interpreted the situations in which the receipt of public benefits was considered relevant to the "public charge," limiting the direct impact of the IIRIRA public charge changes. INS interpreted the change so that only those who were dependent on the government for subsistence either through cash assistance or long-term institutionalization would be considered "likely to become public charges." Use of noncash benefits were not to be considered in determining LPC status, meaning less than 3 percent of immigrants were impacted by the LPC designation. For more on the Gore statement, see Patrick J. McDonnell, "White House to Unveil New Rule on Aid to Non-Citizens," *Los Angeles Times*, May 25, 1999, A3. By and large, only cash-based assistance amounting to the majority of one's income could potentially be disqualifying. For more on INS interpretation see Batalova et al., "Chilling Effects," and INS, "Inadmissibility and Deportability on Public Charge Grounds," *Federal Register* 64, no. 101 (March 26, 1999): 28676–93; and Hester et al., "Historians' Comment on DHS Notice of Proposed Rule." For data on 3 percent impact see https://www.migrationpolicy.org/news/mpi -nearly-half-all-noncitizens-us-could-be- affected-proposed-trump-administration-public.

176. Fox, "The Line Must Be Drawn Somewhere."

Chapter 6: From the Border to the Heartland

1. Skerry, "Is Immigration the Exclusive Responsibility of the Federal Government?"

2. For a more detailed history of federal immigration policy, see Zolberg, *Nation by Design*; Tichenor, *Dividing Lines*; Daniels, *Guarding the Golden Door*; Lee, "A Nation of Immigrants and A Gatekeeping Nation"; Hester, *Deportation*. For a greater discussion of Chinese exclusion, see Lee, *At America's Gates*, and Lew-Williams, *The Chinese Must Go*.

3. The Page Act barred convicted criminals and prostitutes from admission to the United States and would gradually expand the categories of "undesirable" excludable immigrants to include "lunatics," contract laborers, and polygamists, among others. Motomura, *Immigration Outside the Law*, 67.

4. For an overview of major developments in immigration federalism, see Gulasekaram and Ramakrishnan, *The New Immigration Federalism*, 15–56; Tichenor and Filindra, *Raising Arizona v. United States*.

5. *Chy Lung v. Freeman*, 92 U.S. 275 (1875).

6. Kramer, "The Case of the 22 Lewd Chinese Women."

7. Ibid.

8. Meanwhile, the role of states in alienage law was highly contested and is the subject of much scholarship; see introduction for more discussion of alienage law. See also Gulasekaram and Ramakrishnan, *The New Immigration Federalism*, 19–27, for further discussion of these two cases.

9. Lytle Hernández, *Migra!*, 92; Felker-Kantor, *Policing Los Angeles*, 168.

10. McDonald, *Changing Boundaries of Law Enforcement*; Ngai, *Impossible Subjects*; Provine et al., *Policing Immigrants*.

11. McDonnell, "Welfare Law May Affect Police Role, Immigrants," A1.

12. For an excellent history of the LAPD's policing policies and procedures regarding immigrant communities during this period, see "Policing an Internal Border: Constructing Criminal Aliens and Exclusive Citizenship" in Felker-Kantor, *Policing Los Angeles*, 162–189. As Felker-Kantor notes, while the LAPD would formally regulate itself from local enforcement of immigration law, during the 1980s the LAPD would "circumvent these policy limitations within the city's war on drugs and gangs," and "cooperation between the LAPD and INS circumvented both the spirit and the letter of Special Order 40." Felker-Kantor, *Policing Los Angeles*, 163, 186.

13. Oliver, "Court Asked to Halt LAPD Immigration-Status Action," 19.

14. Maxwell, "LAPD Eases Policy Toward Illegal Aliens."

15. Los Angeles Police Department, Special Order 40, http://assets.lapdonline.org/assets/pdf/SO_40.pdf; McDonnell, "Law Could Alter Role of Police on Immigration."

16. Domanick, "Daryl Gate's Downfall."

17. Duffy Memo to Taxi, Box 22, Folder 4, Herman Baca Papers. MSS 0649, Special Collections & Archives, UC San Diego.

18. Baller to Couch Memo "Ad Hoc Committee" dated June 22, 1978, Record Group 4, Box 85, Folder 6, MALDEF Records.

19. Baller to Couch Memo, October 17, 1979, Record Group 4, Box 85, Folder 5, MALDEF Records.

20. May 23, 1978 Memo, Record Group 4, Box 95, Folder 7, MALDEF Records.

21. Memo dated September 13, 1978, Record Group 4, Box 86, Folder 3, MALDEF Records.

22. MALDEF to Bell Letter, January 11, 1978, Record Group 4, Box 95, Folder 8, MALDEF Records.

23. Letters to Bell and Civiletti, April 1978, Record Group 4, Box 86, Folder 3, MALDEF Records.

24. Memo dated September 13, 1978, Record Group 4, Box 86, Folder 3, MALDEF Records.

25. Del Olmo, "Bell Will Warn Police," C1.

26. DOJ Press Release, Record Group 4, Box 86, Folder 5, MALDEF Records.

27. Del Olmo, "Bell Will Warn Police."

28. Crossland Letter, August 9, 1978, Record Group 4, Box 86, Folder 5, MALDEF Records.

29. Perez to MALDEF staff memo dated May 7, 1979, Record Group 4, Box 85, Folder 6, MALDEF Records.

30. Kenneth Schorr Interview, April 25, 2016.

31. Policy Letters Exhibits 1–6 and 9, Record Group 5, Box 1458, Folder "*Gonzales v. Peoria* Trial Exhibits," MALDEF Records.

32. "Walter Craig, Federal Judge; Named to Bench by Kennedy."

33. Girdner, "Local Police Effort to Arrest Aliens Faces Critical Test," *Los Angeles Daily Journal*, March 17, 1983 in Record Group 5, Box 1458, Folder 2 "*Gonzales v. City of Peoria*," MALDEF Records.

34. Schorr Interview, April 25, 2016.

35. Schorr to De Leon Letter dated July 12, 1982, and Schorr to Baller Letter dated June 25, 1982, Record Group 5, Box 1458, Folder 2 "*Gonzales v. City of Peoria*," MALDEF Records.

36. Wong Materials, Record Group 5, Box 1458, Folder 2 "*Gonzales v. City of Peoria*," MALDEF Records.

37. *Gonzales*, 722 F.2d at 474.

38. Schorr to Baller and Moreno Letter, and Moreno to Schorr and Ball Letter, Record Group 5, Box 1458, Folder 1, "*Gonzales v. City of Peoria*," MALDEF Records; Schorr interview April 25, 2016.

39. Senate Amendment 1905 to S.2222 (1982).

40. Girdner, "Local Police Effort to Arrest Aliens Faces Critical Test."

41. "Danger in the Immigration Bill," G4.

42. Subcommittee on Immigration and Refugee Policy of the Committee on the Judiciary, Hearing on September 30, 1982, pp/ 34–35. https://www.loc.gov/law/find/hearings/pdf /00139298160.pdf

43. *Interpreter Releases* 60 (March 4, 1983): 172–173 (quoting guidelines approved by the Attorney General on February 10, 1983).

44. Girdner, "Local Police Effort to Arrest Aliens Faces Critical Test."

45. Kisor, "Enforcing the Immigration and Naturalization Act."

46. "Coast City Spurns Action on Aliens."

47. "Immigration Raids Causing Uproar in Silicon Valley," 1.

48. Ibid.

49. One action of note was a 1989 OLC opinion under President George H. W. Bush in response to a question about an FBI database which restated the earlier opinion that local police could enforce the criminal violations of the INA, but stated that it was "unclear" whether local police could enforce non-criminal federal statutes. https://www.aclu.org/files/images/asset _upload_file438_29970.pdf

50. "Murder Trial Expected to Go to Jury This Week."

51. Younie's blood alcohol level was found in an autopsy to be .21, and the medical examiner testified that he had probably consumed 12 to 13 beers in the three hours before the stabbing. Michelle Linck, "Jury to Decide in Murder Trial," *Sioux County Capital-Democrat*, September 21, 1995, 1.

52. "Guilty Verdicts Returned in Justin Younie Murder Trial,"1.

53. Feder, "The Standoff Over Beef."

54. "Hispanics in Iowa Meatpacking."

55. For more on these changes to meat processing as well as more detail on the specific changes in Iowa, see the essays in Stull, *Any Way You Cut It.*

56. Kandel, "Meat-Processing Firms Attract Hispanic Workers."

57. Grey et al., *The New Iowans.*

58. Carney, "Hispanics in Iowa: A Chorus of Spanish Voices," 1.

59. Ibid.

60. Carney, "Hispanics in Iowa: Both Small Towns and Newcomers Learn to Adapt," 2.

61. Dukes, "A Teen Dead, a Town Tense," M1.

62. Ibid.

63. "Raid at Iowa Lamb prompted."

64. "Sioux City Fatal Hit-And-Run Incident."

65. "Illegal Immigrants Taken from Hawarden Plant."

66. "One Injured, One Killed in Stabbing Incident," 14.

67. "Local Law Enforcement Has No Authority to Arrest Illegal Aliens."

68. Nelson, "Letter to the Editor."

69. McDonald, "Changing Boundaries of Law Enforcement," 6.59.

70. Later Escobedo and Herrarte filed for post-conviction relief on several counts, including deficient counsel's performance and issues with the jury, that were denied.

71. "Herrarte & Escobedo Sentenced to Life Imprisonment," 22.

72. Numerous studies have shown no link between rising immigration levels and crime rates. Three of the most recent include Light and Miller, "Does Undocumented Immigration Increase Violent Crime?"; Nowrastech, "Criminal Immigrants in Texas"; and Bersani, "An Examination of First and Second Generation Immigrant Offending Trajectories."

73. CNN All Politics Iowa State Profile 1996.

74. Carney, "Town Awaits Murder Trial's Start, 2.

75. Fogarty, "Case Spurs Immigration Law Review," 14.

76. Ibid.

77. Kate Thompson, "New Bill Includes Provisions in Memory of Stabbing Victim," *Sioux City Journal*, September 26, 1996.

78. Fogarty, "Senate Cracks Down on Illegal Immigrants."

79. Kaskie, "Letter to the Editor."

80. McDonald, "Changing Boundaries of Law Enforcement," 6.59.

81. Norman, "Immigration Raids Win Praise," 1.

82. Ibid.

83. Norman, "Grassley Lands First INS Office for Iowa," 11.

84. Norman, "Offices Are Coming, One Way or Another."

85. Norman, "Grassley Lands First INS Office for Iowa."

86. Bacon to Bob Barr Letter dated March 9, 1995, Folder Smyrna Immigration and Operation Southpaw, Box 48, Bob Barr Papers, 104th Congress. Annie Belle Weaver Special Collections, Irvine Sullivan Ingram Library, University of West Georgia.

87. Cameron to Newt Memo dated 3/11/96, Folder Immigration, Box 2154, Newt Gingrich Papers, 104th and 105th Congress. Annie Belle Weaver Special Collections, Irvine Sullivan Ingram Library, University of West Georgia.

88. Assistance by State and Local Police in Apprehending Illegal Aliens, 20 Op. O.L.C. 26 (1996).

89. Deputization was to be conducted in writing and with the consent of the governor of that state or the state's chief local official.

90. Norman, "Offices Are Coming, One Way or Another"; Norman, "Harkin: Must Police Also Chase Aliens?" 2.

91. Interview with Kolan Davis, Legislative Assistant to Senator Grassley in William F. McDonald, "Changing Boundaries of Law Enforcement."

92. Norman, "Potomac Fever," 19.

93. Lacey, "Beating Raises Concerns About Policing."

94. Congressman Ganske, *Congressional Record*, March 20, 1996, H2479.

95. Congressman Tom Latham, *Congressional Record*, March 20, 1996, H2480.

96. Congressman Brian Bilbray, *Congressional Record*, March 20, 1996, H2479.

97. Jost, "The States and Federalism."

98. Congresswoman Sheila Jackson-Lee, *Congressional Record*, March 20, 1996, H2478.

99. Congressman Becerra, *Congressional Record*, March 20, 1996, H2477.

100. Norman, "Harkin: Must Police Also Chase Aliens?"

101. Sauder to Barr Letter dated June 30, 1995, Folder Illegal Immigration Task Force, Box 338, Bob Barr Papers, 104th Congress. Annie Belle Weaver Special Collections, Irvine Sullivan Ingram Library, University of West Georgia.

102. Norman, "Immigration Raids Win Praise."

103. Brack, "Immigrants Being Drawn to Midwest," 1.

104. Ibid.

105. Ibid.

106. David Martin Interview, March 21, 2016.

107. NA §287(g)(1), 8 U.S.C. §1357(g)(1).

108. Solórzano, "At the Gates of the Kingdom," 185.

109. Ibid.

110. Ibid.

111. Numerous studies have shown no link between rising immigration levels and crime rates. See Light and Miller, "Does Undocumented Immigration Increase Violent Crime?"; Nowrastech, "Criminal Immigrants in Texas"; and Bersani, "An Examination of First and Second Generation Immigrant Offending Trajectories."

112. McKinnon, "Hatch Addressing Immigration Issues."

113. Janet Reno, Address to "A Summit on Crime—Coming Together for Utah's Future."

114. Ibid.

115. There had recently been an abduction of two Latinos from Pioneer Bar and then a raid of a store, La Diana.

116. Foster, "S.L. Police as INS Agents: Is This a Good Idea?" B1.

117. Ibid.

118. Ibid.

119. Foster, "S.L. Latinos Swayed Councilman," *Salt Lake Tribune*, September 9, 1998, B1. Shawn Foster, "S.L. Police as INS Agents."

120. Foster, "S.L. Latinos Swayed Councilman"; Foster, "S.L. Police as INS Agents."

121. Subcommittee on Immigration and Claims of the House Judiciary Committee, *Field Hearing: Problems Related to Criminal Aliens in the State of Utah*, 105th Congress, 2nd session, July 27, 1998.

122. Kennard complained of jail overcrowding due to individuals being held in local jails pending adjudication by immigration courts.

123. Foster, "SLC Council Says No to Cross-Deputization," C1.

124. Foster, "S.L. Latinos Swayed Councilman."

125. Jane Norman, "Immigrant Policing Project Opposed," *Des Moines Register*, March 2, 1999, 1.

126. For a broader discussion of this transition, see Kalhan, "Immigration Enforcement and Federalism After September 11, 2001."

127. *National Council of La Raza v. Department of Justice*, 411 F.3d 350 (2nd Cir. 2005).

128. Non-Preemption of the Authority of the State and Local Law Enforcement Officials to Arrest Aliens for Immigration Violations, Op. Off. Legal Counsel (July 22, 2002).

129. Harris, *Good Cops*, 7.

130. Cheryl W. Thompson, "INS Role for Police Considered."

131. Ibid.

132. "Local Enforcement of Immigration Laws Through the 287(g) Program," *American Immigration Council*, updated April 2, 2010. http://www.immigrationpolicy.org/just-facts/local -enforcement-immigration-laws-through-287g-program

Epilogue

1. In 2018, the Department of Labor reported that of the 2.5 million farmworkers in the United States, more than half were unauthorized immigrants. Growers and labor unions put this figure at 70 percent. Immigrants make up about 30 percent of the construction labor force and 25 percent of physicians and surgeons. See US Department of Labor, "Findings from the National Agricultural Workers Survey (NAWS) 2015–2016: A Demographic and Employment Profile of the United States Farmworkers," Research Report No 13 (January 2018); "Immigrant Workers in the Construction Labor Force," *NAHB Economics Special Studies*, February 3, 2015; Yash M. Patel, Dan P. Ly, Tanner Hicks, and Anupam Jena, "Proportion of Non–US-Born and Noncitizen Health Care Professionals in the United States in 2016," *Journal of the American Medical Association* 320, no. 21 (2018): 2265–2267.

2. Eduardo Porter, "Illegal Immigrants Are Bolstering Social Security with Billions," *New York Times*, April 5, 2005.

3. Stephen Goss, Alice Wade, J. Patrick Skirvin, Michael Morris, K. Mark Bye, and Danielle Huston, "Effects of Unauthorized Immigration on the Actuarial Status of the Social Security Trust Funds," *Actuarial Note 151* (April 2013), SSA Office of the Chief Actuary, https://www.ssa .gov/oact/NOTES/pdf_notes/note151.pdf

4. Some states like California would pass significant state laws encouraging immigrant immigration, while states like Arizona, Alabama, Georgia, and South Carolina would pass stringent employment verification. See Gulasekaram and Ramakrishnan, *The New Immigration Federalism*. For more on California's expansive immigrant integration and its impact on notions of citizenship, see Colbern and Ramakrishnan, *State Citizenship*. In this way, states have sought to locally define notions of membership and either construct or deconstruct the line between citizens and noncitizens.

5. https://news.gallup.com/poll/244925/immigration-sharply-important-problem.aspx

6. In the years following the period of focus in this book, Gallup has found both a decrease in anti-immigrant sentiment and an increase in those who want to see immigration levels increase.

7. Trump for President Campaign, "Clinton's America," television advertisement, 2016.

8. Douglas S. Massey and Karen A. Pren, "Unintended Consequences of U.S. Immigration Policy: Explaining the Post-1965 Surge from Latin America," *Population and Development Review* 38, no. 1 (March 2012): 1–29.

9. Ibid.

10. "The Obama Record on Deportation: Deporter in Chief or Not?" *Migration Information Source*, Migration Policy Institute, Washington, DC, 20, https://www.migrationpolicy.org /article/obama-record-deportations-deporter-chief-or-not

11. Guidance issued at the time meant that the use of non-cash benefits was not to be considered in determining LPC status, and this would remain the dominant policy for almost twenty years.

BIBLIOGRAPHY

Archival Collections

American Civil Liberties Union Records: Subgroup 3, Regional Offices Files Series, Public Policy Papers, Department of Rare Books and Special Collections, Princeton University Library

Richard Armey Papers, Carl Albert Center, University of Oklahoma, Norman, Oklahoma

Herman Baca Papers, Mandeville Special Collections Library, University of California, San Diego

Bob Barr Papers, 104th Congress. Annie Belle Weaver Special Collections, Irvine Sullivan Ingram Library, University of West Georgia

Carter Domestic Policy Staff Collection, Jimmy Carter Library, Atlanta, Georgia

Governor William P. Clements Jr. Records, Cushing Library, Texas A&M University, College Station, Texas

Domestic Policy Council, Speechwriting, and Office of Communications Collections, William J. Clinton Library, Little Rock, Arkansas

Larry Daves Case file for *Plyler v. Doe*, Miscellaneous Manuscript No. 212, Benson Latin American Collection, General Libraries, University of Texas at Austin

Records of the Department of Justice, National Archives and Records Administration, College Park, Maryland

Federation for American Immigration Reform (FAIR) records, Special Collections Research Center, George Washington University

Newt Gingrich Papers, 104th and 105th Congresses. Annie Belle Weaver Special Collections, Irvine Sullivan Ingram Library, University of West Georgia

Mexican American Legal Defense and Educational Fund (MALDEF) Records, M673, Special Collections and University Archives, Stanford University Libraries

Mountain States Legal Foundation Collection, Hoover Institution Archives, Stanford, California

National Council of La Raza Records, M0744, Special Collections and University Archives, Stanford University Libraries

National Foreign Trade Council (NFTC) records (Accession 2345), Hagley Museum and Library, Wilmington, Delaware

Proposition 187 Campaign Ephemera, University of California, Berkeley, Institute of Governmental Studies

WHORM Subject Files and Staff Files, Ronald Reagan Library, Simi Valley, California

Judge Woodrow B. Seals Papers, Houston Metropolitan Research Center, Houston Public Library, Houston, Texas
Tyler School District Enrollment Records, Tyler ISD Offices, Tyler, Texas
UCLA Television and Film Archive

Databases

Bureau of Labor Statistics Employment
FRED, Federal Reserve Bank of St. Louis

Interviews

Tom Epstein, Political Affairs staff, Clinton White House, January 28, 2016
Ron Haskins, Republican Staff Director, February 17, 2016
David Martin, General Counsel INS 1995–1998, March 21, 2016
Kenneth Schorr, Plaintiffs' Attorney in *Gonzales v. Peoria*, April 25, 2016
Michael Wise, DOJ attorney involved in *Plyler v. Doe*, December 12, 2014

Works Cited

"$13 Billion in Welfare Cuts Restored." In *CQ Almanac 1997*, 53rd ed., 6-31-6-36. Washington, DC: Congressional Quarterly, 1998.
Acuna, Armando. "Capture of Illegal Aliens in Western U.S. Jumps 39%." *Los Angeles Times*, October 2, 1986.
"A National Identity Card?" *Wall Street Journal*, September 2, 1982.
"Alien Employment Bill Approved." *Clovis News-Journal* (Clovis, New Mexico). February 27, 1975, 2.
"American Survey: The Ins and Outs of Immigration Policy." *The Economist*, August 8, 1981.
"Amid Charges, Immigration Bill Dies." *New York Times*, October 12, 1984.
Anderson, Martin. *Revolution: The Reagan Legacy*. 2nd ed. Stanford: Hoover Institution Press, 1990.
"Arizona Roundup." *Gallup Independent* (Gallup, New Mexico). March 2, 1975.
Associated Press. "Clinton Moves to Protect Legal Aliens' Welfare Benefits." *Washington Post*, August 24, 1996.
Ayres, B. Drummond, Jr. "The 1994 Campaign: California; Feinstein Faults Aliens Proposal." *New York Times*, October 22, 1994.
Babcock, Charles R. "Aid for Illegal Aliens' Children: High Court Ruling May Spur Suits against States, Not U.S." *Washington Post*, June 23, 1982, A25.
———. "Justice Officials Move to Control Sensitive Civil Rights Division." *New York Times*, June 4, 1981.
———. "Shifts in Rights Policy and Turmoil at Justice." *Boston Globe*, September 16, 1981.
———. "Treatment of Alien Children in Texas Is Sharply Questioned by High Court." *Washington Post*, December 2, 1981.
Balz, Dan, and Mary Thornton. "U.S. Won't Intervene in Alien School Case." *Washington Post*, September 9, 1981.

———. "As the Hispanic Vote Emerges, Republicans Seek to Christen It." *Washington Post,* July 11, 1981.

———. "Texas Governor Breaks Ranks on Reagan Immigration." *Washington Post,* August 30, 1981.

Barnes, Fred. "GOP Governors Criticize Reagan." *Baltimore Sun,* November 16, 1982.

Batalova, Jeanne, Michael Fix, and Mark Greenberg. "Chilling Effects: The Expected Public Charge Rule and Its Impact on Legal Immigrant Families' Public Benefits Use." Washington, DC: Migration Policy Institute, June 2018.

Belejack, Barbarba. "A Lesson in Equal Protection." *Texas Observer,* July 13, 2007.

Bell, Griffin B., with Ronald J. Ostrow. *Taking Care of the Law.* Macon, GA: Mercer University Press, 1982.

Bell, Jonathan. *California Crucible: The Forging of Modern American Liberalism.* Princeton, NJ: Princeton University Press, 2012.

"Bell Questions Court Decision." *New York Times,* June 20, 1982.

Bernstein, Harry. "U.S Maps Action on Aliens: Cabinet Unit Set Up to Find Illegal Immigration Solution." *Los Angeles Times,* February 22, 1977.

Bernstein, Shana. "Interracial Activism in the Los Angeles Community Service Organization: Linking the World War II and Civil Rights Eras." *Pacific Historical Review* 80, no. 2 (May 2011): 231–267.

Bersani, Bianca E. "An Examination of First and Second Generation Immigrant Offending Trajectories." *Justice Quarterly* 31, no. 2 (2014): 315–343.

"Bill to Curb Illegal Immigration: House Debate Reflects Diversity of Nation." *New York Times,* June 17, 1984.

Bloemraad, Irene, Kim Voss, and Taeku Lee. "The Protests of 2006: What Were They, How Do We Understand Them, Where Do We Go?" In Irene Bloemraad and Kim Voss, eds., *Rallying for Immigrant Rights: The Fight for Inclusion in 21st Century America.* Berkeley: University of California Press, 2011.

Boris, Eileen, and Jennifer Klein. *Caring for America: Home Health Workers in the Shadow of the Welfare State.* New York: Oxford University Press, 2012.

Bornemeier, James. "Putting California Spin on Clinton Policies." *Los Angeles Times,* August 13, 1993.

Bosniak, Linda. *The Citizen and the Alien: Dilemmas of Contemporary Membership.* Princeton, NJ: Princeton University Press, 2006.

———. "Universal Citizenship and the Problem of Alienage." *Northwestern Law Review* 94 (2000): 963.

Brack, Richard. "Immigrants Being Drawn to Midwest." *Des Moines Register,* June 30, 1996.

Brilliant, Mark. *Color America Changed: How Racial Diversity Shaped Civil Rights Reform in California, 1941–1978.* Oxford: Oxford University Press, 2010.

Broder, John M. "Clinton Administration Readies Centrist Strategy." *Los Angeles Times,* November 21, 1994.

Brown, Hana E. "Race, Legality, and the Social Policy Consequences of Anti-Immigration Mobilization." *American Sociological Review* 78, no. 2 (April 2013): 290–314.

Brownstein, Ronald. "Wilson Proposes U.S. Version of Prop. 187 Immigration." *Los Angeles Times,* November 19, 1994.

Burdman, Pamela. "Democrats Blame Wilson for Immigration Problem." *San Francisco Chronicle*, September 20, 1994.

Bush, George H. W. *Statement on the Signing of the Immigration Act of 1990*. November 29, 1990.

"Bush vs. Clinton: What Would Be Best Immigration Policy?" *Los Angeles Times*, October 26, 1992.

Calavita, Kitty. *California's "Employer Sanctions": The Case of the Disappearing Law*. Research Report Series, no. 39. La Jolla: Center for U.S.-Mexican Studies, University of California, San Diego, 1982.

———. "Employer Sanctions Legislation in the United States: Implications for Immigration Policy." In Wayne A. Cornelius and Ricardo Anzaldua Montoya, eds., *America's New Immigration Law: Origins, Rationales and Potential Consequences*. La Jolla: Center for U.S.-Mexican Studies, University of California, San Diego, 1983.

———. "The New Politics of Immigration: 'Balanced-Budget Conservatism' and the Symbolism of Proposition 187." *Social Problems* 43 (1996): 284–305.

Cannon, Lou. "Hispanic Voter's Reaction to Signing Aliens Bill Hard to Predict." *Washington Post*, June 21, 1984.

Caplan, Lincoln. *The Tenth Justice: The Solicitor General and the Rule of Law*. 1st ed. New York: Knopf, 1987.

Cárdenas, Gilberto. "United States Immigration Policy toward Mexico: An Historical Perspective." *Chicana/o Latina/o Law Review* 2 (1975): 66–91.

Carney, Tom. "Town Awaits Murder Trial's Start." *Des Moines Register*, September 12, 1995, 2.

———. "Hispanics in Iowa: A Chorus of Spanish Voices." *Des Moines Register*, July 2, 1995.

———. "Hispanics in Iowa: Both Small Towns and Newcomers Learn to Adapt." *Des Moines Register*, July 6, 1995.

"Carter Unveils Illegal-Alien Proposals; Unions, Businessmen Criticize Package." *Wall Street Journal*, August 5, 1977.

Chavez, Leo R. *The Latino Threat: Constructing Immigrants, Citizens, and the Nation*. Palo Alto, CA: Stanford University Press, 2008.

———. *Anchor Babies and the Challenge of Birthright Citizenship*. Palo Alto, CA: Stanford University Press, 2017.

Chetty, David Grusky, Maximilian Hell, Nathaniel Hendren, Robert Manduca, and Jimmy Narang. "The Fading American Dream: Trends in Absolute Income Mobility Since 1940, Executive Summary." *Science* 356, no. 6336 (2017): 398–406, 2017.

"Clinton Maps Ideas from Inner City to Persian Gulf." *Los Angeles Times*, August 14, 1992.

Clinton, William J. "1995 State of the Union." Speech, Washington, DC, January 24, 1995. http://millercenter.org/president/clinton/speeches/speech-3440

CNN All Politics Iowa State Profile 1996. http://www.cnn.com/ALLPOLITICS/1996/states/IA/IA00.shtml

"Coast City Spurns Action on Aliens." *New York Times*, September 11, 1983.

Cobble, Dorothy Sue. *The Sex of Class: Women Transforming American Labor*. Cornell Paperbacks. Ithaca, NY: Cornell University Press, 2007.

Cochran, Mike. "'Outsider' Lawyers, Texas Town Duel on Civil Rights." *Los Angeles Times*, October 26, 1980.

Cody, Edward. "US Beckons Mexicans as Economy Falters." *Washington Post*, June 22, 1986.

Cohodas, Nadine. "Combination of Penalties, Amnesty: Congress Clears Overhaul of Immigration Law." *CQ Weekly* (October 18, 1986): 2595–2596.

Colbern, Allan, and S. Karthick Ramakrishnan. "Citizens of California: How the Golden State Went from Worst to First on Immigrant Rights." *New Political Science* 40, no. 2 (2018): 353–367.

———. *State Citizenship: A New Framework for Rights in the United States.* Cambridge: Cambridge University Press, 2020.

Commission on Population Growth and the American Future. *Interim Report.* Washington, DC: Government Printing Office, 1971.

"Congress Clears Overhaul of Immigration Law." In *CQ Almanac 1986*, 42nd ed., 61–67. Washington, DC: Congressional Quarterly, 1987.

Congressional Quarterly Weekly Report. January 14, 1995. Congressional Record, March 20, 1996, H2477–80.

Cortés, Michael Eduardo. "Policy Analysts and Interest Groups: The Case of Immigration Reform." PhD Diss., University of California, Berkeley, 1992.

Countryman, Matthew J. *Up South: Civil Rights and Black Power in Philadelphia.* Philadelphia: University of Pennsylvania Press, 2005.

Cowie, Jefferson R. *Capitol Moves: RCA's Seventy-Year Quest for Cheap Labor.* Ithaca, NY: Cornell University Press, 1999.

———. *Stayin' Alive: The 1970s and the Last Days of the Working Class.* New York: New Press, 2012.

Craig, Jim. "Lulac Head Thinks Officials Made Deal in Alien Court Case." *Houston Post*, September 10, 1981.

Crewdson, John M. "Hispanics Angered as U.S. Bars Brutality Charges against Police." *New York Times*, July 10, 1979.

"Curbing Illegal Immigration," *Chicago Tribune*, January 16, 1977.

"Danger in the Immigration Bill." *Los Angeles Times*, May 16, 1982.

Daniels, Rodger. *Guarding the Golden Door: American Immigration Policy and Immigrants since 1882.* New York: Hill & Wang, 2004.

Davidson, Adam. "Do Illegal Immigrants Actually Hurt the U.S. Economy?" *New York Times Magazine*, February 12, 2013.

Davis, Martha F. *Brutal Need: Lawyers and the Welfare Rights Movement, 1960–1973.* New Haven, CT: Yale University Press, 1993.

Decker, Jefferson. *The Other Rights Revolution: Conservative Lawyers and the Remaking of American Government.* Oxford: Oxford University Press, 2016.

Del Olmo, Frank. "Chavez Union Does a Turnabout, Opposes Alien Worker Bill." *Los Angeles Times*, March 27, 1973.

———. "Illegal Alien Union Targets." *Los Angeles Times*, January 30, 1975.

———. "Dole Hits Plan to Penalize Employers of Illegal Aliens." *Los Angeles Times*, September 25, 1976.

———. "Bell Will Warn Police." *Los Angeles Times*, June 22, 1978.

———. "Labor Leaders Seeking to Avert Latino Boycott." *Los Angeles Times*, July 17, 1984.

DeParle, Jason. "Welfare Plan Seeks Limit on Benefits." *New York Times*, May 12, 1994.

Dillin, John. "For Democrats in California, There's No Ducking the Touchy Issue of Immigration." *Christian Science Monitor*, June 1, 1984.

Dittmer, John. *Local People: The Struggle for Civil Rights in Mississippi*. Urbana: University of Illinois Press, 1994.

Domanick, Joe. "Daryl Gate's Downfall: L.A. Changed, but He—and His Department—Would Not." *Los Angeles Times*, April 18, 2010.

Dugger, Celia W. "In Surge to Be Americans, Thousands Take Oath." *New York Times*, July 5, 1997.

———. "Giuliani Uses Conference to Rally Immigrant Cause." *New York Times*, June 10, 1997.

———. "New Alliances and Attitudes on Aid." *New York Times*, August 1, 1997.

Dukes, Jennifer. "A Teen Dead, a Town Tense: Hawarden Fears that Racial Tension Will Boil Over." *Des Moines Register*, January 16, 1995.

Durand, Jorge, Douglas S. Massey, and Fernando Charvet. "The Changing Geography of Mexican Immigration to the United States: 1910–1996." *Social Science Quarterly* 81, no. 1 (March 2000): 1–15.

Edelman, Peter. "The Worst Thing Bill Clinton Has Done." *The Atlantic*, February 1997.

Edley, Christopher. Testimony before the US Commission on Civil Rights, Presentation on Civil and Human Rights Implications of U.S. Southwest Border Policy. November 14, 2002, http://www.usccr.gov/pubs/migrant/present/trans.htm

Ellis, Virginia, and Patrick McDonnell. "Suit Targets U.S. Cuts in Aid for Immigrants." *Los Angeles Times*, March 27, 1997.

Elsasser, Glen. "Wider Demands for Illegal Aliens Seen." *Chicago Tribune*, June 20, 1982.

Engelberg, Stephen. "G.O.P.'s Voice on Aliens Roars to Challenge the Party." *New York Times*, December 8, 1994.

Epstein, Lee, and Karen O'Connor. "A Legal Voice for the Chicano Community: The Activities of the Mexican American Legal Defense and Educational Fund, 1968–1982." In Rodolfo O. De la Garza, ed., *The Mexican American Experience: An Interdisciplinary Anthology*. Austin: University of Texas Press, 1985.

Feder, Barnaby J. "The Standoff Over Beef." *New York Times*, October 17, 1995.

Feldman, Paul. "Prop 187: Immigrant Measure Foes Open Drive." *Los Angeles Times*, August 19, 1994.

Felker-Kantor, Max F. *Policing Los Angeles: Race, Resistance and the Rise of the LAPD*. Chapel Hill: University of North Carolina Press, 2018.

Fine, Janice, and Daniel Tichenor. *Worker Centers: Organizing Communities at the Edge of the Dream*. Cornell Paperbacks. Ithaca, NY: ILR Press/Cornell University Press, 2006.

———. "A Movement Wrestling: American Labor's Enduring Struggle with Immigration, 1866–2007." *Studies in American Political Development* 23 (April 2009): 84–113.

Fink, Leon. *The Maya of Morganton: Work and Community in the Nuevo New South*. Chapel Hill: University of North Carolina Press, 2003.

———. "Labor Joins *La Marcha*: How New Immigrant Activists Restored the Meaning of May Day." In Nida Flores-González and Amalla Pallanes, eds., *¡Marcha!: Latino Chicago and the Immigrant Rights Movement*. Urbana: University of Illinois Press, 2010, 109–119.

Fitzgerald, Randy. "Welfare for Illegal Aliens?" *Reader's Digest*, June 1994.

Fix, Michael E., and Jeffrey S. Passel. "Immigration and Immigrants: Setting the Record Straight." *The Urban Institute*, May 1994.

Fogarty, Thomas A. "Case Spurs Immigration Law Review." *Des Moines Register*, June 18, 1995.

———. "Senate Cracks Down on Illegal Immigrants." *Des Moines Register*, April 24, 1996.

Foley, Neil. *Mexicans in the Making of America*. Cambridge, MA: Harvard University Press, 2014.

Foster, Sean. "S.L. Police as INS Agents: Is This a Good Idea?" *Salt Lake Tribune*, October 13, 1997.

———. "S.L. Latinos Swayed Councilman; He Voted Against INS Plan After Foes Packed Meeting." *Salt Lake Tribune*, September 9, 1998.

———. "SLC Council Says No to Cross-Deputization." *Salt Lake Tribune*, September 2, 1998.

Fox, Cybelle. *Three Worlds of Relief: Race, Immigration, and the American Welfare State from the Progressive Era to the New Deal*. Princeton, NJ: Princeton University Press, 2012.

———. "Unauthorized Welfare: The Origins of Immigrant Status Restrictions in American Social Policy." *Journal of American History* 102, no. 4 (March 2016): 1051–1074.

Fox, Cybelle, and Thomas Guglielmo. "Defining America's Racial Boundaries: Blacks, Mexicans, and European Immigrants, 1890–1945." *American Journal of Sociology* 118, no. 2 (2012): 327–379.

Fujiwara, Lynn. *Mothers Without Citizenship: Asian Immigrant Families and the Consequences of Welfare Reform*. Minneapolis: University of Minnesota Press, 2008.

Gabaccia, Donna R. "Nations of Immigrants: Do Words Matter?" *The Pluralist* 5, no. 3 (2010): 5–31.

———. "Is Everywhere Nowhere? Nomads, Nations, and the Immigrant Paradigm of United States History." *Journal of American History* 86, no. 3 (December 1999): 1115–1134.

Gallup, George. "Illegal Aliens' Job Prohibition Favored 6 to 1." *Washington Post*, April 24, 1977.

Georges, Christopher, and David Rogers. "Senate Delays Cutoff in Immigrant Aid but Is Divided on Long Term Spending." *Wall Street Journal*, May 8, 1997.

Germani, Carla. "Hispanic Demand: Scuttle Immigration Bill." *Christian Science Monitor*, July 19, 1984.

Gerstle, Gary. *American Crucible: Race and Nation in the Twentieth Century*. Princeton, NJ: Princeton University Press, 2001.

———. "The Immigrant as Threat to American Security: A Historical Perspective." In Elliott R. Barkan, Hasia Diner, and Alan M. Kraut, eds., *From Arrival to Incorporation: Migrants to the U.S. in a Global Era*. New York: New York University Press, 2007.

"Gingrich Changes Mind, Backs Immigrant Benefits." *Chicago Tribune*, January 10, 1995.

Girdner, Bill. "Local Police Effort to Arrest Aliens Faces Critical Test." *Los Angeles Daily Journal*, March 17, 1983.

Glickman, Charles. "Dispute over Antibias Hiring Clause in New Immigration Law." *Christian Science Monitor*, November 26, 1986.

Gonzales, Sylvia Alicia. *Hispanic American Voluntary Organizations*. Westport, CT: Greenwood Press, 1985.

Goodman, Adam. *The Deportation Machine: America's Long History of Expelling Immigrants*. Princeton, NJ: Princeton University Press, 2020.

Gordon, Andrew, and Trevor Stack. "Citizenship Beyond the State: Thinking with Early Modern Citizenship in the Contemporary World." *Citizenship Studies* 11, no. 2 (2007): 117–133.

Gorney, Cynthia. "Hispanic Delegates Split Over Call for Boycott on First Ballot Tonight." *Washington Post*, July 18, 1984.

Gottron, Martha V. "Illegal Alien Curbs: House Action Stalled." *Congressional Quarterly Weekly Report*, March 20, 1976.

Grey, Mark A., Anne C. Woodrick, Michele Yehieli, and James Hoelscher. *The New Iowans, A Companion Book to the PBS Miniseries "The New Americans."* Iowa Center for Immigrant Leadership and Integration, University of Northern Iowa, 2003.

Grier, Peter. "US Politicians Court Hispanics—but Come Bearing Few Gifts." *Christian Science Monitor,* April 30, 1984.

"Guilty Verdicts Returned in Justin Younie Murder Trial." *Ireton Examiner,* September 28, 1995.

Gulasekaram, Pratheepan, and S. Karthick Ramakrishnan. *The New Immigration Federalism.* Cambridge: Cambridge University Press, 2015.

Gutiérrez, David G. *Walls and Mirrors: Mexican American, Mexican Immigrants and the Politics of Ethnicity.* Berkeley: University of California Press, 1995.

Gutiérrez, Elena R. *Fertile Matters: The Politics of Mexican-Origin Women's Reproduction.* Austin: University of Texas Press, 2008.

Harris, David A. *Good Cops: The Case for Preventive Policing.* New York: New Press, 2005.

Havermann, Judith. "Civil Rights Groups, N.Y. Mayor Challenge Welfare Cutoff for Legal Immigrants." *Washington Post,* March 27, 1997.

———. "Republicans Start to Break Ranks on Welfare Cutoff for Legal Immigrants." *New York Times,* April 20, 1997.

"Herrarte & Escobedo Sentenced to Life Imprisonment." *Siouxland Press,* November 8, 1995.

Hester, Torrie. *Deportation: The Origins of U.S. Policy.* Philadelphia: University of Pennsylvania Press, 2017.

Hester, Torrie, Hidetaka Hirota, Mary E. Mendoza, Deirdre Moloney, Mae Ngai, Lucy Salyer, and Elliott Young. "Historians' Comment on DHS Notice of Proposed Rule 'Inadmissibility on Public Charge Grounds' FR 2018–21106." October 5, 2018.

"High Court Hears Views on Free Schooling for Alien Children." *New York Times,* December 2, 1981.

Higham, John. *Strangers in the Land: Patterns of American Nativism, 1860–1925.* Revised edition. New Brunswick, NJ: Rutgers University Press, 2002.

Hines, Craig. "Issue of Illegals' Schooling before High Court This Week." *Houston Chronicle,* November 29, 1981.

Hing, Bill Ong, and Kevin R. Johnson. "The Immigrant Rights Marches of 2006 and the Prospects for a New Civil Rights Movement." *Harvard CR-CLL Review* 42 (2007).

Hirota, Hidetaka. *Expelling the Poor: Atlantic Seaboard States and the Nineteenth-Century Origins of American Immigration Policy.* Oxford: Oxford University Press, 2017.

"Hispanics in Iowa Meatpacking." *Rural Migration News* 1, no. 4 (October 1995). https://migration.ucdavis.edu/rmn/more.php?id=66

HoSang, Daniel. *Racial Propositions: Ballot Initiatives and the Making of Postwar California.* Berkeley: University of California Press, 2010.

Houseman, Alan W., and Linda E. Perle. "Securing Equal Justice for All: A Brief History of Civil Legal Assistance in the United States." Edited by Center for Law and Social Policy, Washington, DC, 2007.

Hower, Joseph E., and Joseph A. McCartin. "Marshall's Principle: A Former Labor Secretary Looks Back (and Ahead)." *Labor: Studies in Working-Class History of the Americas* 11, no. 4 (2014): 91–107.

Hutchinson, Dennis J. "More Substantive Equal Protection? A Note on *Plyler v. Doe.*" *Supreme Court Review* (1982): 167–194.

"Ideas & Trends: Government Pulls Back on Two School Cases." *New York Times*, September 13, 1981.

"Illegal Aliens." *CQ Almanac 1977*, 33rd ed., 573–575. Washington, DC: Congressional Quarterly, 1978. http://library.cqpress.com/cqalmanac/cqal77-1203618

"Illegal Aliens: Bill to Bar Them Is Under Pressure." *Times Standard* (Copley, California). February 22, 1972.

"Illegal Immigrants Taken from Hawarden Plant." *Hawarden Independent*, November 24, 1994.

"Immigrant Workers in the Construction Labor Force." *NAHB Economics Special Studies*, February 3, 2015.

"Immigration Raids Causing Uproar in Silicon Valley." *Los Angeles Daily Journal*, August 2, 1984.

Interpreter Releases 60 (March 4, 1983): 172–173.

Jackel, Donna. "Law's Effect on Kin Dims New Citizens' Joy." *Rochester Democrat and Chronicle*, April 9, 1997.

Jacobson, Robin Dale. *The New Nativism: Proposition 187 and the Debate over Immigration.* Minneapolis: University of Minnesota Press, 2008.

Jasinowski, Jerry J. "Immigration: Save Reform." *Washington Post*, August 1, 1984.

Johnson, Kevin R. "The New Nativism: Something Old, Something New, Something Borrowed, Something Blue." In Juan Perea, ed., *Immigrants Out!: The New Nativism and the Anti-Immigrant Impulse in the United States.* New York: New York University Press, 1997.

Jones, Clayton. "Reagan Answer to Mexican 'Illegals'—Let Them In and License Them." *Christian Science Monitor*, November 12, 1980.

Jost, Kenneth. "Cracking Down on Immigration." *CQ Researcher* 5 (February 3, 1995): 97–120.

———. The States and Federalism." *CQ Researcher*, (September 13, 1996): 793–816.

"Justice Reportedly to Back Illegal Alien's Free Education." *Houston Post*, October 12, 1979.

Kalhan, Anil. "Immigration Enforcement and Federalism After September 11, 2001." In Ariane Chebel d'Appollonia and Simon Reich, eds., *Immigration, Integration, and Security: America and Europe in Comparative Perspective.* Pittsburgh, PA: University of Pittsburgh Press, 2008.

Kalman, Laura. *Right Star Rising: A New Politics, 1974–1980.* 1st ed. New York: W.W. Norton, 2010.

Kandel, William. "Meat-Processing Firms Attract Hispanic Workers to Rural America." *Amber Waves* (USDA Economic Research Service Magazine), June 1, 2006.

Kanstroom, Daniel. *Deportation Nation: Outsiders in American History.* Cambridge, MA: Harvard University Press, 2007.

Kaskie, Sherry. "Letter to the Editor." *Hawarden Independent*, February 2, 1995.

Katz, Michael. *In the Shadow of the Poorhouse: A Social History of Welfare in America.* 10th anniversary ed. New York: Basic Books, 1996.

Kaufman, Michael T. "Former Rep. Peter W. Rodino Jr. Is Dead at 95." *New York Times*, May 9, 2005.

Keely, Charles B. "Immigration Recommendations of the Commission on Population Growth and the American Future." *International Migration Review* 6, no. 3 (Autumn 1972): 290–294.

Kelly, Lee. "Legal Aid Still Open." *Longview-News Journal* (Longview, TX), February 4, 1982.

Kemerer, Frank R. *William Wayne Justice: A Judicial Biography.* 1st ed. Austin: University of Texas Press, 1991.

Kisor, Raymond M. "Enforcing the Immigration and Naturalization Act: Cooperation and Support on the Federal, State and Local Levels." *National Sheriff* (October–November 1984): 34–36.

Klarman, Michael J. *From Jim Crow to Civil Rights: The Supreme Court and the Struggle for Racial Equality*. Oxford: Oxford University Press, 2006.

Kornbluh, Felicia. *The Battle for Welfare Rights: Politics and Poverty in Modern America*. Philadelphia: University of Pennsylvania Press, 2007.

Kornbluh, Felicia, and Gwendolyn Mink. *Ensuring Poverty, Welfare Reform in Feminist Perspective*. Philadelphia: University of Pennsylvania Press, 2018.

Kovach, Bill. "Eased Immigration Laws Altering the Ethnic Profile of America." *New York Times*, June 14, 1971.

Kramer, Paul A. "The Case of the 22 Lewd Chinese Women." *Slate Magazine* (April 13, 2012).

Krikorian, Greg, and Dave Lesher. "Huffington Declares Support for Prop. 187." *Los Angeles Times*, October 21, 1994.

Kruse, Kevin M., and Julian E. Zelizer. *Fault Lines: A History of the United States Since 1974*. New York: W.W. Norton, 2019.

Kulish, Nicholas, and Mike McIntire. "Why an Heiress Spent Her Fortune Trying to Keep Immigrants Out." *New York Times*, August 14, 2019.

Kumbala, Tendayi. "Bill on Illegal Aliens Called 'Discriminatory.'" *Los Angeles Times*, February 4, 1973.

La Raza Organizational History. http://www.nclr.org/index.php/about_us/history/initiation _of_research_policy_efforts/#sthash.YOAhBFiU.dpuf, accessed March 1, 2014.

Lacey, Marc. "Beating Raises Concerns About Policing." *Los Angeles Times*, April 9, 1996.

Laffer, Arthur B. "Curbing Illegals Would Hurt Them and U.S. Economy." *Los Angeles Times*, August 14, 1984.

LaFranchi, Howard. "Courting the Hispanic Vote; Neither Candidate a Clear Winner." *Christian Science Monitor*, July 11, 1988.

Landsberg, Brian K. *Enforcing Civil Rights: Race Discrimination and the Department of Justice*. Studies in Government and Public Policy. Lawrence: University Press of Kansas, 1997.

Lassiter, Matthew D. "Political History Beyond the Red-Blue Divide." *Journal of American History* 98, no. 3 (December 2011): 760–764.

Latham, Nicholas. *Ronald Reagan and the Politics of Immigration Reform*. Westport, CT: Praeger, 2000.

"Legislator Charges Committee Fixed." *Redlands Daily Facts* (Redlands, CA). March 16, 1972.

Le May, Michael C. *Anatomy of a Public Policy: The Reform of Contemporary American Immigration Law*. Westport, CT: Praeger, 1994.

Lee, Erica. *At America's Gates: Chinese Immigration during the Exclusion Era, 1882–1943*. Chapel Hill: University of North Carolina Press, 2003.

———. "A Nation of Immigrants and a Gatekeeping Nation: American Immigration Law and Policy." In Reed Ueda, ed., *A Companion to American Immigration*. Malden, MA: Blackwell, 2006, 5–35.

———. *America for Americans: A History of Xenophobia in the United States*. New York: Basic Books, 2019.

Lew-Williams, Beth. *The Chinese Must Go: Violence, Exclusion, and the Making of the Alien in America*. Cambridge, MA: Harvard University Press, 2018.

Lesher, Dave, and Eric Lichtblau. "O.C. Group Helps Fuel Anti-Immigrant Furor." *Los Angeles Times*, August 30, 1993.

Light, M. T., and Miller, T. "Does Undocumented Immigration Increase Violent Crime?" *Criminology* 56 (2018): 370–401.

"Local Law Enforcement Has No Authority to Arrest Illegal Aliens." *Hawarden Independent*, January 25, 1995.

Los Angeles Police Department, Special Order 40, http://assets.lapdonline.org/assets/pdf/SO _40.pdf

Lytle Hernández, Kelly. *Migra!: A History of the U.S. Border Patrol*. Berkeley: University of California Press, 2010.

Malone, Julia. "Hispanic Groups Foresee Backlash, Ease Opposition to Immigration Bills." *Christian Science Monitor*, April 2, 1985.

Marcus, Ruth. "Clinton Assails California Proposal to Cut Illegal Immigrant Services; Democratic Strategist Says Measure May Spur Turnout." *Washington Post*, November 6, 1994.

Marro, Anthony. "Carter Aides to Map New Policy on Aliens." *New York Times*, April 4, 1977.

Martinez, Gebe, and Doreen Carvajal. "Creators of Prop. 187 Largely Escape Spotlight Ballot: From Secret O.C. Location, Political Novices and Veterans Spawn Strong Drive Against Illegal Immigration." *Los Angeles Times*, September 4, 1994.

Massey, Douglas S., Jorge Durand, and Nolan J. Malone. *Beyond Smoke and Mirrors: Mexican Immigration in an Era of Economic Integration*. New York: Russell Sage Foundation, 2002.

Maxwell, Evan. "LAPD Eases Policy Toward Illegal Aliens: Officers Won't Question Status Except in Serious Crimes." *Los Angeles Times*, March 21, 1979.

McCartin, Joseph A. *Collision Course: Ronald Reagan, the Air Traffic Controllers, and the Strike that Changed America*. Oxford: Oxford University Press, 2011.

McDaniel, Ann. "Justice Dept. Pulling Out of Alien Case." *Dallas Times Herald*, September 9, 1981.

McDonald, William F. *Changing Boundaries of Law Enforcement: State and Local Law Enforcement, Illegal Immigration, and Transnational Crime Control* (final report). Washington, DC: National Institute of Justice, 1999.

McDonnell, Patrick J. "Welfare Law May Affect Police Role, Immigrants." *Los Angeles Times*, September 30, 1996.

McKinnon, Courtney. "Hatch Addressing Immigration Issues." *Daily Universe* (BYU), June 12, 1997.

McWilliams, Rita. "Bias Issue Blocks Aliens Bill Conference." *Washington Times*, September 17, 1984.

———. "Hispanics Tell Democrats to Halt Immigration Bill." *Washington Times*, September 13, 1984.

Merid, Kevin, and Judith Havemann. "Gingrich Softens Stance Against Aliens' Benefits; Speaker Suggests GOP Will Revisit Welfare Question." *Washington Post*, January 10, 1995.

Miller Center. "Interview with Ray Marshall." University of Virginia, May 4, 1988. http:// millercenter.org/president/carter/oralhistory/ray-marshall. Accessed July 1, 2016.

Miller, Martin. "Creators Set Prop. 187 for National Stage, Immigration: O.C. Backers Say Groups in 18 States Have Sought Advice." *Los Angeles Times*, November 10, 1994.

Minian, Ana Raquel. *Undocumented Lives: The Untold Story of Mexican Migration*. Cambridge, MA: Harvard University Press, 2018.

Molina, Natalia. *Fit to Be Citizens? Public Health and Race in Los Angeles, 1879–1939*. Berkeley: University of California Press, 2006.

Motomura, Hiroshi. *The Curious Evolution of Immigration Law: Procedural Surrogates for Substantive Constitutional Rights*, 92 Columbia Law Review 1625, 1627 (1992).

———. *Americans in Waiting: The Lost Story of Immigration and Citizenship*. Oxford: Oxford University Press, 2007.

———. *Immigration Outside the Law*. Oxford: Oxford University Press, 2014.

"Murder Trial Expected to Go to Jury This Week." *Sioux Center News*, September 19, 1995.

Murphy, Alice. "Pete Tijerina Firing Requested by Ford." *San Antonio Express*, March 21, 1970.

Mydans, Seth. "A New Tide of Immigration Brings Hostility to the Surface, Poll Finds." *New York Times*, June 27, 1993.

Nelson, Lynne. "Letter to the Editor." *Hawarden Independent*, February 2, 1995.

Newton, Jim. "The Brennan Memos." *Slate Magazine*, January 11, 2007.

Ngai, Mae M. *Impossible Subjects: Illegal Aliens and the Making of Modern America*. (Part of Politics and Society in Twentieth-Century America series). Princeton, NJ: Princeton University Press, 2004.

Norman, Jane. "Immigration Raids Win Praise." *Des Moines Register*, May 17, 1996.

———. "Grassley Lands First INS Office for Iowa." *Des Moines Register*, March 12, 1996.

———. "Harkin: Must Police Also Chase Aliens?" *Des Moines Register*, March 22, 1996.

———. "Offices Are Coming, One Way or Another." *Des Moines Register*, March 17, 1996.

———. "Potomac Fever." *Des Moines Register*, April 14, 1996.

Nowrastech, Alex. "Criminal Immigrants in Texas: Illegal Immigrant Conviction and Arrest Rates for Homicide, Sex Crimes, Larceny and Other Crimes." Cato Institute, Immigration Research and Policy Brief 4 (February 2018). https://object.cato.org/sites/cato.org/files/pubs/pdf/irpb-4-updated.pdf. Accessed June 2, 2019.

O'Connor, Karen, and Lee Epstein. "A Legal Voice for the Chicano Community: The Activities of the Mexican American Legal Defense and Educational Fund, 1968–1982." In Rodolfo O. De la Garza, ed., *The Mexican American Experience: An Interdisciplinary Anthology*. Austin: University of Texas Press, 1985.

Oleszek, Walter J. *The Use of Task Forces in the House* (CRS Report No. RS20421). Washington, DC: Congressional Research Service, 1999.

Olivas, Michael A. *No Undocumented Child Left Behind: Plyler v. Doe and the Education of Undocumented Schoolchildren*. New York: New York University Press, 2012.

Oliver, Myrna. "Court Asked to Halt LAPD Immigration-Status Action." *Los Angeles Times*, December 11, 1979.

"On Not Blaming Immigrants First." *Washington Post*, May 9, 1994.

"One Billion Americans?" *New York Times*, March 21, 1971.

"One Injured, One Killed in Stabbing Incident." *Des Moines Register*, January 15, 1995.

"O'Neill Blocks Immigration Bill in House." *CQ Almanac 1983*, 39th ed., 287–292. Washington, DC: Congressional Quarterly, 1984. http://library.cqpress.com/cqalmanac/cqal83-1198947

Orleck, Annelise. *Storming Caesars Palace: How Black Mothers Fought Their Own War on Poverty.* Boston, MA: Beacon, 2005.

Parker, Kunal M. *Making Foreigners: Immigration and Citizenship Law in America. 1600–2000.* New York: Cambridge University Press, 2015.

"Party Ratifies Conservative Platform." *New York Times,* August 22, 1984.

Payne, Charles M. *I've Got the Light of Freedom: The Organizing Tradition and the Mississippi Freedom Struggle.* Berkeley: University of California Press, 1995.

Pear, Robert. "O'Neill Says Bill on Illegal Aliens Is Dead for 1983." *New York Times,* October 5, 1983.

———. "Bill on Aliens a Divisive Issue for Democrats." *New York Times,* April 22, 1984.

———. "Reagan Raises New Obstacles to House Bill on Immigration." *New York Times,* August 9, 1984.

———. "Talks Break Down on Alien Measure." *New York Times,* September 27, 1984.

———. "White House Calls House Immigration Measure Unacceptable." *New York Times,* July 26, 1984.

———. "Law Sets Off Dispute on Legal Alien's Jobs Rights." *New York Times,* November 23, 1986.

———. "New Restrictions on Immigration Gain Public Support, Poll Shows." *New York Times,* July 1, 1986.

———. "President Signs Landmark Bill on Immigration." *New York Times,* November 7, 1986, A12.

———. "The Nation; Deciding Who Gets What in America." *New York Times,* November 27, 1994.

———. "Clinton Will Seek Spending to Curb Aliens, Aides Say." *New York Times,* January 22, 1995.

———. "Welfare Bill Cleared by Congress Now Awaits Clinton's Veto." *New York Times,* December 23, 1995.

———. "G.O.P. Governors Seek to Restore Immigrant Aid." *New York Times,* January 25, 1997.

———. "GOP Backing Off Deal to Restore Aid to Immigrants." *New York Times,* June 4, 1997.

Perea, Juan F., ed. *Immigrants Out! The New Nativism and the Anti-Immigrant Impulse in the United States.* New York: New York University Press, 1997.

Perrotti, Rosanna. "Resolving Policy Conflict: Congress and Immigration Reform." PhD Diss., University of Pennsylvania, 1989.

Perry, Leah. *The Cultural Politics of U.S. Immigration: Race, Gender and the Media.* New York: New York University Press, 2016.

Pew Research Center. "Modern Immigration Wave Brings 59 Million to U.S., Driving Population Growth and Change Through 2065: Views of Immigration's Impact on U.S. Society Mixed." Washington, DC, September 2015

Pitti, Stephen J. *The Devil in Silicon Valley: Northern California, Race and Mexican Americans.* Princeton, NJ: Princeton University Press, 2002.

Podger, Pamela. "Ballot Measures Attract Big Money." *Fresno Bee,* October 17, 1994.

Porter, Eduardo. "Illegal Immigrants Are Bolstering Social Security with Billions." *New York Times,* April 5, 2005.

"Presidential Statement: Carter Proposes Illegal Aliens Legislation." *CQ Almanac 1977*, 33rd ed., 43-E–45-E. Washington, DC: Congressional Quarterly, 1978. http://library.cqpress.com/cqalmanac/cqal77-863-26256-1200549

Press Conference. "A Summit on Crime—Coming Together for Utah's Future." Salt Lake City, Utah, June 30, 1997. https://www.justice.gov/archive/ag/speeches/1997/06-30-1997a.pdf

Price, Jorjanna. "Texas to Appeal Aliens Decision." *Houston Post*, July 23, 1980.

Provine, Doris Marie, Monica W. Varsanyi, Paul G. Lewis, and Scott H. Decker. *Policing Immigrants: Local Law Enforcement on the Front Lines*. Chicago: University of Chicago Press, 2016.

Purdum, Todd. "Clinton in a Box as a Welfare Bill Edges Closer." *New York Times*, July 26, 1996.

Radford, Jynnah, and Luis Noe-Bustamante. "Facts on U.S. Immigrants, 2017." Pew Research Center, June 3, 2019.

"Raid at Iowa Lamb Prompted . . ." *Hawarden Independent*, November 24, 1994.

Ramakrishnan, Karthick, and Allan S. Colbern. "The 'California Package' of Immigrant Integration and the Evolving Nature of State Citizenship." *Policy Matters* 6 (3): 1–19.

Rangel, Jesus. "Rise in Status Gives a Hispanic Group Growing Pains." *New York Times*, June 25, 1984.

Reaves, Gayle. "Legal Aid Fights Its Bitter Success." *Austin American-Statesman*, August 23, 1981.

Rector, Robert, and William Lauber. "America Is Becoming a Deluxe Retirement Home." *The Social Contract*, April 1995. http://www.thesocialcontract.com/pdf/six-one/retireme.pdf

Reese, Ellen. *They Say Cut, We Say Fight Back! Welfare Activism in an Era of Retrenchment*. New York: Russell Sage Foundation, 2011.

Reid, T. R. "O'Neill Exercised Power, Bars Immigration Bill." *Washington Post*, October 5, 1983.

Reimers, David M. *Still the Golden Door: The Third World Comes to America*. 2nd ed. New York: Columbia University Press, 1992.

———. *Unwelcome Strangers: American Identity and the Turn Against Immigration*. New York: Columbia University Press, 1998.

Reinhold, Robert. "A Welcome for Immigrants Turns to Resentment." *New York Times*, August 25, 1993.

Reno, Janet. Address to "A Summit on Crime—Coming Together for Utah's Future." Salt Palace Ballroom, Salt Lake City, Utah, June 30, 1997. https://www.justice.gov/archive/ag/speeches/1997/06-30-1997c.pdf

Richards, David. *Once Upon a Time in Texas: A Liberal in the Lone Star State*. Focus on American History Series. 1st ed. Austin: University of Texas Press, 2002.

Richter, Kelly K. "Uneasy Border State: The Politics and Public Policy of Latino Illegal Immigration in Metropolitan California, 1971–1996." PhD Diss., Stanford University, 2014.

San Miguel, Guadalupe. *Chicana/o Struggles for Education: Activism in the Community*. University of Houston Series in Mexican American Studies. 1st ed. College Station: Texas A&M University Press, 2013.

Sandalow, Marc. "Republicans Battle Over Immigration for 'Soul of Party.'" *San Francisco Chronicle*, November 22, 1994.

Schmos, Diana Jean. "In Recession, Illegal Aliens Find a Cold Reception on L.I." *New York Times*, February 14, 1992

Schrag, Peter. *Not Fit for Our Society: Immigration and Nativism in America*. Berkeley: University of California Press, 2010.

Schwarz, Carl E. "Employer Sanctions Law: The State Experience as Compared with Federal Proposals." In Wayne A. Cornelius and Ricardo Anzaldua Montoya, eds., *America's New Immigration Law: Origins, Rationales and Potential Consequences*. La Jolla: Center for U.S.-Mexican Studies, University of California, San Diego, 1983.

Sciolino, Elaine. "Clinton Says U.S. Will Continue Ban on Haitian Exodus." *New York Times*, January 15, 1993.

"Sending a Message on Immigration." *Washington Post*, May 14, 1984.

Shapiro, Margaret. "Angry Hispanic Activists Declare Immigration Bill a Lost Cause." *Washington Post*, June 16, 1984.

Shogren, Elizabeth. "Clinton Unveils Welfare Reform." *Los Angeles Times*, June 15, 1994.

Sierra, Christine Marie. "The Political Transformation of a Minority Group: The Council of La Raza, 1965–1980." PhD diss., Stanford University, 1983.

———. "Latino Organizational Strategies on Immigration Reform: Success and Limits in Public Policymaking." In Roberto E. Villarreal and Norma G. Hernandez, eds., *Latinos and Political Coalitions: Political Empowerment for the 1990s*. Westport, CT: Praeger, 1991.

———. "In Search of National Power: Chicanos Working the System on Immigration Reform, 1976–1986." In David Montejano, ed., *Chicano Politics and Society in the Late Twentieth Century*. Austin: University of Texas Press, 1999.

Simpson, Alan K. "The Politics of Immigration Reform." *International Migration Review* 18, no. 3 (October 1, 1984): 486–504.

"Sioux City Fatal Hit-And-Run Incident Shows Possible Hawarden Connection." *Hawarden Independent*, November 25, 1993.

Skerry, Peter. "Is Immigration the Exclusive Responsibility of the Federal Government?" *Publius: The Journal of Federalism* 25, no. 3 (Summer 1995): 71–85.

Smith, Hendrick. "Texas Looming as a Close Battle between President and Reagan." *New York Times*, October 9, 1980.

Smothers, Ronald. "Texas Caucuses Spotlight Role of Hispanic Voters." *New York Times*, May 4, 1984.

Solórzano, Armando. "At the Gates of the Kingdom." In Elzbieta M. Gozdziak and Susan F. Martin, eds., *Beyond the Gateway, Immigrants in A Changing America*. Oxford: Lexington Books, 2005.

Sontag, Debora. "Calls to Restrict Immigration Come from Many Quarters." *New York Times*, December 13, 1992.

Southworth, Ann. *Lawyers of the Right: Professionalizing the Conservative Coalition*. Chicago: University of Chicago Press, 2008.

Soysal, Yasemin. *The Limits of Citizenship: Migrants and Postnational Membership in Europe*. Chicago: University of Chicago Press, 1995.

"Sponsor Skeptical About Passage of Illegal Alien Hiring Measure." *Greely Daily Tribune* (Greely, Colorado). April 16, 1971.

Sracic, Paul. *San Antonio v. Rodriguez and the Pursuit of Equal Education: The Debate over Discrimination and School Funding.* Lawrence: University Press of Kansas, 2006.

Stall, Bill, and Patrick J. McDonnell. "Wilson Urges Stiff Penalties to Deter Illegal Immigrants."
Los Angeles Times, August 10, 1993.

———. "Reagan Forces Have Eye on Texas." *New York Times,* September 22, 1980.

Stefanic, Jean. "Funding the Nativist Agenda." In Juan Perea, ed., *Immigrants Out!: The New
Nativism and the Anti-Immigrant Impulse in the United States.* New York: New York University
Press, 1997.

Stein, Judith. *Pivotal Decade: How the United States Traded Factories for Finance in the 1970s.* New
Haven, CT: Yale University Press, 2010.

Stevens, William K. "Education of Aliens at Issue in Texas." *New York Times,* March 13, 1980.

Stowers, Carlton. "Alien Issue Triggers Uneasiness in Tyler." *Dallas Morning News,* September 14,
1977.

Stull, Donald D., Michael J. Broadway, and David Griffith, eds. *Any Way You Cut It: Meat Processing and Small Town America.* Lawrence: University Press of Kansas, 1995.

Subcommittee on Immigration and Claims of the House Judiciary Committee. *Field Hearing:
Problems Related to Criminal Aliens in the State of Utah.* 105th Congress, 2nd session, July 27,
1998.

Subcommittee on Immigration and Refugee Policy of the Committee on the Judiciary, *Hearing
on September 30, 1982,* 34–35. https://www.loc.gov/law/find/hearings/pdf/00139298160.pdf

Suro, Roberto. "California's SOS on Immigration." *Washington Post,* September 29, 1994.

———. "GOP Would Deny Legal Immigrants Many U.S. Benefits." *Washington Post,*
December 24, 1994.

Sutton, Charles. "Illegal Immigrants Swamp State." *Independent* (Long Beach, California).
April 15, 1970.

Taylor, Paul, and Milton Coleman. "Minority Blocs Step Up Pressure for Platform
Modifications." *Washington Post,* July 17, 1984.

Taylor, Stewart, Jr. "Conflict over Rights of Aliens Lies at Supreme Court's Door." *New York
Times,* September 28, 1981.

Teles, Steven M. *The Rise of the Conservative Legal Movement: The Battle for Control of the Law.*
Princeton, NJ: Princeton University Press, 2010.

"Text of President Clinton's Welfare Announcement." *New York Times,* August 1, 1996.

"The Rights of Illegal Aliens." *Washington Post,* June 18, 1982.

Thompson, Cheryl W. "INS Role for Police Considered." *Washington Post,* April 4, 2002.

Tichenor, Daniel J. *Dividing Lines: The Politics of Immigration Control in America.* Princeton
Studies in American Politics. Princeton, NJ: Princeton University Press, 2002.

———. "Strange Bedfellows: The Politics and Pathologies of Immigration Reform." *Labor:
Studies in Working-Class History of the Americas* 5, no. 2 (2008): 39–60.

Tichenor, Daniel J., with Alexandra Filindra. "*Raising Arizona v. United States*: Historical
Patterns of American Immigration Federalism." 16 *Lewis & Clark Law Review* 1215 (2012):
1223–1234.

Tilly, Chris. "Short Hours, Short Shrift: The Causes and Consequences of Part-Time
Employment." In Virginia L. duRivage, ed., *New Policies for the Part-Time and Contingent
Workforce.* Armonk, NY: M.E. Sharpe, 1992.

Tolchin, Martil. "O'Neill, in a Reversal, Supports Immigration Bill." *New York Times*, December 1, 1983.

Trout, Hillary, and Phil Kuntz. "GOP May Reconsider Proposal to Deny Benefits to Legal Aliens, Gingrich Says." *Wall Street Journal*, January 10, 1995.

University of Texas at Austin. Bureau of Business Research. "Texas Fact Book 1980." Austin, TX: Bureau of Business Research.

"U.S. Asks to Join in Court Challenge of Texas Tuition Law for Illegal Aliens." *Washington Post*, January 17, 1980.

US Congress Senate Committee on the Judiciary. Subcommittee on Immigration and Refugee Policy. *Proposed Regulation Changes for Refugee Assistance: Hearing Before the Subcommittee on Immigration and Refugee Policy of the Committee on the Judiciary*, US Senate, 97th Congress, Second Session, February 9, 1982. Washington, DC: US Government Printing Office, 1983.

"US, in Shift, Says Alien Case a Texas Issue." *Boston Globe*, September 9, 1981.

Vargas, Zaragoza. *Labor Rights Are Civil Rights: Mexican American Workers in Twentieth-Century America*. Politics and Society in Twentieth-Century America. Princeton, NJ: Princeton University Press, 2007.

Verboon, Jon. "U.S. Will Leave Alien Tuition to Court." *Houston Chronicle*, September 9, 1981.

"Walter Craig, Federal Judge; Named to Bench by Kennedy." *New York Times*, July 3, 1986.

Watson, Dan. "Aliens Get No Protection from Court in School Suit." *Dallas Morning News*, September 16, 1977.

Weaver, R. Kent. *Ending Welfare as We Know It*. Washington, DC: Brookings Institution Press, 2000.

"Welfare Bill Clears under Veto Threat." *CQ Almanac 1995*, 51st ed., 7-35-7-52. Washington, DC: Congressional Quarterly, 1996. http://library.cqpress.com/cqalmanac/cqal95-1100649

West, Richard. "State Measure to Ban Hiring of Illegal Aliens Signed into Law: Reagan Places Signature on Bill Making Violation by Employer Misdemeanor Carrying Minimum Fine of $200." *Los Angeles Times*, November 9, 1971.

———. "Tyler Illegal Alien Students Receive Stay of Deportation." *Dallas Morning News*, September 17, 1977.

Westoff, Charles F. "The Commission on Population Growth and the American Future: Its Origins, Operations, and Aftermath." *Population Index* 39, no. 4 (October 1973): 491–507.

Wiker, Tom. "A Success Story: Building Hispanic Voter Strength." *New York Times*, October 14, 1984.

Wilentz, Sean. *The Age of Reagan: A History, 1974–2008*. New York: Harper, 2008.

Winter, Catherine. "A Supreme Court Case 35 Years Ago Yields a Supply of Emboldened DACA Students Today." *APM Reports*, August 21, 2017.

Wishnie, Michael J. "Prohibiting the Employment of Unauthorized Immigrants: The Experiment Fails." *University of Chicago Legal Forum*, 2007, 193–217.

Wolf, Richard. "Food Stamp Loss Takes Toll." *USA Today*, January 28, 1998.

Wong, Carolyn. *Lobbying for Inclusion: Rights Politics and the Making of Immigration Policy*. Palo Alto, CA: Stanford University Press, 2006.

Wong, Tom K. *The Politics of Immigration: Partisanship, Demographic Change and American National Identity*. Oxford: Oxford University Press, 2017.

Wroe, Andrew. *The Republican Party and Immigration Politics: From Proposition 187 to George W. Bush*. London: Palgrave Macmillan, 2008.

Zelizer, Julian E. *Jimmy Carter*. The American Presidents Series. 1st ed. New York: Times Books, 2010.

Zelizer, Julian E., and Meg Jacobs. *Conservatives in Power: The Reagan Years*. Boston, MA: Bedford, 2011.

Zolberg, Aristide R. *Nation by Design: Immigration Policy in the Fashioning of America*. Cambridge, MA: Harvard University Press, 2006.

Zong, Jie, and Jeanne Batalova. "Frequently Requested Statistics on Immigrants and Immigration in the United States." *Migration Information Source*, April 27, 2016. http://www.migrationpolicy.org/article/frequently-requested-statistics-immigrants-and-immigration-united-states#Current%20and%20Historical%20Numbers%20and%20Shares

Zumbrun, Ronald. "Life, Liberty and Property Rights." Chapter 2 in Lee Edwards, ed., *Bringing Justice to the People: The Story of the Freedom-Based Public Interest Law Movement*. Berwyn Heights, MD: Heritage Books, 2004.

INDEX

287(g) program, 11, 160–64, 169

abortion, 27, 132
Abreu, Jan Tomas, 137
activism: affirmative action and, 17, 50;
anti-immigrant sentiments and, 4, 12,
62, 105–6, 108, 111, 120, 168; benefits
and, 104–6, 108, 111, 120–21, 126–27, 140;
California and, 14, 120–22; Carter and,
34, 43, 50, 145, 181, 186n10; Chicano rights
organizations and, 67; civil rights and,
12 (*see also* civil rights); conservatives
and, 3–4, 14, 27–28, 43, 59, 127; East Texas
Legal Services and, 20–21; education and,
13–20; enforcement and, 145–46, 161, 165;
Equal Protection Clause and, 9, 14–15,
33–38, 40, 42, 48–49, 51, 54, 56; eugenics
and, 71; Federation for American Immigration Reform (FAIR) and, 58, 71–72,
113; *Griggs v. Duke Power* and, 54;
Immigration and Naturalization Service
(INS) and, 16–17, 24–25; Latinos and, 10,
95, 161; liberals and, 4, 14, 27, 58–59, 61, 82,
167; Mexican American Legal Defense
and Education Fund (MALDEF) and, 13,
47, 49; Mexicans and, 10, 17, 95, 106, 146;
Miliken v. Bradley I and, 54; Mountain
States Legal Foundation (MSLF) and,
28–29, 40–41, 53; Pacific Legal Foundation
(PLF) and, 28; *Plyler v. Doe* and, 9, 13–15,
19, 50, 59, 167; pro-immigration, 16, 80,
136, 141; Reagan and, 14, 27–28; regulation
and, 15; *Swann v. Charlotte-Mecklenburg*

Board of Education and, 54; Texas and,
13–26, 29; unauthorized immigrants and,
15–17, 24, 28, 104; unions and, 3, 20–21, 47,
73; US Supreme Court and, 14–17, 23; *Yick
Wo v. Hopkins* and, 15
Ad Hoc Coalition, 78–79
Ad Hoc Committee on the Police Enforcement of Immigration Laws, 146
affirmative action, 17, 50
AFL-CIO, 21, 66–68, 76–77, 87, 94–95
Agricultural Council of California, 67
Agricultural Research Act, 140
agriculture: California and, 67, 76, 110;
employer sanctions and, 61, 64–69,
76, 83, 86, 92–93, 101–2; labor and, 7,
20, 61, 64–67, 69, 76, 83, 86, 92–93, 101–2,
110, 137, 140; Mexicans and, 7, 64,
110; National Council of Agricultural
Employers (NCAE) and, 86, 100–1;
protectionism and, 110; seasonal work
of, 65; Secretary of Agriculture and, 137;
Texas and, 20, 66; United Farm Workers
(UFW) and, 66–68, 73, 79, 87, 101; US
Department of Agriculture and, 140
Aguirre, Edward, 48
Aid to Families with Dependent Children
(AFDC), 36, 38, 107–8, 111–12, 119, 132
alienage rights, 5, 14–15, 97, 105, 169, 180n14
Alien and Sedition Acts, 179n10
Allianza Latina, La, 162
Almond, Lincoln, 137
al Qaeda, 164
American Bar Association, 91, 149

A NOTE ON THE TYPE

This book has been composed in Arno, an Old-style serif typeface in the classic Venetian tradition, designed by Robert Slimbach at Adobe.

CPSIA information can be obtained
at www.ICGtesting.com
Printed in the USA
JSHW020027190123
36417JS00004B/5

9 780691 203331